Philosophy and
Feminist Thinking

Philosophy and Feminist Thinking

Jean Grimshaw
Senior Lecturer in Philosophy and Cultural Studies
Bristol Polytechnic

University of Minnesota Press   Minneapolis

Published by the University of Minnesota Press
2037 University Avenue Southeast, Minneapolis MN 55414.
Published simultaneously in Canada
by Fitzhenry & Whiteside Limited, Markham.
Printed in Great Britain.

Library of Congress Cataloging-in-Publication Data

Grimshaw, Jean.
    Philosophy and feminist thinking.

    Bibliography: p.
    Includes index.
    1. Feminism. 2. Feminism—History. 3. Women as
    philosophers. I. Title.
    HQ1154.G75   1986   305.4′2   86-6993
    ISBN 0-8166-1545-4
    ISBN 0-8166-1546-2 (pbk.)

Contents

Preface

This book is an exploration into some tensions in feminist thinking and their relationship to philosophy. I believe these tensions to be central to contemporary feminist debate; they have certainly been central to my own engagement with feminism. And the first debt I owe is to all those women without whose work a book like this could not exist. Where I criticise, I have sometimes also learned the most.

I would like to thank all the women with whom I have regularly participated in philosophical discussion for their critical interest and support, including Alison Assiter, Caroline Bailey, Paula Boddington, Judith Hughes, Mary Midgley, Ann Payne, Anne Seller, Margaret Whitford and others. Most especially, I thank Morwenna Griffiths for her encouragement and for the care with which she read and commented on much of the book in draft.

My thanks are also due to John for his interest, and for various invaluable forms of support, such as putting a word-processor my way and helping with the production of the typescript in ways that made the process easier and less stressful than I could have imagined.

I would have been unable to write the book without funding for time relief from the Bristol Polytechnic Research Committee, and without the encouragement of my colleagues Anne Beezer and Martin Barker and their generosity in coping with the extra pressures that sometimes resulted from my temporary absences.

I have written this book in the hope that it might provide a resource for those who share something of my own engagement with feminism or philosophy, or both, to explore some questions raised by their meeting. The Italian philosopher, Antonio Gramsci, wrote: 'It is essential to destroy the widespread prejudice that philosophy is a strange and difficult thing just because it is the specific intellectual activity of a particular category of specialists or of professional and systematic philosophers', (Selections from the Prison Notebooks, 1971, p.323). I have tried to show not only that questions about women are central to philosophy but that philosophical problems arise out of the tensions and contradictions in women's lives and out of the varieties of feminist thinking and practice, and that they are central to feminism as well as to philosophy.

Jean Grimshaw
September 1985

Introduction

The impetus for this book came from two sources. The first was an increasing awareness of the way in which so many philosophers seemed either to ignore women or to hold them in contempt and to regard them as inferior to men, and a belief that it is important to take seriously what philosophers have said about women. The second was an increasing awareness of and interest in what seem to me to be some central tensions in feminist thinking and in the relationship between these tensions and philosophical theories and traditions.

It surprises me now that as a philosophy undergraduate I did not even really notice the things that philosophers said about women. I did a degree in which I studied a conventional list of 'Great Philosophers'. At no point, not even in the study of moral and political philosophy, was it pointed out to me that most of the philosophers on undergraduate reading lists *did* say something about women. If I read what they wrote about women, it was never a question for consideration; thus, when reading Plato's *Republic,* I discussed his view of knowledge, of justice, of democracy, but never his opinions about women and the family. If a philosopher wrote a separate treatise on women, it was never an object of study; thus I read Mill on liberty, but not on the subjection of women. I even managed to read what Rousseau wrote about the education of Emile, but entirely omitted what he said about Sophie.

When one does begin to notice, it is not hard at all to find evidence of the ways in which philosophers have devalued women, spoken of them contemptuously, relegated them to inferior and subordinate status. It is, however, extremely hard to find much in the way of discussion or recognition of

1

this fact in mainstream philosophy. A smattering of articles on gender-related issues began to appear in mainstream philosophical journals around the late 1960s, and there has been a steady trickle since then. But the content of most philosophy courses scarcely acknowledges the existence of such issues, let alone their importance, and the books that are written for these courses reflect this absence.

It is important to ask why this is so. One reason is the fact that there are so few women teaching philosophy. But this is not the only reason, since women themselves (including myself as an undergraduate) may not recognise the importance of questions about women in philosophy. Another reason is that it has sometimes been assumed that questions about women were not really 'philosophical'. A decade or so ago it was common in British philosophy to make a sharp distinction between 'first order' and 'second order' questions. First order questions were supposed to be substantive ones, such as empirical questions about reality or what the world was like, or moral questions about how we should behave or what our principles should be. Second order questions were supposed to consist of 'conceptual analysis', in which philosophers analysed the language we used to talk about reality or about morals. And I think it was tacitly assumed that questions about women were either empirical (what are women like or how are they treated?) or moral (how should we treat them?), hence they weren't properly philosophical, or of the 'second order' variety.

This sharp distinction between first and second order questions is not now so generally accepted; thus moral philosophers do not now, on the whole, assume that we can talk about, say, the concept of 'morality' without bringing in substantive moral questions. But questions about women still seem very peripheral to mainstream academic philosophy.

An additional reason for this may be a certain sort of liberal complacency (coupled perhaps with a little embarrassment). Of course, it is supposed, no one holds views like that about women any more (least of all intelligent, liberal-minded philosophers), so they are not really worth discussing. But this view is tenable only if you make two assumptions. The first is that the sorts of attitudes to women held by philosophers in the past *are* dead or disappearing, and there might be good reason to question that. The second is that such attitudes are a mere question of 'prejudice', supposedly belonging to a past age, so that we can, in effect, simply delete all the passages where philosophers have said embarrassing things about women, ignore them as unfortunate relics of the past and go about our philosophical business as usual. But this supposes that it is always possible to *isolate* what a philosopher says (or implies) about women from the rest of their philosophy, to cut it out and leave the rest intact. And it is this in particular that needs to be questioned.

The task of simply documenting instances of misogyny in philosophy is fairly easy once one starts on it, and it is an essential preliminary. But there are more difficult questions that need asking. Are there cases where a philosophical view or theory would have had to be different if a different view of women had been adopted? Are there cases in which philosophical views or theories which are not *apparently* 'about' women at all are nevertheless inflected or influenced by a view of gender and gender relationships? Are there senses in which such theories can be seen as 'male' or 'masculine'?

A number of philosophers (mainly, though not exclusively, women) have begun to look at past philosophers and philosophical theories with these questions in mind, though their work is still often read only by feminists and rarely made generally accessible to philosophy students. Detailed studies have been made, for example, of the treatment of women in past political philosophy, and the new light this may cast on our understanding of the work of such philosophers as Plato, Descartes or Locke.[1] But feminist philosophers have also begun to try to develop a more general account of ways in which philosophy might be seen as 'male'. Some have argued that it is possible to identify in philosophy a cluster of views about knowledge, reason, human nature and the self which can be seen as expressing a typically or characteristically 'male point of view' that has tended to dominate philosophy. And they

have argued that it might similarly be possible to express a
female point of view, that there might be a 'female voice' in
philosophy which has yet to be really heard. One of the
objectives of this book is to examine the idea of male and
female 'voices' or points of view in philosophy and to ask
whether there are grounds for supposing not only that much
of philosophy is gender-inflected but that it is possible to
identify more general themes and concerns which can in
some way be seen as male or female.

Feminist thinking is, as I shall argue later, both anchored
in and, in various ways, critical of certain major
philosophical traditions. It confronts some important
tensions and contradictions which arise both out of women's
lives and out of the concepts and theories which feminists
have used to try and express and understand such tensions. I
am not aiming in this book to give a comprehensive or
detailed account of what individual philosophers have said
about women, or to give a full description of the theories in
which their views about women are located. Nor am I aiming
to offer a detailed survey of feminist theory. Other books
have gone a long way towards providing such accounts, and I
have referred to these in the Bibliography. Neither, on the
other hand, do I want simply to discuss discrete or separate
'topics' assumed to be of interest to feminists. There are,
again, other books which provide such discussion.[2] What I
hope to do, rather, is discuss what seem to me to be some of
these central themes and tensions in feminist thinking, and
their relationship to philosophy.

To talk of such 'tensions' is to suggest that feminist
thinking may confront concerns which it is difficult to see
how to reconcile, and may sometimes take directions which
either are or may appear to be in contradiction to each
other. Thus a concern for women's autonomy and
independence may lead to the conceptualising of such needs
in terms of a theory in which it is difficult to conceptualise
human interdependence; conversely, a concern to stress the
capacities of women for caring or empathy with others may
lead to the conceptualising of such capacities in terms of a
theory in which there seems to be little space for the needs of
the individual self. Such concerns and tensions are not, of

course, merely theoretical; they are also practical and political. Thus the tension between one's own needs and the demands of care for others is a central one in women's lives. But practical and political concerns may be conceptualised in different ways, and in the course of trying better to understand the situation of women, feminists have drawn on various political and philosophical theories and traditions which are themselves in tension or conflict with each other. At the same time, they have also been critical of many of these traditions.

I aim to explore some of these tensions, and in particular to look at those which centre on the idea of a specifically female philosophical viewpoint or perspective. Women have wanted autonomy, and have appealed to philosophical theories to express this, but some women have also argued that many conceptions of 'autonomy' are male-defined. They have wanted equality with men and have fought against their exclusion from theories put forward by men and from institutions dominated by men. But they have also expressed a profound ambivalence about that from which they have been excluded, and they have criticised the values and priorities which they have thought to be a function of the maleness of those theories and institutions. It is this ambivalence that has given rise both to the complexity of the relationship of feminism to philosophy and to the view that women have their own distinctive values, priorities and point of view, and that the aim of a feminist philosophy should be to put these forward. This book, therefore, has two main concerns. The primary one is to identify and discuss what seem to me to be central tensions in feminist thinking, and the way in which these have involved both a use and a critique of philosophical theories. And the second is to ask whether and in what sense philosophical views can be seen as 'male' or 'female', and to enquire into the implications this might have for feminist philosophical thinking.

1 Feminism and Philosophy

FEMINISM

It is not uncommon for people to ask the question 'What *is* feminism' and expect to be given a brief and clear definition in a sentence or so, which would enable them to look quickly at ideas, arguments, political convictions or programmes, and so forth, and say at a glance whether they should count as 'feminist'. I think that this is mistaken, and I shall start by explaining why.

Feminist ideas did not of course spring into being out of nowhere in the late 1960s, with the rise of the contemporary Women's Liberation Movement. They have a long history, some of which has sometimes been obscured by the tendency for the writings of women to be marginalised or consigned to invisibility or oblivion.[1] The consequence has been that those feminist writers whose works *are* relatively well known sometimes appear as isolated voices. In fact, however, there has been a strong tradition of feminist argument since at least the eighteenth century, and at no point have feminist writings or arguments disappeared entirely.

Eighteenth-century feminists such as Mary Wollstonecraft were concerned to question beliefs about women which they saw as false or damaging, and social practices which they saw as unjust and discriminatory. They raised questions about women's rights, about women's capacities and abilities, about the dependence of women on men, about the relationships that obtained, or ought to obtain, between women and men. But there are two related conditions of the

possibility of raising such questions. First, there has to be
what can be called 'social space' for the raising of such
questions; social conditions have to allow the possibility of at
least conceiving of a different way of life for women, or a
different way of regarding social relationships. Second,
there must be available some way of *conceptualising* the
situation of women as unjust and oppressive. And the
particular forms that feminist questions and concerns take
depend largely on changes in these things.

There were two things which made possible the more
systematic emergence of a tradition of feminist thinking in
the eighteenth century. First, there were the upheavals in
modes and methods of production and in social relationships
which were the consequence of what has become known as
the 'Industrial Revolution'; the decline of the old pattern of
a rural subsistence economy, in which production was
centred on the household or small community. The growth
of an urban economy, and the associated development of
capitalism, led to the increasing importance of an influential
middle class, many members of whom had in their lives both
the possibility of leisure and of the choice of a career or
profession. This led to an increasingly sharp split between
'home' and 'work', and a resultant tension in the lives of
many middle-class women.[2] Their lives were no longer
dominated by the exigencies of subsistence agricultural and
domestic production. But at the same time, their economic
dependence on men was increased, and they were more or
less totally excluded from most of the professions and
occupations that were open to men.

The second factor which underpinned the emergence of
feminist thinking was the growth of egalitarian political
ideals. European politics and political thought in the
eighteenth century was dominated by the fight against
absolute monarchy, aristocracy and political tyranny. The
question which preoccupied many political philosophers was
that of the rights and powers of states or governments over
their subjects, and of the grounds of political obligation.
Why should one obey the ruler? Where should the
legitimate authority of the ruler end? Not all political
philosophers who asked these questions came up with

democratic or egalitarian answers. Thus the seventeenth-century philosopher Hobbes produced in his *Leviathan* a legitimation of absolute monarchy. Others, such as John Locke, argued in favour of a form of representative government based on property ownership. But the ideas that were most influential in the emergence of feminism were the libertarian and egalitarian political ideals that underlay the American and French Revolutions; conceptions of the 'Rights of Man', not only to property, but, as stated in the American Declaration of Independence, to 'life, liberty and the pursuit of happiness'.

Who this 'Man' was who possessed these rights was a question that could not be long avoided. For one thing, many early conceptions of the 'Rights of Man' simply meant property-owning man, and it took a long struggle before a principle such as that of universal male suffrage was accepted. But what was abundantly clear was that the 'Rights of Man' did not include woman.

Political egalitarian ideals stressed the themes of liberty, justice and equality. But there was also a stress not merely on an individual's political rights and freedoms but also on his autonomy as a *rational* being, one who could act on the clear light of reason and preserve his independence of mind and ability to make autonomous judgements. And, just as women were politically excluded from the 'Rights of Man', so they were normally (as in many previous philosophies) excluded from rationality. Unlike men, they were beings who had the potential for neither rationality nor autonomy.

The 'agenda' for the writings of Mary Wollstonecraft was set not merely by her own experiences of unhappiness and oppression but by the central themes of the political and philosophical beliefs and controversies of her time. The main targets of her attack were the philosophers Edmund Burke and Jean-Jacques Rousseau. Burke had written a political and philosophical critique of the libertarian and egalitarian ideals underlying the French Revolution. Wollstonecraft wrote a defence of these ideals called *A Vindication of the Rights of Man,* and in all her philosophical writings she espoused passionately the doctrine of 'natural rights'. The birthright of man, she argued, was a degree of liberty compatible with the liberties of other individuals. And what gave men these rights was the power of reason, which Wollstonecraft distinguished from mere 'sense' or 'sensual taste' and saw as the quality which distinguished human beings from 'brutes'.

In *A Vindication of the Rights of Woman,* Wollstonecraft argued that there was no sound or logical reason for excluding women from political rights, or regarding them as incapable of reason. One of her main targets here was Rousseau. In his political philosophy, Rousseau's supreme value was that of freedom; servitude of any form was what most degraded man. In the *Discourses* Rousseau presented his analysis of how and why human servitude had come about, and in the *Social Contract* he offered a conception of a form of government in which it would be possible for a citizen both to follow the 'general will' and at the same time to obey himself alone. In *Emile* Rousseau discussed the sorts of principles that he thought should underly the education of the boy Emile; above all, he thought it essential that Emile should preserve his independence of mind and spirit. His virtues were to be those of hardiness of body and mind, independence of the judgements and opinions of others, and a carefully nurtured autonomy and self-sufficiency.

But when Rousseau turned to write about the education of the girl Sophie, Emile's companion-to-be, it was a very different story. Sophie was to be educated with the sole aim of pleasing Emile. Everything that she did or learned was to be undertaken with the aim of making her a pleasing companion who would be compliant and obedient to Emile, always virtuous and chaste. Her abilities to reason were only inportant insofar as they contributed to this. Virtue or excellence was quite different for a woman than for a man. And it was this idea above all that Wollstonecraft rejected. Human virtues or excellence, she argued, should be just that; human, and not dependent on sex. If, as Wollstonecraft thought, the most important and distinctively human characteristic was that of reason, then it was in no way justifiable to exclude women from the exercise of this capacity or to set up a different standard of excellence for women. Wollstonecraft believed that there was much truth in the accusations made by men that women were often irrational, swayed by sense and feeling; and she somctimes evinced an irritation bordering on contempt for what she saw as the limitations of her own sex. But she ascribed these limitations to the circumstances of women's lives and their lack both of education and motivation to improve themselves by developing their rational capacities. Wollstonecraft believed strongly in the possibility of the improvement or perfectibility of human beings by the exercise of reason.

Since the time of Wollstonecraft, feminist questions and concerns have always had a dialectical relationship to dominant or influential philosophical or political traditions; they have both used but also been critical of them. Wollstonecraft asked why the 'Rights of Man' did not include women. But there were many questions asked by later feminists which could not easily be raised within the tradition of thought which shaped her work. She did not, for example, ask questions about class and assumed the existence of domestic servants in the lives of middle-class women. She did not ask questions about sexuality, and despite her own extremely difficult and unhappy experiences of marriage and childbearing, did not really ask questions about the institution of marriage as such. Her conception of the 'human nature' which she thought both men and women should realise is one in which sex and gender are seen as 'accidental' or contingent factors which are irrelevant to becoming fully 'human'.

The tradition of liberal, egalitarian thinking in which Wollstonecraft's work was anchored has been, and remains, central to feminism. It still underlies many political programmes such as that of achieving equal rights or equal opportunities for women. But there are two other traditions which are of equal importance in understanding the development of feminist thinking. They are the traditions of Marxism and psychoanalysis. Marxism made possible the idea of women as an oppressed *class,* and it raised questions about the relationship of women's oppression to class oppression. It made possible the discussion of 'ideology'; of the ways in which theories about human nature or social relationships might be used to legitimate the interests of a ruling or dominant group, and thereby justify or reinforce oppression, and the ways in which liberal or egalitarian political ideals might themselves sometimes serve to disguise the existence of other forms of inequality or oppression. Freud's theories raised questions about sexuality and identity, and about the psychological construction of masculinity and femininity which have been central to twentieth-century feminism.

Feminists have of course often criticised the theories of Freud and Marx, frequently to the extent of denying that they are relevant or useful at all to understanding the situation of women.[3] Others have argued that a Marxist or psychoanalytic framework of ideas can, if suitably modified, provide crucial insights into the subordination of women and into the construction of ideologies of masculinity and feminity.[4] But traditions such as Marxism and psychoanalysis are in tension with each other, not just with feminism. Some tensions in feminist thinking can be seen as related to the tensions and contradictions within the traditions of thought against which feminist ideas have to be understood. But feminists have often argued that the problem with such traditions is not simply that they do not always provide adequate answers to the questions they ask, but that they omit or marginalise important questions which need to be asked if the situation of women is to be understood or changed.

I have argued that changing social conditions led to the possibility of raising questions about women's situation. They lead also to the prominence of particular questions at particular times; to the centrality in feminist thinking of certain issues or concerns. A central concern of twentieth-century feminism, for example, has been the question of the role of women as mothers, and a central criticism that feminists have made of all the traditions of thinking that I have mentioned has been of their failure to see motherhood as a *problem*, their tendency simply to confine women to it or regard it as the special province of women without question.[5]

The removal of production from the home and women's

confinement to the home in the nineteenth century led to the increasing definition of women (or at least middle-class women) as mothers. Mothering was above all what women *did*, and many of the most dominant nineteenth- and twentieth-century images of women have centred around woman as mother. Now, working-class women had undertaken wage-labour since the inception of the Industrial Revolution, but during the twentieth century, women began to enter the workforce in increasing numbers. The decline of infant mortality and the increasing availability of more or less efficient contraception, made it possible for women to devote much less of their lives to having or rearing children, or even to consider having none at all, without necessarily forgoing a sexual relationship with a man.

Much of the libertarian political critique of the 1960s was anti-family. Prominent figures such as the psychiatrist R.D. Laing, moved from arguing in *Sanity, Madness and the Family* (with A. Esterson, 1964) that certain particular sorts of family nexus oppressed some of the family members, to arguing, in his *The Politics of Experience* (1967), that all parental relationships were oppressive, were violence masquerading as love. Popular tracts such as *The Greening of America,* by Charles Reich (1970) depicted middle-class family life as repressed and 'uptight'. Many experiments in collective or communal living were undertaken. All of these things coalesced with the criticisms that some women had been making for a long time that women were 'trapped' within the family and by their responsibilities for mothering; and when, frequently, in the radical politics of the 1960s, women were *still* left holding the baby and doing all the domestic chores, many women exploded with anger. And there has been since then a strand in feminist thinking which rejects motherhood and everything associated with it as the basic mechanism of women's subordination. Shulamith Firestone (1970) argued that while women continued to bear babies, they would inevitably be subordinate and oppressed, and that the solution lay in extra-uterine reproduction and new forms of communal living. More recently Jeffner Allen (1984) has argued that motherhood annihilates women, and that it should, at least for a time, be totally rejected: 'A mother is she whose body is used as a resource to reproduce men and the world of men...Motherhood is dangerous to women because it continues the structure within which females must be women and mothers, and, conversely, because it denies to females the creation of a subjectivity and world that is open and free' (p.315). To become a mother at all is to capitulate to patriarchy: 'identification with any single aspect of the motherhood continuum, is an identification with every aspect of the motherhood continuum, for no single aspect exists as separate from the whole of its context' (p.320). To be a mother is to obliterate one's freedom to choose and define oneself and one's own life.

Many women, however, continued to wish to be mothers, and many girls saw and continue to see their futures largely in terms of marriage and motherhood, partly at least because the sorts of paid labour available to many women seem only to be something one would undertake out of necessity, and if motherhood is an option, it seems a preferable one. But the wish to bear a child was something which was faced also by women who identified strongly with feminism. Many younger feminists, who were perhaps in their twenties in the 1960s, became conscious of the desire to have a child in the 1970s, and of the fact that the time in which to do so might be running out. Quite a large number of feminist activists and writers had a child in their thirties, often as a 'single parent'. And many, of course, made a conscious decision not to.

The publication in 1976 of Adrienne Rich's book *Of Woman Born* marked, I think, something of a watershed in feminist thinking. Rich distinguished between motherhood as 'experience' and motherhood as 'institution', and she asked whether the experience of bearing and caring for children did not, despite its frequent isolation and oppressiveness, give women certain strengths and capacities, as well as rewards. Since the publication of Rich's book, a great deal has been written by feminists about mothering, and much of it has been a response not merely to the conflicts and problems about their role as mothers that women have faced but also to the recognition that being dismissive or derogatory about motherhood can be divisive, and alienating and threatening to women who have spent much of their lives being mothers.

Women have indeed often lacked the sort of access to power and material resources that men have had, and they have been victims of male power and brutality. But a picture of history which presents it solely as 'man-made' and woman as mere victim is not *so* different from the sort of history (often rightly criticised by feminists) which relegates 'women' to a brief chapter or a few footnotes. Writers such as Adrienne Rich have argued that despite the constraints and limitations of their lives, women have often developed female networks of skills, friendship and support which have sometimes taken the form of an implicit critique of the priorities of the 'public' male world from which they were largely excluded or in which they were relatively powerless. Women's 'world' may often have been small scale, concerned largely with the care of children and the physical and emotional maintenance of household or family. But a number of feminists have argued that the historical concerns and priorities of women have provided a source for a female critique of the values and concerns of the 'public' world which has been mainly the preserve of men; for a typically or distinctively female approach to ethical questions, to questions about knowledge and to questions about political goals and the means by which these should be achieved.

The debate about women's mothering thus points, I think, to a central tension in feminist thinking, and to the reason why it is impossible to offer a brief definition of feminism. There are many feminists who have wanted, as far as possible, to see women as genderless 'persons', as sexless bearers of 'human' rights. Wollstonecraft, as I have said, argued that virtue was the same in a woman as in a man. There are of course occasions when sex *has* to be seen as relevant to campaigns for women's rights; thus the fact that women and not men become pregnant means, for example, that special provision needs to be made for this in any legislation concerning equal rights or opportunities or sexual discrimination. Nevertheless, the fundamental programme of many feminist campaigns has been that women should be allowed to participate or compete with men on equal terms, and that women's failure to do this should be blamed on the injustices from which they have suffered, and their own psychological 'conditioning' to avoid competing with men.

But there is also an important strand in feminist thinking which has wanted to stress the importance of male/female difference and which wants in some way to celebrate rather than deny this difference. Some feminists have felt strongly that what is needed cannot be conceptualised simply in terms of justice or equality for women, but that in some way women are in a position that may hopefully enable them to offer a critique, not only of the injustice done to them but also of the ways in which male-dominated institutions and beliefs and social practices are more generally oppressive or damaging. Programmes, it is argued, which simply aim at 'equal rights' for women, or which adhere to some supposedly 'universal' ideal of human nature, fail to recognise the ways in which such ideals are usually *male* ones or the ways in which the social practices and institutions within which women want equality express or reflect a male point of view. Many feminist writers have therefore tried to offer an analysis of what it means to talk about a belief or a theory or a social practice as 'male', and what this 'maleness' consists in. And they have tried to give an account of a 'female point of view'; thus it has been argued that women think differently from men about moral issues, that there is a typically or distinctively *female ethic* whose values and concerns and priorities are different from male ones. It has been argued that women *reason* differently and that there is an approach to knowledge which can be seen in some way as female. It has been argued that women think about questions of *self* and problems of *identity* in a different way. And it has been argued that the importance of identifying such female views or perspectives is not merely that they should be given parity of esteem, as it were, with male views, but that they provide a basis for a critique of the ways in which male views have tended to be damaging, dangerous and destructive.

Conceptions of a distinctively female perspective are sometimes linked to a belief in some ultimate biologically based differences between men and women. More commonly, though, they are related to a conception of differences in male and female *experience* of the world, which it is thought give rise to different values, priorities and fundamental concerns. Thus it has been argued, for example, that women's experience both of mothering and of being mothered by women, gives rise to priorities which challenge male tendencies to subordinate 'personal' considerations to 'abstract' causes, or to regard violence and destruction as legitimate means for achieving ends.

Now there are immense problems with the ideas of distinctively male or female points of view which surface constantly in feminist writing. How does one try, in the first place, to set about identifying these, and is there any evidence that there *is* such a thing as a typically female point of view? Talk of male and female points of view constantly runs, in particular, into the following dangers.

1. The danger of a 'false universalism'; that is, the too easy assumption that it is possible to talk about 'men' or 'women' as such, without sufficient regard to things like historical difference, class difference, ethnic difference, and so forth.
2. The danger of idealisation of the idea of a female point of view; the idea that women are somehow naturally virtuous and men naturally wicked, or that insofar as there *are* things which might plausibly be identified as characteristically female qualities, that these have remained totally 'uncorrupted' or undistorted by women's frequent powerlessness and dependence. Sometimes, too an idealisation of femaleness is combined with an image of women as *totally* degraded by 'patriarchy', as mere victims, living in servitude or slavery.
3. The idea that women are locked into female experience which is self-authenticating, a female 'reality' which is self-validating and quite exclusive of male 'reality'. Linked with this is the belief that virtually all previous thought is 'male' and should therefore be rejected; that a women's point of view is almost spontaneously self-generating from female experience.

Furthermore, even if it can be argued that there are some

characteristically female qualities, priorities or concerns, the
problem always arises of how to conceptualise or describe
these. The story of female difference is, after all, an old one.
Time and again supposed differences between women and
men have been marked by such dichotomies or polarisations
as emotion/reason, concrete/abstract, universal/particular,
in ways that were not only conceptually questionable but
served to justify or reinforce views of male superiority, or
beliefs that the male exemplified 'true humanness' more
than the female.

The sorts of questions and tensions that I have described
above are reflected both in women's lives and in feminist
thinking. Women are faced with choices and conflicts which
often create profound tension and ambivalence. They feel
unjustly treated and excluded, yet may have profound
doubts about the value of that from which they are excluded.
Motherhood may be the source of great joy, yet also the site
of the most intense conflicts and frustrations. The demands
of care and love for others can seem absolute, but so also can
the demands of self for autonomy, for privacy, for space to
pursue one's own goals. Feminist thinking is anchored in
these sorts of experiences of women, and itself faces the
same tensions and contradictions.

My aim in this book is to explore some of these tensions
and contradictions, and the ways in which they are both
anchored in and suggest a critique of some traditions of
philosophical thinking. In particular, I want to ask whether a
sense can be given to the idea of female difference, a
feminist approach to philosophical problems, which avoids
the sorts of dangers and difficulties which I have mentioned
above (and shall discuss further later): which neither
idealises women nor assumes some overgeneralised and
ahistorical view of a 'woman's voice'. And I want also to try
to give a sense to the idea of the 'maleness' of philosophy
without lapsing into ahistorical generalisations about things
such as 'masculinity', and without distorting or
oversimplifying the history of philosophy itself.

It might, however, still be insisted that despite the
varieties of feminist theory and practice, there must be
something which distinguishes a feminist position or

viewpoint, some essential condition such a viewpoint must fulfil before it can be described as 'feminist'. In a way, I think this is right, but before I say in what way, I will describe two approaches to this question which I think are mistaken.

The first mistake is to restrict the term 'feminist' to someone whose beliefs, practices or life-style follow a very specific pattern; and the reason it is a mistake is that it is both divisive and tends to imply that clear answers are available where it would usually be better to recognise how problematic both the questions and the answers are. The term 'feminist' has sometimes become something like an honorary label, which is ascribed or denied on the basis of whether someone's views or practice coincide closely with that of a particular group, and it has led to questions about whether or not someone is 'really' a feminist which are divisive and exclusive. Such divisiveness and exclusiveness is sometimes a consequence of a particular theoretical view; thus, if one believes that to be a mother or to have a sexual relationship of any kind with a man is inevitably to 'sell out to patriarchy', to be totally co-opted by 'the system', then a woman who does either of these things cannot 'really' be a feminist. And I think the right response to such views is not only to point to their divisiveness but also to criticise the crudity and specious clarity of the analyses of women's situation that they present.

But there is a kind of response to this narrowness and exclusiveness which is itself just as problematic. An example is the approach of Janet Radcliffe Richards in her book, *The Sceptical Feminist* (1980).[6] Radcliffe Richards is aware of the differences among feminists and rightly worried by the divisiveness of conceptions of feminism which tie it too closely to particular beliefs or practice. But her response is to try to establish what can be called a 'consensual' version of feminism; that is to say, one on which all 'reasonable' people might be able to come to agree. And she hopes in this way to make feminism more acceptable and 'attractive'.

Feminists, Radcliffe Richards argues, are often seen as committed to particular *theories* about what kinds of thing are wrong with women's situation, whose fault it is and what

should be done to put matters right. They are also often seen
as committed to particular *ideologies and activities,* such as
the forswearing of feminity of appearance, belief in the
oppressiveness of families, and so forth. These sorts of
things, however, she regards as *inessential* to feminism.
What is *essential* to feminism is simply the belief that women
are badly treated and that they suffer from systematic social
injustice because of their sex.

Now I think it is right to say that for any viewpoint to
count as feminist it must believe that women have been
oppressed and unjustly treated and that something needs to
be done about this. But it does not follow from this that any
consensus is available as to the precise forms this oppression
or injustice takes, or as to how they should be remedied.
Radcliffe Richards distinguishes between the 'general' belief
that women are badly treated and 'particular' beliefs about
why this is so. The trouble is, however, that if one tries to
make out a 'general' or 'essential' case for feminism which is
supposed to be attractive to all 'reasonable' people, one of
two things will happen. Either this consensual version of
feminism will be empty or it will support a particular point of
view under the guise of a neutral or uncommitted
'reasonableness'. The reasons are as follows. Any belief that
women are badly or unjustly treated is quite empty and
useless as a basis for action unless one spells out the
particular forms one thinks this injustice or bad treatment
has taken. But the 'facts' about injustice to women do not
just lie to hand, available on inspection to any 'reasonable'
observer. What one regards as reasonable, what one sees as
harmful to women, what directions one sees for change,
depends on the concepts and theories which are used
(explicitly or implicitly) to make sense of experience, to try
and understand the situation of women. And in Radcliffe
Richards' book, what tends to happen is that conclusions
which are in fact the outcome of particular ways of
understanding social relationships and particular political
choices are misleadingly presented *as if* they were the
outcome of a neutral and consensual 'reasonableness'.
(Thus, for example, she argues that since parents *choose* to
have children, there is no good reason why others should

pay for them, and that welfare benefits should be means-tested.) But this is not, as she suggests, a merely 'reasonable' solution which somehow transcends politics; it is directly in line with a view of the state, of welfare, of the ways in which human needs should be met which is necessarily a political one.

Feminism is, therefore, a response to a belief that women have been oppressed and unjustly treated, and sometimes also to a belief that they have available to them more than to men certain resources for developing a critique of the damaging and destructive aspects of human institutions and social relationships, and for tracing the links between these things and the subordination of women to men. But the nature of this response varies, and cannot be delineated in an ahistorical or consensual way. This is not a counsel of despair. Feminists can and do make common cause on many things; conceptions of the nature of women's oppression and the strategies needed to change it intersect at many points. Thus feminists of very different persuasions have made common cause on issues such as abortion, welfare rights, equal opportunities and opposition to discrimination, the provision of adequate nursery care, and so forth. But the tensions in feminist thinking reflect, as I have said, the tensions in women's lives and the changing and varied nature of women's experience, and there is not, nor do I think there is likely to be, any unanimity in the results of efforts to resolve these tensions. What is required, I think, is a resolute effort to recognise and resolve them, combined with a recognition of the difficulty and complexity of so doing, and a respect for those strategies of resolution which might differ from one's own.

PHILOSOPHY

Just as it is not possible to give a brief definition of feminism, so it is not possible to define philosophy in a sentence or so. The conception of philosophy as a relatively autonomous 'discipline' with its own professionals or specialists is a relatively recent one, and is partly at least a function of the modern development of institutions of higher education, especially universities, in the nineteenth century. Before the nineteenth century there was not the same sharp distinction made, for example, between 'philosophy' and 'science'. In medieval philosophy, it would not have been possible to distinguish sharply between philosophy and theology. There have been great historical changes in the lives and roles of those who are usually now seen as 'philosophers', and their own conceptions of their intellectual activities have varied immensely.

Nevertheless, despite such historical changes, I think it is clearly possible and useful to see some historical continuities and common threads in the questions to which philosophers have addressed themselves. And it seems to me that there are three groups of questions, three sorts of concerns to which philosophers have addressed themselves which are of central relevance to feminism. To talk of a 'group' of questions should not be taken to imply that the questions always have the same background or meaning when asked in different historical periods. One cannot assume, for example, that concepts such as 'body' or 'mind' have a constant meaning throughout history, or that when Plato asked questions about human knowledge and reason his concerns were exactly the same as those of Hume or Kant. Despite this, however, I think that certain central concerns of philosophy can be identified.

First, philosophers have been concerned to ask questions about human knowledge and human reason. They have asked what sorts of things human beings can know, and how they can come to know them; how true knowledge can be distinguished from mere belief or opinion. They have asked about the relationship of the knower to what is known. They have asked about the nature of human reason, and about its limits; about the relationship between reason and faith, and between reason and human passions or desires.

Second, they have asked questions about human nature. What is it that particularly distinguishes human beings from other animals, and what capacities are most distinctively human? Which human potentialities are the most important or desirable to develop? How should we think about the human soul or the human self? Is it possible to identify the most basic or fundamental desires, needs or motivations of human beings?

Third, they have asked questions about the goals or well-being both of social life and of individual human beings. What constitutes human well-being or happiness, and is happiness important in human life? What are the virtues to which human beings should aspire? What is a 'good' society, and what sorts of social and political arrangements are likely to be most conducive to this? How is the good of individual human beings related to the good of society as a whole?

Identifying the central concerns of philosophy in this sort of way means that it is not always possible to make absolutely sharp distinctions between those who are or are not 'philosophers'. Take the work of Freud, for example. Freud is not usually seen as a 'philosopher', but as a psychoanalyst. Yet his work constantly raises questions about human reason, human nature and the human self and the constraints these place on human social arrangements. Sharp demarcations between academic disciplines are often a function of the need, given institutional academic structures, to demarcate particular territories for academic expertise. In this book, whilst I shall discuss the work of those conventionally seen as 'philosophers', I shall also include where relevant the work of others who have addressed themselves to the sorts of questions that I have outlined above.

When asking questions about human reason or human virtue or the nature of the good society, philosophers have mostly tried to come up with substantive answers to these questions. That is to say, they have thought it their task to try to set up or define norms or standards of what virtue or reason is, or of how human beings should live. The reason it is important to note this is that, at least in the English-speaking academic world, there has been an influential tradition in the twentieth century which has thought of philosophy rather differently. And this view of philosophy has underpinned some conceptions of the relationship between feminism and philosophy. So I want now to outline it and explain why I disagree with it.

The best way of understanding this view is to look at an example, and I have chosen a book called *Problems of Political Philosophy* by D. Raphael. The revised edition of the book was published in 1976, and it is a textbook-style introduction to political philosophy.

The first chapter is called 'What Is Political Philosophy', and in it Raphael sets out his conception of philosophy. He argues that although political philosophers are best known for their attempts to describe the ideal state, this enterprise is not really central to what they have tried to do. Rather, they have been primarily concerned with the critical evaluation of beliefs and the clarification of concepts. The critical evaluation of beliefs involves the attempt to give rational grounds for accepting or rejecting beliefs which we might normally take for granted. But there are, Raphael says, two sorts of criteria for judging beliefs or systems of beliefs. The first is whether they are internally consistent or coherent. The second is whether they accord with the facts. And, he argues, 'While philosophers are well qualified to test consistency, they are in no special position to say what the relevant facts are. Their speciality is clear thinking, not factual investigation' (p.8).

So what sort of 'clear thinking' is it that philosophers are supposed to be especially good at? Raphael sees their job (and his book) as an exercise in the clarification of concepts. The objective is that we will all be clear about the meanings of the words that we use and so be less prone to fall into muddles and confusion. The task has several aspects. Raphael mentions *analysis,* or specifying the 'elements' of a concept, such as offering a definition of 'the state'. Then there is *synthesis,* or the showing of logical relations between concepts. Finally, there is *improvement,* which Raphael sees as the process of recommending a definition or use that will assist clarity or coherence and enable us to talk much more clearly about the state or about democracy, liberty or equality. The job of philosophy is *not* to decide between competing ideals of politics or political life, and Raphael sees philosophy and the philosopher as politically neutral. And he compares philosophy to house-cleaning; it clears away the mental rubbish and confusion that has accumulated. And, as with house-cleaning, there is not a great deal to be seen for the philosopher's labours; it is just that everything is a bit tidier. Fortunately for the career prospects of philosophers, however, just as houses need cleaning often, so does 'mental clearance' need to be done regularly: 'Cleaning the house is not a job that can be done once and for all. You have to do it every week. The mere business of living continues to produce more rubbish, which has to be cleared regularly' (p.16).

What are the assumptions that lie behind this view of philosophy? One of the most important is concealed by Raphael's use of the word 'we'. He is interested in how people might be able to resolve their political disagreements. Some disagreements may, he thinks, be about 'the facts', and these result simply from lack of information. People may also disagree about their political ideals or values; thus, he says, some people may 'rate' liberty more highly than equality. But he sees a lot of disagreement as arising from the sort of confusion that philosophy can sort out. If only we all did enough conceptual house-cleaning, we might all at least agree about the meanings of the words that we use.

But who are 'we'? To bring out the problems here, consider Raphael's definition of the state. The state, he says, is an association which is organised for the pursuit of specified common purposes, and it has certain agreed functions: 'Its primary function is to settle and prevent conflict or, to put it another way, the keeping of order and the maintenance of security' (p.46). In addition to that: 'The newer, positive function of the modern state may be described as the promotion of welfare and justice' (p.48). Raphael therefore sees the state as organised so as to increase the well-being of its members and make the distribution of rights among them more fair. While the state has coercive powers, its power is quite different from that of 'armed robbers or bullies', since it is based on the rule of law. Raphael therefore argues that the state operates in 'our' interests, and that we need it to guard against the effects of human weakness and individual crime or irresponsibility. He recognises that there might be unjust laws, but sees this as a remediable and accidental defect. By and large, the state does us good.

Now all of this is presented as a piece of 'neutral' conceptual or philosophical analysis; it is supposed to tell us what we *mean* by 'the state', but not to adopt any particular political viewpoint. Compare Raphael's view of the state, however, with that of Harold Laski. The state, Laski (1934) argued, is not a neutral umpire, arbitrating impartially between competing groups: 'It does not stand over and above the conflicting groups judging impartially between them. By its very nature, it is simply coercive power used to protect the system of rights and duties of one process of economic relationship from invasion by another class which seeks to change them in the interests of another process' (p.118). The welfare policies of modern capitalist states, Laski argued, were simply concessions made by the ruling class in order to preserve its own power as far as possible.

Laski is writing here from a Marxist perspective. The Marxist tradition sees state power as a repressive instrument used in the interests of the ruling class. And it offers a very different picture of society from that of Raphael. Raphael writes, for example, about the 'communities' and 'associations' that people belong to, as if the relationships between people were all voluntarily and consensually chosen. He dismisses any notions that institutions themselves might be oppressive with the simple assertion that individual human beings are not all that nasty. The notion that some groups of people might oppress other groups, or that such oppression might be a structural feature of a social system and not merely a local or accidental distortion or the result of individual 'nastiness', does not enter into Raphael's scheme of things.

Now, no amount of 'mental house-cleaning' is going to resolve this sort of dispute about the state. It is indeed an important philosophical task to map out and investigate the meanings and associations that particular concepts have in certain contexts; to be clear, for example, about the way Raphael himself is using the concept of 'the state'. But Raphael assumes a sharp distinction between 'facts' and values'; as if we can all *first* agree about the meanings of the words that we use, and *then* go on to consider the facts. But 'facts' are not separable from 'values' in this sort of way. Consider, for example, the situation in Northern Ireland, or the Greenham protest against Cruise missiles. What often happens is that there is a *dominant* discourse in which events are described, the language, perhaps, of 'terrorists' and 'gunmen', of 'extremists' and 'agitators', of 'hysterical women' or 'filthy lesbians', and that this language is used in institutionally powerful contexts *as if* it were simply common sense and based on an assumed consensual 'right-mindedness'. Those who differ are then presented as irrational, as unbalanced, as extreme (rather as Raphael dismisses as simply muddle-headed those who see state power as oppressive).

The important thing to grasp is that the discussion of 'meanings' or of 'concepts' cannot be divorced from consideration of the 'facts' to which they apply. Thus to describe someone as a 'terrorist' is *already* to have made a political judgement or evaluation of the situation; to define the state as that which acts in 'our' interests is *already* to have committed oneself to a particular view of society.

Philosophers have indeed often asked questions about meaning and attempted to offer definitions of knowledge, justice, liberty, and so forth. In the dialogues of Plato, Socrates is constantly asking questions such as 'What is justice?' – and trying to show how the first definitions offered by his friends are inadequate. But Plato's view of 'justice' was based on the idea of hierarchy, both in the individual soul and in the state. The 'just' state was one in which different classes or orders of people fulfilled their proper functions, and the 'just' soul was one in which the lower aspects obeyed the higher. Such a view of 'justice' is quite different, for example, from a view which sees a just society as one in which people can compete with others on equal terms for the desirable things of life. But such views of what 'justice' is are not intelligible simply as opinions about the meanings of a word, which can be discussed in abstraction from 'facts' or from 'values'. They are only intelligible in the light of certain understandings of social relationships and of human nature, and in the light of certain

beliefs about desirable social goals. There is no 'real' or
'fundamental' meaning of 'justice' or of 'the state' which
some process of 'conceptual analysis', all by itself, can
discover.

Now some conceptions of the relationship between
feminism and philosophy have operated with a view of
philosophy which is very similar to that of Raphael. I
referred previously to Janet Radcliffe Richards' book, *The
Sceptical Feminist* (1980); here is what she says about
feminism and philosophy:

> Feminism on the whole is still relatively little concerned with philosophy.
> It tends to be preoccupied with debates about what might broadly be
> called factual matters: the history of women's oppression, differential
> treatment of girls and boys, the effect expectation has on performance,
> economics and power, women's role in children's books, male sexual
> fantasy, anthropological studies of women, political methods and so on.
> Disagreements are of a kind to be decided by further empirical evidence.
> Philosophical questions, in contrast with these questions about matters of
> fact, can be classified roughly as those whose solution has nothing to do
> with empirical matters, but depends on reasoning; on techniques like
> finding contradictions, showing what follows from what, exposing
> ambiguities, working out presuppositions, clarifying confusions and so on.
> These techniques are rather neglected in feminism, but they are extremely
> important: they are needed to deal with the most fundamental issues [p.4]

Radcliffe Richards therefore sees philosophy as a matter of
technique; of learning how to think clearly and argue
logically. Philosophy can clean up the conceptual house of
feminism; it can sort out the muddles and confusions from
which feminist arguments suffer, since feminists are so often
not clear about the meanings or implications of the concepts
they use and the views that they hold. This conception of
philosophy is identical to that of Raphael. And, as in the
case of Raphael, Richards' approach to philosophy leads to
her presenting political conclusions as if they were the
outcome of a supposedly neutral or apolitical philosophical
analysis.

Similarly, it leads sometimes to an uncritical acceptance of
the sorts of terms in which issues are currently or
commonsensically discussed. Thus, in a chapter entitled
'The unadorned feminist', she argues, among other things,

that the rejection of 'femininity' of appearance by some feminists is misguided. It is, she argues, simply an unfortunate fact of nature that some women are more beautiful than others, even if standards of beauty in the past have been too high and should come down. It is also a fact of nature that men will tend to make for physically attractive women, and there is nothing wrong about that (provided that the men care about the women's other qualities as well). All men, she suggests, other things being equal, would really prefer their women to look like the centre-fold from *Playboy*.

In a comment on this chapter, Radcliffe Richards (1982) writes as follows: 'It is concerned not with current or any other ideals of sensuality...but with logical questions about sensuality and such things in general' (p.42). By 'logical questions', she presumably means questions about what the concept of 'sensuality' does or does not entail, about what its relationships are with other concepts. And the mistake she makes is to suppose that there *is* some 'real' or 'essential' meaning of a term like 'sensuality', which can be discussed by philosophers in abstraction from any of its historical manifestations.

Meanings are not just *given*; they are not timeless things which have a 'logic' which can be investigated by a process of dehistoricised conceptual analysis.[7] Consider, for example, the concept of sexuality. Freud devoted a great deal of his work to discussing the concept of sexuality. And he should, I think, be read as making a *proposal* about what we should take the word 'sexuality' to mean (in much the same sense as Plato was making a proposal about the meaning of 'justice'). He was neither simply offering a definition of what he took the word 'sexuality' to mean nor simply describing empirical discoveries about its nature. He was, rather, proposing that in the light of a complex array of discoveries and investigations in such things as biology, psychoanalysis and child observation, we should redefine the word by reorganising the phenomena. Thus Freud's theories suggest that we should see things in new ways (e.g. the relation between adult 'perversions' and modes of infantile sexuality), that we should notice things which had not been

noticed before, see as important that which had previously
been seen as unimportant.

Radcliffe Richards is using a form of discourse about
sexuality, sensuality, attractiveness, and so forth, that is
closely related to conceptions of sexual relationships as a
kind of 'market' in which we all 'make for' the most
attractive people and compete for them, and in which the
ways in which women are supposed to 'attract' men are quite
different from the ways in which men 'attract' women. And,
again, it is indeed important to understand and analyse how
such terms are used in these ways. But because of her
assumption that concepts such as 'sensuality' have some sort
of timeless and ahistorical logic ('sensuality as such'), what
she tends to do is see as 'facts of nature' things which are,
rather, the product of certain forms of social relationships
and of the sorts of discourse to which these give rise. And
what she fails to recognise is the need for any real critique of
the sorts of language in which issues about sexuality and
sensuality are discussed; the way, for example, in which in
much current discourse, notions of sensuality and of
conventional feminity are conflated, or in which the
asymmetries of notions of sexual 'attraction' often define
men as sexual predators who hunt women.

An essential task for a feminist approach to philosophy,
therefore, is to consider critically the sorts of discourse in
which issues important to women are discussed, and the
sorts of concepts which are assumed to be relevant or central
to those issues. Consider, for example, the debate about
abortion. It has often been pointed out how loaded the
language of those who oppose abortion is; the use, for
example, of words such as 'killing' and 'murder', and the
assumption of the 'selfishness' of the woman who does not
want to bear the child. But language which does not appear
to be loaded like this may nevertheless serve to conceal
crucial issues under the guise of an abstract moral argument.

A good example of this is the approach to the ethics of
abortion suggested by the philosopher Richard Hare (in
Baker and Elliston, 1975). Sometimes arguments about
abortion have centred around the question of whether or not
the foetus is a person. Sometimes they have centred around

the concept of 'rights': does the foetus have rights, and if so
how are these to be weighed against the rights of the
mother? Hare rejects both of these approaches. He argues
that the concept of 'rights' is too problematic and that of a
'person' too indeterminate to serve as a basis for arguing
about the morality of abortion. But he proposes another
principle which he thinks can serve as a guide, and it is a
version of what he calls 'the golden rule' – that we should do
to others what we would wish them to do to us (or what we
are glad they once did to us). Therefore, he suggests, if we
are glad we are alive, we are enjoined not to terminate any
pregnancy which will result in the birth of a person having a
life like ours; and even if we are *not* glad we are alive, there
is still no reason for aborting those who would or might be
glad.

I discussed earlier the way in which Raphael refers to what
'we' think and what is in 'our' interests in his discussion of
the state, and suggested that this sort of use of 'we' may
serve to conceal the fact of differences in power, or the
oppression of one social group by another. Very similarly,
throughout his article on abortion, Hare refers to what 'we'
ought to do, and to the principles on which 'we' ought to
decide. He writes almost as if *both* men and women bore
children, and at no point does he discuss the sorts of radical
asymmetry between the social situations of men and women
which make the abortion issue such a crucial one. There is
no discussion of the reasons why women often want
abortions, of the conditions in which they may often have to
bring up children, often with sole responsibility for them.
There is no discussion of the power structures which operate
in the question of abortion, of the control exercised by the
(mostly male) medical profession. As Mary Daly has argued
(Daly,1973, pp.106-14), arguments about abortion which
see it simply as a question of moral principle usually make
hidden false assumptions. In particular, they assume that
men and women have equal roles in the reproductive
process, that women have an equal voice with men in the
decisions that most affect their lives, that women have free
choice in their sexual behaviour and its consequences and
that they have adequate and safe means of birth control.

These false assumptions, these absences from the argument of these features of women's situation, are hidden behind Hare's 'we'. 'We' are assumed to be a community of equals who have simply to make moral decisions. Abstracted from the argument is all reference to the ways in which we are *not* in fact equal, and to the ways in which decisions about abortion have to be made in the concrete circumstances of women's lives.

In her chapter on abortion, Janet Radcliffe Richards does in fact recognise that the sorts of 'moral' arguments put forward against abortion may sometimes be seen as a cover for other things. They might, for example, be seen as a rationalisation of a male desire to control women in general and their fertility in particular. There are many cases where ideas and arguments can be seen as providing a rationalisation for the interests of a powerful or dominant group in this sort of way. Thus, for example, the arguments of many doctors from the nineteenth century onwards about the incompetence and inferiority of midwives, or the need for highly technologised intervention in the processes of birth, may often be seen as a rationalisation for the attempt to establish and maintain the control or hegemony of a male-dominated medical profession. There are also cases where beliefs may be seen as a defence against the fears of a group. Barbara Ehrenreich (1983) has suggested, for instance, that the strong moral opposition to abortion which is maintained by many women may be read as based on a fear that sexual freedom for women, especially in conditions of economic uncertainty or insecurity, will undermine 'the family' and further erode male responsibility for its support.

Feminism therefore needs a critical relationship to the language in which issues are discussed, but this critical relationship is not just a question of 'clear thinking', conceived of merely as technique. Of course feminists need to think clearly, but they also need to be critical of some conceptions of what 'thinking clearly' amounts to. In particular, they need to be critical of those prevalent or dominant or 'commonsense' forms of discourse which appear to set the only possible parameters in which an issue can 'reasonably' be discussed but which in fact operate to disguise inequality or reinforce oppression or subordination. It may be 'commonsense' to suppose that state power is exercised in 'our' interests or that men will always 'make for' attractive women; but underlying such prevalent or commonsense views are concepts and beliefs that can be challenged and assumptions that may be concealed and need bringing out into the open. The view that philosophy is merely a question of 'techniques' of clear thinking, and that philosophical discussion can be aimed at clarifying concepts without reference to questions of 'fact' or of 'value', has an inbuilt tendency to remain uncritical of current or commonsense concepts and beliefs.

I think, too, that there is another consequence of the conception of philosophy as technique. Richards writes that up until now feminists have been relatively little concerned with philosophy, and her conception of philosophy suggests that it is something that feminists can either take or leave (except that they had better take it if they want to think clearly). But I think that this radically misrepresents the relationship between feminism and philosophy. For one thing, a historical look at feminist thinking shows how this has (as in the case of Mary Wollstonecraft) been anchored in philosophical traditions which put forward views of reason, of human nature, and so forth. Philosophy is not something which feminists can just take or leave; philosophical questions are an intrinsic aspect of feminist thought and action. I have argued that philosophical theories and philosophical proposals about meaning cannot be understood in isolation from the beliefs about human beings and human society or the visions of human well-being and the good society on which they depend. But the reverse is also true. That is to say, the 'facts' about the situation of women cannot even be identified, let alone understood, without the concepts and theories which articulate these facts and make sense of them to us.

Feminists are necessarily concerned with the sorts of questions about human nature, human knowledge and reason, and human potentialities and well-being which have been the concern of philosophers. Feminist arguments have used concepts such as liberty, justice, equality, oppression and liberation, concepts of human nature and the self, of male and female nature, which are closely related to philosophical and political traditions. The varieties of feminist practice presuppose different views of these things, however implicitly. There are no 'facts' about women which simply speak for themselves in advance of some form of conceptual organisation. In this sense feminists cannot avoid engaging with philosophical questions and issues.

To say that feminism necessarily engages in this way with philosophy is not of course to say that the institutionally based ways in which philosophy is studied and practised should not be criticised. I have already mentioned, for example, the frequent absence of any recognition or discussion of gender-related issues in philosophy courses. But many feminists have been critical and suspicious of 'theory' in general, and of academic theorising in particular.

These criticisms and suspicions have a number of sources. The most important, I think, is the way in which many women have found that theories put forward by 'experts' (mostly male) are often signally discrepant with their own experience. Thus women have been told how they do (or should) experience sexuality, motherhood, domestic labour. They have been told by male experts how they should bring up their children. They have been told (indirectly) by historians that their lives are of little significance and often worth not much more than a passing reference. They have been told that they are sick, or at least not truly feminine, if they question or fail to conform to the norms which have been supposed to govern women's lives. It is therefore not surprising that contemporary feminism has stressed the importance of women's experience and the ways in which this may be used to challenge theories which seem to offer false or distorted accounts of it. The stress on experience has also led to the distrust of an élitism of expertise, of any division of labour in which there are some who are the experts, the skilled, who know more, especially since those who 'know' have so often been men.

In Chapter 3, I shall discuss some problems concerning the notion of 'experience' and the way in which it has figured in some feminist discourse. The feminist emphasis on experience has also sometimes led to a belief that the domination of intellectual enquiries such as philosophy by males has led to their being 'male' in form and content. Philosophy, it has been argued, has been based on male experience of the world; it is male created and male dominated, and its concerns and theories have therefore reflected a male view of the world. It is this conception of philosophy as male that I shall now turn to look at.

2 The 'Maleness' of Philosophy

The idea that a discipline such as philosophy might be 'gendered' in some way is one that has been explored in a considerable amount of feminist writing; it is one, too, that is still often greeted with great scepticism. I think that it is right to say that much of philosophy has been 'male' in some important senses, but it is not at all easy to say what those senses are. So in this chapter I shall explore what it might mean to talk of the 'maleness' of philosophy and look at some ways of describing and explaining this 'maleness' that seem to me to be problematic.

There are two things to note at the outset, both of which are true, but neither of which establish the 'maleness' of philosophy in any really important sense. The first is that most of the practitioners of philosophy have been, and still are male. There may well be female philosophical work which has been relegated to oblivion and not survived, and there have certainly been women who had an interest in philosophy but were prevented by institutional arrangements from making the most of that interest. Nevertheless, the dominance of males is clear. But it does not follow from this *alone* that philosophical theories can be seen as male in any interesting sense; that if women had done more philosophy they would have done it differently; that any sort of distinctively male perspective or viewpoint can be identified.

Second, there is no doubt about the way in which most male philosophers have devalued women, believed them to be inferior or held them in contempt. The history of the views of male philosophers about women is a dreary one of misogyny which is easy to document. Here are some examples:

As between male and female, the former is by nature superior and ruler, the latter inferior and subject.
Aristotle   *Politics*

Women are directly fitted for acting as the nurses and teaches of our early childhood by the fact that they are themselves childish, frivolous and short-sighted; in a word, they are big children all their life long.
Schopenhauer   *On Women*

Here at its origin we grasp one of the most fundamental tendencies of human reality – the tendency to fill... A good part of our life is passed in plugging in holes, in filling empty places, in realising and symbolically establishing a plenitude...It is only from this standpoint that we can pass on to sexuality. The obscenity of the feminine sex is that of everything which 'gapes open'.
Sartre   *Being and Nothingness*

Sentiments such as these, or similar, can be reduplicated from the work of many male philosophers.[1] But again, this sort of misogyny is not in itself enough to establish the 'maleness' of philosophy in any philosophically important sense. The reason is this. Not *all* views that philosophers hold about *anything* are necessarily of relevance to interpreting or understanding their philosophical theories. Berkeley, for example, held views about the health-giving properties of tar water, which it would be implausible to see as connected to his philosophical idealism. It is not easy to see how Bertrand Russell's opinions about marriage could be seen as relating to his theory of knowledge. In other words, one cannot simply *assume* that the opinions philosophers hold about women affect or are integral to the rest of their philosophical work. A case has to be made out for this.

How, then, might one begin to make out such a case? The most useful starting point, I think, is to consider the ways in which women have been *excluded* by many philosophers from philosophical ideals of such things as human nature and morality, and the inconsistencies and problems this may generate in their theories. Sometimes this exclusion is absolutely explicit. Sometimes, however, a philosophical theory or ideal may *appear* to be 'genderless'; that is, it may make no reference at all to women or men, and may purport to be about all human beings. In such cases, what needs asking is whether this appearance is in any way misleading, and whether there is any reason to believe that the theory implicitly excludes women. If it does, what would happen if one tried to *include* women, and what does this show about the theory? Could it have remained just the same? I want now to look at some examples of what happens if these questions are asked. I stress that they are merely examples; the same questions should of course be asked of other theories and philosophers as well.

THE EXPLICIT EXCLUSION OF WOMEN FROM PHILOSOPHICAL THEORIES

In the work of many philosophers, conceptions of what is a good life for human beings are anchored in conceptions of what it is to be 'fully human'. Sometimes this humanness has been characterised by trying to identify what are seen to be the *distinguishing* marks of human beings – those things which differentiate human beings from other species. Aristotle is a case in point. Much of his philosophy is based on the assumption that everything which exists can be seen as existing for a reason or an end. To understand this end, we have to identify the *function* of a thing, and its function resides in its nature, in that which distinguishes it from other things and makes it the sort of thing that it is. Aristotle assumes that, just as the individual parts of the human body have a function, or just as the harp player has a function – namely, to play the harp as well as possible – so human beings have a function, which is to develop their special talent or excellence. We will find what this function is when we find what it is that distinguishes human beings from other species.

The mere act of living, Aristotle says, the facts of nurture and growth and the experience of sensations, are shared by humans with other species. What distinguishes human beings is their reason. Hence, he concludes, the function of human beings is to exercise their non-corporeal faculties or 'soul' in accordance with a principle of reason. And central to the capacity for reason is the faculty of speech. So, he says, in the *Politics:*

Nature, as we say, does nothing without some purpose, and she has endowed humans alone among animals with the power of speech. Speech is something different from voice, which is possessed by other animals also and used by them to express pain or pleasure, for their nature does indeed enable them not only to feel pleasure and pain but to communicate their feelings to each other. Speech, on the other hand, serves to indicate what is useful and what is harmful, and so also what is just and what is unjust. For the real difference between humans and animals is that humans alone have perceptions of good and evil, just and unjust. [p.60]

So the distinguishing mark of human beings lies in their power of reasoning, which is related to the faculty of speech. It is 'according to Nature'; that is to say, it is consonant with the function or special mark of humanness that the body should be ruled by the soul:

The living creature consists in the first place of mind and body, and of these the former is ruler by nature, the latter ruled...It is clear that it is both natural and expedient for the body to be ruled by the soul, and for the emotional part of our Nature to be ruled by the mind, the part which possesses Reason [p.68]

There were however, according to Aristotle, certain classes of human beings who were excluded from the full exercise of human reason; namely, slaves and women. Slaves he regarded basically as a form of property: 'Any piece of property can be regarded as a tool enabling a man to live, and his property is an assemblage of such tools; a slave is a sort of living piece of property, and like any other servant is a tool in charge of other tools' [p.64]. The life of a slave is simply a means to an end, that of enabling the master to pursue a life of freedom and virtue among the other male citizens of the city state or polis. The life of a woman was similarly functional; the wife of a male citizen was needed to produce heirs and, like slaves, to play a part in providing the necessities of life. Aristotle also expressed this by saying that the family or household (to which women and slaves were confined), existed 'for the sake of' the *polis*. It was an inferior though necessary form of association, whose rationale lay in its providing the means for free males to live a life devoted to intellectual and political pursuits. Aristotle, however, recognised a difficulty with his exclusion of women and slaves from the life of reason, and the way in which he tried to cope with it is revealing of the assumptions from which he starts.

The problem is this. Women and slaves are, after all, human beings. They do not lack speech, and the adequate performance of their functions will surely require capacities for reason, and perhaps certain virtues. Here is how he expresses the problem:

About slaves, the first question to be asked is whether, in addition to their virtues as tools or servants, they have another and more valuable one. Can they possess restraint, courage, justice, and every other condition of that kind, or have they in fact nothing but the serviceable quality of their persons? The question may be answered in either of two ways, but both present a difficulty. If we say that slaves have these virtues, how then will they differ from free men? If we say that they have not, the position is anomalous, since they are human beings and share in reason. Roughly the same question can be put in relation to wife and child. [p.94]

Aristotle's solution to this problem is to argue that the *type* of knowledge possessed by slaves (and presumably, women) was a special type. The fully rational part of the soul, the 'deliberative faculty' was not present at all in slaves and was ineffective in females. The knowledge and virtue of slaves and women consisted in knowing how to be ruled and how to perform their allotted tasks, and this did not qualify as fully rational.

Now this view of women and slaves, combined with Aristotle's belief that it is 'natural' for the rational part of the soul to rule the irrational, generates an anomaly in Aristotle's philosophy and points to some assumptions that underly it. The anomaly has been discussed in detail by Elizabeth Spelman (1983), and it arises as follows. Aristotle compared the rule of the mind over the body to the rule of a master or free man over a slave. He believed that there was a class of 'natural rulers'; that is to say, those whom nature had intended to rule. But he did *not* believe that everyone who was born into this natural ruling class necessarily possessed the qualities of mind and character to fit them for this task. There were free males in whom the rational part of the soul did *not* rule. In the case of such people, Aristotle would argue that the rational part of the soul *should* rule the irrational, that it was natural and fitting that this should be so. He could not, however, argue this in the case of women or slaves, since this would be undermining the sharp distinction between the rulers and those who should be ruled. This is tantamount, Spelman suggests, to saying that women are by nature unnatural. What Aristotle does is to offer a general theory of human nature and about the proper relationship between body and soul, and then simply excludes certain classes of human beings from this 'human nature' in ways which cannot be explained at all within the theory, and which generate the sort of anomaly I have described above.

The whole of Aristotle's political philosophy is based on the assumption that one class of human beings — namely free males — should lead a life that he sees as self-justifying or as lived for its own sake, and that others should lead a life that is merely a means to this. And he consistently regards women as defective, inferior beings, almost as a degenerate form of human life. This comes out very clearly in his biology. Aristotle believed that the female supplied the 'matter' in conception, and he thought this to consist of the menstrual fluid. The male, on the other hand, supplied the 'form' or 'soul', via the emission of semen. He believed the male to be superior in possessing more 'vital heat' than the female; semen, he thought, was a 'concoction' of the blood which was superior in all respects (though analagous to) the menstrual fluid. Females were inferior because of their inability to 'concoct' semen. Female embryos were inferior to male ones; if a girl child was born, it was an indication of the inferiority of the state of the uterus. Aristotle regarded the female state as being a sort of deformity, although one which occurred in the ordinary course of nature. Aristotle, of course, did not have available to him modern biological knowledge about conception. But the assumption of the inferiority of the female in no way follows from his purely biological assumptions; these would have been quite compatible with the assumption of an equally important part played by both males and females in conception.[2]

Aristotle therefore sees women as inferior and deficient. But there is sometimes a tension between this and the fact that he also wants to see women (and, of course, slaves) as fitted or suited for the roles that they play. This tension is very common in the history f philosophy. On the one hand, women are seen as inferior, as lacking whatever capacities it is supposed exemplify some ideal of excellence. On the other hand, women are seen as possessing their *own* virtues, or their *own* special forms of skill or excellence. These special female virtues or skills are seen as necessary for the female role. They may also (though not in the case of Aristotle) be seen as charming or delightful or valuable, they may even sometimes be praised to the skies, and not apparently or officially regarded as inferior at all. If one reads such views of women, however, in the context of more general assumptions about human nature or morality or social life, it is usually the case that women's virtues are seen as lesser, and that the fullest or truest forms of excellence are reserved for men. Conversely, if one reads some philosophical accounts of these in the light of a philosopher's views about women, it can be argued that they are 'gendered', even though they may not on the face of it appear to refer only to men or make a distinction between the sexes. And I want now to illustrate this by looking at the relationship between Kant's view of morality and his views about women.

THE IMPLICIT EXCLUSION OF WOMEN FROM PHILOSOPHICAL THEORIES

Kant wrote a paper, which is not, I think, very often brought to the attention of students, called 'Of the Distinction between the Beautiful and the Sublime in the Interrelations of the Two Sexes'. In it, he differentiates sharply between male and female characteristics and abilities. Here is a list of the ways in which Kant describes men, and the sorts of characteristics and capacities that he ascribes to them (or, rather, potential characteristics, since Kant does not think that all men actually exemplify them): noble; deep; sublime; surmounting difficulties; deep meditation; sustained reflection; laborious learning; profundity; abstract speculation; fundamental understanding; reason; universal rules; capable of principles. And here is a list of those he thinks applicable to women: delicate; beautiful; modest; sympathy; compassion; fair; charming; finer feeling; study of humankind (especially man); pleasant diversions; sense; sensitivity; feelings; benevolence; complaisance; particular judgements; incapable of principles.

There are a number of things which are unclear about Kant's account of women in this paper. First, it is not clear to what extent he is saying that women are *unable* to reason in ways that men can, and to what extent he is saying that they *should* not. Sometimes he explicitly picks out what he sees as female disabilities; thus he says that he does not believe the 'fair sex' to be capable of principles. At other times he writes as if he believes that women are *capable* of intellectual pursuits, but must not distort or pervert their femininity by pursuing them. Thus he suggests that if a woman fills her head full of Greek or mechanics, she might as well have a beard; that is to say, she will be a freak or monstrosity. This ambivalence about whether it is supposed that women are *incapable* of certain intellectual pursuits or whether it is supposed that they will simply spoil their femininity if they pursue them, is common both in philosophy and elsewhere.

The second thing which is unclear is whether Kant is or is not saying in this paper that women are inferior. He would himself, I think, have resisted very strongly the suggestion that he believed women to be *generally* inferior to men. He intended to talk about what he saw as the *complementary* virtues of each sex. If accused of believing women to be inferior, Kant would, I think, have replied that he thought women were simply different, with their own particular virtues, without which the world would be a bleak place.

It is at this point that there is a need to place this essay about women in the context of other aspects of Kant's work, especially his moral philosophy. One question that Kant tried to answer was that of what gave an action what he called 'moral worth'. Human beings do many things for many different reasons; Kant saw the moral worth of an action as residing in the motives out of which an action was performed, and he believed that only a certain sort of motive could qualify as truly moral. Here is what he says about 'moral worth' in *Groundwork of the Metaphysic of Morals* (Paton, 1948):

To help others where one can is a duty, and besides this there are many spirits of so sympathetic a temper that, without any further motive of vanity or self-interest, they find an inner pleasure in spreading happiness around them, and can take delight in the contentment of others as their own work. Yet I maintain that in such a case an action of this kind, however right and however amiable it may be, has still no genuinely moral worth. It stands on the same footing as other inclinations – for example, the inclination for honour, which if fortunate enough to hit on something beneficial and right and consequently honourable, deserves praise and encouragement, but not esteem; for its maxim lacks moral content; namely, the performance of such actions, not from inclination, but *from duty*. Suppose then that the mind of this friend of man were overclouded by sorrows of his own which extinguished all sympathy with the fate of others, but that he still had the power to help them in distress, though no longer stirred by the need of others because sufficiently occupied with his own; and suppose that, when no longer moved by any inclination, he tears himself out of this deadly insensibility and does the action without inclination for the sake of duty alone; then for the first time his action has its genuine moral worth. Still further; if nature had implanted little sympathy in this or that man's heart; if (being in other respects an honest fellow) he were cold in temperament and indifferent to the sufferings of others – perhaps because, being endowed with the special gift of patience and robust endurance in his own sufferings, he assumed the like in others, or even demanded it; if such a man (who would in truth not be the worst product of Nature) were not exactly fashioned by her to be a philanthropist, would he not still find in himself a source from which he might draw a worth far higher than any that a good natured temperament can have? Assuredly he would. It is precisely in this that the worth of character begins to show – a moral worth and beyond all comparison the highest – namely that he does good, not from inclination, but from duty. (pp.63-4)

I am not aiming here to discuss the reasons why Kant thought that the only truly moral actions were those which were performed out of duty. What I want to point out is the striking similarity between what he says about moral worth and what he elsewhere characterises as masculine, and the striking lack of connection between the virtues he ascribes to females and what he describes in the passage above as the highest form of character. Sympathy, feeling, sensitivity, compassion, are all seen as irrelevant to the moral worth of an action. Kant is not in fact saying that the possession of these things *detracts* from the moral worth of an action. Thus a moral person can be a compassionate one as well. But it is only insofar as a person acts out of duty that they can be described as moral.

To act out of duty, for Kant, necessarily involved acting out of *principle,* and one of the main aims of his moral philosophy was to try and identify a universal principle which could serve as the cornerstone for all morally right action. But he did not see females as capable of acting on principle. If we therefore map some central features of Kant's moral philosophy onto what he says elsewhere about women, the notion that he is simply talking about female *difference* wears a little thin. If women are incapable of principles, then they are incapable of the highest form of virtue, and are therefore inferior to men.

There is a clear sense, then, in which aspects of Kant's moral philosophy might be seen as 'masculine'. Like Aristotle, he in effect excludes women from a philosophical ideal, this time of 'moral worth'. Aristotle overtly and explicitly excludes women, and runs into difficulties in trying to make this exclusion coherent and justifiable. Kant's exclusion is implicit; he does not even discuss the question of gender directly in his main writings on moral philosophy. But in a way Kant's exclusion of women is less arbitrary than that of Aristotle. And the reason is that the ideal of moral worth *itself* encapsulates qualities seen as paradigmatically masculine, and excludes those seen as feminine. A conception or ideal of what it is to be masculine is written into a philosophical theory or ideal.

This is common in the history of philosophy, and I will give one more example here. It comes not from the work of a male philosopher at all, but from Simone de Beauvoir. *The Second Sex* (1949) is one of the most influential and perceptive feminist books ever written and is a source of immensely powerful and detailed analysis of the processes by which women are schooled into subordination to, and dependence on, men. But de Beauvoir (following her mentor and companion, Jean-Paul Sartre), posited an ideal of autonomy and independence for women which can be seen, like Kant's theory of moral worth, to encapsulate an ideal of masculinity. Here is what she says about the upbringing of boys:

The great advantage enjoyed by the boy is that his mode of existence in relation to others leads him to assert his subjective freedom. His apprenticeship for life consists in free movement towards the outside world; he contends in hardihood or independence with other boys; he scorns girls. Climbing trees, fighting with his companions, facing them in rough games, he is aware of his body as a means for dominating nature, and as a weapon for fighting...He undertakes, he invents, he dares. [1972, p.307]

Girls, de Beauvoir argues, are denied this autonomy, they are taught instead to please others and to bend their will to that of others. They are taught coquetry and compliance, never to assert themselves or act independently. The upbringing of the boy, however, is not seen as problematic, and throughout *The Second Sex* de Beauvoir tends to regard the qualities and capacities which she sees as masculine as those which women should emulate or strive to attain.

A recognition of the relationship between ideals of such things as morality or autonomy and conceptions of masculinity and femininity should prompt some important questions. If it is a question of specific capacities or abilities, it is often very much to the point simply to argue or produce evidence that women are as capable as men; that they can, for example, do Greek or mechanics just as well as men, given the opportunity. If it is a question, however, of a more general cluster or syndrome of abilities or personality characteristics, such as those discussed by Kant or de Beauvoir, then we can ask why things such as sympathy or compassion should be regarded as of less value than abstract notions of duty, and whether there is not something distorted or restrictive about conceptions of moral worth or autonomy which exclude characteristics seen as female in this sort of way.

One approach to this sort of question is simply to argue that both men and women should *share* masculine and feminine characteristics. A good example of this sort of aproach is a book by Karl Stern called *The Flight from Woman* (1965). In this book, Stern discusses what he calls the 'female principle', which he sees as that of receiving, nurturing, nourishing, dependence on others, intuition and non-reflective relations with the world. He contrasts this with the 'male principle' of activism and intellectualism, which avoids feeling and stresses the life of reason. Stern was a psychiatrist and suggested that at the bottom of many neuroses among men lay a rejection of the feminine in themselves, a shying away from tenderness, dependence, feeling and passivity.[4] He saw the need for a re-evaluation of the 'feminine' and a recognition of the 'bisexuality' of each person.

The trouble with a view like that of Stern is that it still leaves uncriticised the whole association of particular qualities with the masculine and others with the feminine. In an article on Kant's moral philosophy, Larry Blum (1982) notes that Kant's list of feminine characteristics incorporates a wide range of very *differing* sorts of things (and the same is true of that of Stern). In particular, some of the 'virtues' that Kant ascribes to women seem to be *solely* to do either with pleasing or with being submissive to men. Thus the 'virtues' of charm and compliance are seen as virtues because they render women obedient and docile and pleasing in men's eyes. Blum asks why characteristics such as sympathy or sensitivity or compassion should be seen as intrinsically associated with obedience or docility. Similarly, Stern associates such things as tenderness and receptivity with dependence and passivity. Why cannot sensitivity, compassion and tenderness be associated with strength rather than weakness, independence rather than dependence, self-confidence rather than obedience or docility? De Beauvoir sees autonomy, freedom and self-definition as linked to an intrusive or aggressive style, to domination and subjugation, to fighting and violence, to competitiveness and scorn for others. Why should autonomy not be compatible with a *rejection* of domination and aggression, with a recognition of human interdependence, and of the need for care of others?

A response to the gender inflection or masculinism of philosophical theories should involve, I think, neither merely the assertion that women too should be seen as included under or capable of whatever norms are suggested by the theory, nor merely the assertion that what is seen as feminine should be valued too, or given equal status with what is seen as male. Rather, what is needed is a critique of the polarisation of masculine and feminine qualities, and in particular a critique of the way in which such qualities may be interpreted or clustered.

Later in the book I shall discuss in detail the idea of a 'female ethic' – the idea that there are certain values and characteristics which are typically or distinctively female and which in some way provide a corrective to, or grounds for, a critique of the male values and characteristics which are seen as having been dominant. Here I will simply note the importance of recognising that, even if there are good reasons for supposing that women do tend to differ psychologically from men in certain ways, these differences have often arisen in situations where women have been powerless and dependent. Consider, for example, Kant's view of the female virtue of sensitivity. According to Kant, women are especially good at understanding and interpreting human behaviour, particularly male behaviour. Now in a situation where a woman is totally dependent on a man for her support, and would be destitute without him, it may well be of crucial importance to her to please him constantly and to develop a sensitivity which is devoted to 'reading' his behaviour constantly in order to anticipate and meet his slightest whim. In a context like this, a virtue such as sensitivity may come to be associated with fear, with constant self-denial, with a feeling that the wishes of others must always be given priority.

Similarly, the self-assertion of a man, his conception of himself as autonomous, may sometimes (as de Beauvoir's account suggests) involve contempt for others, a tendency to be blind to their needs or wishes, an aggressive style, a projection of self which denies its own dependence on others. The problem, which is both a practical and political one and a philosophical one, is how to give an account of virtues such as sensitivity to others, or qualities such as autonomy, which avoid the distortions arising from situations of power or powerlessness. There is a tendency sometimes in feminist thinking, as I shall try to show later, either to idealise what are thought to be female qualities, or simply to throw them overboard in some way as a mere relic of oppression, and I think that both these tendencies should be resisted.

In the case of Aristotle, therefore, women are explicitly excluded from his norm of human nature, and the result is an anomaly, an inconsistency in his theory. In the case of Kant, there is no inconsistency; but that is because it can be argued that a conception of masculinity is built into the theory in the first place. And the question that needs asking is not merely why women should be excluded, but whether what they are excluded from represents an ideal of morality which we should accept, and whether the omission of characteristics seen as feminine leads to a distortion that needs correcting.

THE PROBLEM OF INCLUDING WOMEN IN PHILOSOPHICAL THEORIES

Could women be included in an Aristotelian theory of human nature or a Kantian theory of morality? To some extent I think that they could; Kant could, without inconsistency, have retained his view about 'moral worth', but changed his view of women. The case of Aristotle is more complex. If he had allowed women too the status of rational beings, it would have made impossible one of the major premises of his political theory; namely, the belief that some classes of human beings were destined to perform menial (and reproductive) labour in order that others might lead a life free from these things. In other words, Aristotle's philosophy could not remain unchanged if women were regarded as equal to men. One anomaly might have been removed, but it would have been at the cost of undermining the foundations of his whole political theory. Much the same is true of the political philosophy of John Locke.[5]

Locke assumes several things about women. He assumes a 'natural' inequality of the sexes, and a 'natural' authority of husband over wife. 'Natural' is here opposed to that which is a result of specific social arrangements; thus, to talk of 'natural' authority or inequality is to talk of that which is assumed to be given, a fact of nature, and not amenable to change. Locke sees the dependence of women on men, and the authority of men over women, as arising from the fact that women have the role of bearing children. He sees this role as necessarily generating female economic dependence on men and loss of autonomy with respect to the right to control property. When Locke discusses women, he in fact discusses married women; he assumes that women will marry and have children, and that their reproductive and marital role is the only important aspect of their lives that needs discussion.

In his political philosophy in general, Locke aimed to establish the rights of citizens against the arbitrary powers of absolute monarchs or tyrants who thought they could dispose of the lives and property of their subjects at will. He was particularly concerned about the question of property. What gave a man (and it is only men that Locke was talking about) a right to appropriation, to property, was, Locke thought, the fact that he had contributed by his labour to the product. And Locke was concerned to defend the exclusive right of males to hold on to and dispose of their property as they wished – normally to their legitimate heirs. The 'natural rights' that he defended were those of life, liberty and property; the property was to be under the individual control of male heads of families.

Unlike men, however, women did not, in Locke's view, have the right to dispose of the fruits of their productive labour and the theory that the contribution of labour generates a right to appropriation is forgotten in their case. The right to appropriation is only a male right. Women had, according to Locke, certain very limited rights over the property they might have brought into a marriage with them, but they were to have no legal say at all in the disposition of any of the products of their own or their husband's labour during the marriage.

Locke would, as I have said, have justified this economic dependence and powerlessness of women as necessitated by their childbearing function. Lorenne Clark (1979) has argued, however, that this sort of appeal to the 'naturalness' of women's subordination to men really serves to conceal the true importance to Locke's political philosophy of the dependence of women. The point is, she argues, that the objective of ensuring male control over property *requires* keeping women in an inferior and dependent position, and, especially, requires male control over reproduction. If men are concerned to pass on their property to their legitimate heirs, they will see a need for a guarantee of the legitimacy of those heirs, and this can only be achieved if women are restricted within monogamous marriage and deprived of any autonomy outside it.

Equality in marriage, Clark argues, and the economic independence of women, is not compatible with a system of property distribution based on an exclusive male right to dispose of family property. If women were to be independent, such a system would be bound to collapse. But since Locke's political philosophy proposes just such a system, it could not consistently recognise the equality of women. In other words, the inequality and dependence of women is a structural feature of Locke's political theory, and of the objectives that this theory was intended to achieve. It is not an 'accidental' or peripheral feature which can be easily removed, leaving the rest of the theory intact. It is not a question of mere 'prejudice' against women, which can easily be discounted. And it is surprising how, in most of the 'standard' commentaries on Locke, this is not discussed at all. It is common to find discussion of problems in Locke's theory of how we 'consent' to government, in his view of property rights, in his theory of natural rights. But one of the most fundamental and integral features of his political philosophy, namely the exclusion of women, has apparently eluded the notice of most commentators.

I have argued that while the fact that most philosophers have been men and that many of them have expressed misogynistic views about women is not enough to establish that any of the theories they have put forward are masculine in any philosophically important sense, there are nevertheless important ways in which many philosophical theories *can* be seen as masculine. First, many of them exclude women, explicitly or implicitly. Second, some philosophical ideals and theories encapsulate ideals of masculinity; masculinity is, as it were, written into them. Third, the views that philosophers have held about women may sometimes be integral to the rest of their work; that is to say, the theories they put forward may, for example, be premised on a belief in the dependence and subordination of women, and may be incompatible with seeing women as equal to men.

A considerable amount of work has been done by feminist philosophers which has, I think, conclusively established these things, and shown as well how neglected they have been in most philosophical commentary and discussion, and how different the history of philosophy might look if they were taken into account. But some philosophers have made broader and rather different claims about the relationship between masculinity and philosophy, and it is these that I now want to look at.

IS THERE A TYPICALLY MALE POINT OF VIEW IN PHILOSOPHY?

The senses I identified above in which a philosophical theory might be seen as masculine do not necessarily imply any sort of historical constancy or similarity in the sorts of ideals of masculinity which may get written into philosophical theories. They do not necessarily imply that there are, throughout the history of philosophy, specific themes or views which can be seen as *typically* male. Nor do they suggest any particular sorts of reasons why male philosophers might hold the sorts of views that they do. It is the suggestion that there are such typically male beliefs or points of view, coupled with a theory as to why males hold them, that has characterised some recent feminist work.

The maleness of philosophy is not always seen as residing

in any explicit exclusion of women or genderisation of philosophical theories, nor in the intentions of philosophers. Take, for example, the philosophy of Descartes. As Genevieve Lloyd (1984) has pointed out, Descartes' belief that there was a distinctive method of reasoning which, if followed by any human being, would guarantee the discovery of truth, was in many ways egalitarian in intent. Descartes had no intention of excluding women (and one of his main philosophical correspondents was a woman). He wrote in the vernacular, not in Latin, which was in itself a way of expressing a belief that arriving at the truth did not depend on following the institutional procedures of the medieval schools, from which, of course, women had been excluded. And it is not easy to see an ideal of masculinity or femininity as written into Descartes' theory of knowledge in the way I have suggested it is in Kant's view of morality. The fact that women did not in practice have equal opportunities to men, and that the mind/body distinction which characterised Descartes' work has been used in more explicit theories of male/female difference, might therefore be seen as extraneous to Descartes' work, and as not justifying a view that Descartes' philosophy is in itself masculine in any way.

Descartes philosophy has, however, been seen as a prime example of a typically or paradigmatically male point of view in philosophy, despite his egalitarian intentions and despite the lack of evidence that any particular theory of masculinity is encapsulated in his view of knowledge. And I want now to look at how this has been argued.

I shall start by discussing an article by Sheila Ruth (1981) since I think it brings out clearly the general form of such arguments. Ruth argues that professional philosophers – including women who have identified with the male tradition – have tended to 'think like men'; that is to say, they have espoused theories or points of view which can be seen as typically male. But what does it mean to say that someone 'thinks like a man'? The answer that Ruth gives to this question is as follows.

First, she identifies what she sees as Western dichotomies or polarisations between the masculine and feminine. The masculine involves such qualities as competitiveness, aggression, power, dominance and courage. The ideal woman, on the other hand, is supposed to be tender, receptive and emotional, but not aggressive, dominant or intelligent. And since Western culture has placed an imperative on men not to be like women, men devalue and despise what is seen as feminine.

Second, Ruth argues that there are connections between these conceptions of masculinity and femininity and philosophical theories. I have already argued myself that there are cases in which such connections can be traced, using the example of Kant. Ruth's argument concerns not just the work of particular philosophers, however, but the whole of Western philosophy. She suggests that it is possible to identify dichotomies and oppositions in the history of philosophy which can be seen as based on the polarity between male and female, and a shunning of or contempt for the female. So, she says:

Flight from woman is flight from feeling, from experiencing, from the affective; it is flight into distance. It is mind–body split, priority of cognition over feeling, fear of ambiguity (loss of control), preference for deduction over induction, faith in systems rather than responses, pre-occupation with logic to the detriment of aesthetics, and so on. [1981, p.47]

Third, Ruth argues that the maleness of philosophy is related to male *experience* of the world.

Men and women express their consciousness not only in what they think, but in how they think. Men think, perceive, select, argue, justify, malely. *What* they have thought, *how* they have thought, world views and *Lebenswelten* imbedded necessarily in a male consciousness, become manifest in their intellectual constructions, their philosophies. That is perhaps as it should be. What should not be is the raising of these male constructs to the status of universals – the identification of male constructs with all allowable constructs, so that women cannot 'legitimately' think, perceive, select, argue etc. from their unique stance. [1981, p.47]

Now, there are some questions which arise from what Ruth says here that I shall return to in a later chapter; in particular, the notion of a radical split between the experience or 'stance' of women and men, and the belief that there are quite distinct male and female views of reality.

Here I want to consider what sort of male experience of the world might be thought to underlie what are identified as typically male points of view. Ruth does not say much about this. A number of other writers have done so, however, and have relied heavily on a particular theory of male experience which is based on the psychoanalytic work of Nancy Chodorow. So I shall now outline this theory and show how it has been used to give an account of the maleness of philosophy.

Object Relations Theory and Male Experience

The version of psychoanalytic theory which is used by Nancy Chodorow in her book *The Reproduction of Mothering* (1978) is known as 'object relations' theory.[6] Like Freud, object relations theorists see the period of infancy and early childhood as crucial in the development of the human self, and, like him, they stress the importance of unconscious mental processes. Unlike Freud, however, who saw the psychic development of human beings to be the result of the interplay between instincts, especially sexual instincts, and culture, object-relations theorists reject the absolute primacy of sexuality and the Freudian notion of instincts. Rather, they see the human self as something constructed out of social relationships; the term 'object relations' is used to signify the belief that aspects of these relationships become internalised, become 'internal objects' for the self, helping to constitute its very nature.

At birth, it is argued, the human infant is not yet a self. It is not fully capable of distinguishing itself from others or from the physical world, and there are as yet no clear boundaries between self and others or between self and the world. The process of becoming a self is one of drawing such boundaries, of differentiation and individuation, of learning both that one is a separate self, and learning what sort of self one is. This process happens via the development of such things as motor and manipulative skills, but most importantly via relationships with other human beings, especially those responsible for early primary care in infancy. The ways in which a person (largely unconsciously) comes to experience her or himself *as* a self will be crucially dependent on the nature of those early relationships.

Object relations theorists see this process of increasing differentiation and individuation as fraught with problems; in particular, that of achieving a balance between the necessary dependence on adults and need for psychic security, and the move towards separation and autonomy and the sense of self as an effective agent in the world. This can give rise to intensely conflicting and ambivalent emotions: fears of desertion and aloneness, but also hatred at what are seen as attempts to thwart moves towards separation. Fears of dependence can lead to the development of overrigid ego-boundaries, where other people are perceived as a threat and as needing to be controlled or dominated, and where there is a constant stress on one's autonomy and separation from others. Fears of autonomy or separation can lead to regression towards infantile forms of dependence and to an inability to develop a sense of oneself as an effective agent or as fully separate from others.

Most object relations theorists (such as the British psychoanalyst D. W. Winnicott) simply assumed that the early primary caretaker would be the mother, and they were not primarily interested in the question of gender differentiation in the psychic development of boys and girls. Chodorow, however, placed the question of gender differentiation at the centre of her work and asked how the psychoanalytic framework of object-relations theory might be used, with some modifications, to explain psychological differences between the development of men and women.

In a social system where mothers provide almost exclusive early care, children of both sexes have a primary relationship with the mother. It is in relation to her that an infant's sense of self will at first develop, and out of the initial sense of oneness with her that the processes of separation and individuation must begin. Chodorow argues that, given this initial relationship to the mother, and the father's absence from most primary care, boys tend to have a harder time establishing their identity as males. To achieve an identity as male is to be *different* from the mother, the person who is the ubiquitous presence in his early life and on whom he is at first totally emotionally and physically dependent. He has to define himself as like the 'absent' father, whose role in his life is so different, and who is 'out' and 'away' most of the time. Masculinity, membership of the community of men, is something over and against daily life, to be achieved in opposition to it, in escaping from the female world of the household. Given also the cultural stress on the importance and superiority of male pursuits and activities, the male develops a need to deny the power of women (and to fear it) – to devalue women and to assert his autonomy and separateness, to repress the early infantile experience of near-symbiotic relatedness to a woman. Becoming female, however, is a very different process. The girl, because of her continuing tie to the mother, cannot and does not need so thoroughly to repress her infantile experience or her relational capacities. She is more likely to define herself in relation to others. While she too may turn to her father for 'protection' from her mother, for escape from the initial sense of oneness, she continues to look to the concrete example of her mother as a model for her gender identity. Chodorow argues that, in the tones and nuances of their relationships with their children, mothers tend to regard and treat boys as 'other'; they are more likely to perceive girls almost as an extension of themselves, as not 'separate' in quite the same way as boys.

There are many questions that can be asked about Chodorow's account of gender differentiation,[7] but one is of particular importance here. It is not always clear how far Chodorow sees her thesis about psychological difference between males and females as depending on the existence of a particular sort of child-care or family life, or how far she sees it as dependent *simply* on the fact that women have been mainly responsible for the care of infants. I do not think that Chodorow really intends to put forward a thesis about the psychic development of males and females in all historical periods, and she criticises Freud, for example, for failing to recognise the historical specificity of the constellation of family relationships that he saw as underlying the Oedipus complex. On the other hand, there are points at which it is not difficult to read Chodorow as arguing that it is simply women's responsibility for child-care which is the crucial factor in the different psychic development of males and females. On this reading, Chodorow's work can be seen as suggesting an extremely sweeping sort of thesis about typical male and female development; and it is the one which seems to have been adopted in a number of recent accounts of masculinity in philosophy.

One of the most explicit of such accounts is that given by Jane Flax (1983). She argues that the psychic qualities of maleness which have resulted from infant upbringing being largely the responsibility of women have left their mark on philosophy; much of philosophy can be seen as the work of 'the patriarchal unconscious'. In her analysis of the work of individual philosophers, she is careful to make clear that she is not intending to present an account of any philosophers' work which sees their theories merely as the outcome of individual psychological characteristics or dilemmas. So the fact that Rousseau's mother died when he was an infant, and that he was brought up by his father and then by a whole succession of other caretakers, and that his childhood in no way fits the sort of 'nuclear family' model of Chodorow's account, does not invalidate the view that his philosophy can be seen as 'male'. Philosophy, Flax suggests, can be seen as a stream of social consciousness:

Thinking is a form of human activity which cannot be treated in isolation from other forms of human activity, including the forms of human activity which in turn shape the humans who think. Consequently philosophies will inevitably bear the imprint of the social relations out of which they and their creators arose...The very persistence and continuing importance of certain philosophies and philosophic issues can be treated as evidence of their congruence with fundamental social experiences and problems. Philosophy must at least resonate with central social and individual wishes and offer some solution to deeply felt problematics. [1983, pps 248-9].[8]

Flax argues that the fundamental social experiences and problems with which philosophy resonates are male, since philosophy has largely been produced by males and since males have had the power to have their ideas socially validated. And she puts forward an account of these fundamental male experiences which is based on that of Chodorow. Thus, she says:

The boy by age five will have repressed the 'female' parts of himself, his memories of his earliest experience and many relational capacities. He will have developed the 'normal contempt' for women that is a fundamental part of male identity under patriarchy...The boy deals with the ambivalence inherent in the separation-individuation process by denial (of having been related), by projection (women are bad; they cause these problems), and by domination (mastering fears and wishes for regression by controlling, depowering and/or devaluing the object). [1983, p.253]

So what are the characteristics of philosophical theories that Flax sees as answering to or resonating with male social experiences and problems. The following are the main ones she identifies.

1. A denial of the social and interactive character of human development; a stress on the separateness or isolation of human beings.
2. Forms of individualism which stress autonomy; for example, the autonomy of the individual will or the autonomy of the knower and the radical separation of the knower from what is known.
3. Oppositions between mind and body, reason and passion, reason and sense.
4. Themes of mastery, domination and control of the body, the passions or the senses; and fears about loss of control.
5. Fear of women and of anything that is seen to be associated with them; sexuality, nature, the body.
6. Devaluation of all that is associated with women, and a need not to be dependent on it.

Flax discusses the way in which these sorts of themes can be found in the work of four philosophers, Plato, Descartes, Hobbes and Rousseau. Plato is unusual among philosophers in that he allowed women a position of equality with men as 'Guardians' or rulers of his ideal state. The precise nature and implications of this apparent 'feminism' of Plato has been the subject of considerable debate (see, for example, Okin (1980) and Elshtain (1981)). Flax, however, does not discuss this aspect of Plato's philosophy. Instead she notes the themes of control of the passions and distrust of the senses, and the fear of disorder and chaos which underlay the static unity of the ideal state that Plato presented in the *Republic*. She notes his ideal of love as uncorrupted by materiality or the body, and of knowledge as being of the unchanging world of Forms, free from the shifting illusions of the senses. She discusses the imagery of the cave in the *Republic:* 'The imagery of the cave in the *Republic;* the world of shadows, of the Unconscious and of the womb, which the light of reason cannot penetrate or dispel, reveals the fear of regression to that pre-verbal state when feelings, the needs of the body and women (mothers) rule' (1983, p.257). She reads many aspects of Plato's philosophy as a *defence* against infantile wishes, and against women and all that is associated with them. And she argues similarly about Descartes. 'Descartes' philosophy can also be read as a desperate attempt to escape from the body, sexuality and the wiles of the Unconscious' (1983, p.258). Descartes' image of the self as created and maintained by thought, and as not dependent on any material thing, replicates, she suggests, a typically male fear of regression to an infantile state and a loss of autonomy and independence.

As for Hobbes and Rousseau, despite the differences between them, both, she argues, deny in different ways the primary relatedness to and dependence on the (female) caretaker in infancy. Of Hobbes' view of human beings in the state of nature, she says: 'It is only possible to view people in this way if an earlier period of nurturance and dependence is unsatisfactory and/or denied and repressed' (1983, p.261). Hobbes' human beings are rather like greedy infants locked into illusions of infantile omnipotence, and Hobbes' sovereign, the Leviathan, is rather like an externalised superego, whose task it is to restrain these infantile wishes. In Rousseau's philosophy, she points to his intense dislike and fear of dependence of any form, which he thought necessarily led to servitude and inequality. And she notes his fear of the power of women and his belief that this had at all costs to be restrained by patriarchal authority in the family.

There is no doubt about the fact that in the work of the philosophers discussed by Flax, women are seen as either subordinate or inferior or both. But these ways differ a great deal. And I think the problem with the sort of analysis of the maleness of philosophy that is given by Ruth or by Flax is that it tends to distort or do violence to history in general and the history of philosophy in particular. There are historical problems and complexities in talking about ideals of masculinity or femininity and about male experience and psychological development, and in generalising about 'Western philosophy' which I think are glossed over. I want now to discuss these, and then to explain what implications I think they have for the idea of specifically male or female points of view in philosophy.

Problems in Talking about Ideals of Masculinity or Femininity

Sheila Ruth's account of the maleness of philosophy suggests that it is possible to identify 'Western' conceptions of masculinity in a fairly straightforward way. But I think this should be questioned, for two reasons. First, conceptions of masculinity or femininity are complex and shifting things; they have varied historically and are not at all monolithic or homogeneous. Second, I think it can be argued that the sort of interest we ourselves have in the psychological characterisation of masculinity and femininity is itself historically relatively recent.

There is of course plenty of evidence, apart from common experience, that ideals of masculinity and femininity are different. An example of such evidence is provided by the *Hite Report* on male sexuality (Hite, 1981b). Shere Hite and her colleagues devised questionnaires which were answered, often in great detail, by over 7,000 men of widely varying classes, ages and ethnic groups. When asked what they understood by 'masculinity' or 'being a man', the most commonly referred to characteristics were: being self-assured, unafraid, in control, self-sufficient, not dependent. The next most frequently mentioned were qualities of success, dominance, leadership, being a good provider. When asked what they admired most about women, however, the qualities most often mentioned, apart from physical characteristics, were: being helpful, loving, nurturing, sweet, supportive.

However, there is also evidence that conceptions of masculinity may vary – according to class, for example. In a book called *Learning to Labour,* Paul Willis (1977) described a rebellious (and male) 'counter-school culture' in a school in the Midlands. The conception of masculinity adhered to by these boys stressed such things as toughness, 'making' girls and boasting of sexual prowess, but it also included a contempt for academic or book work, a belief that only manual labour was 'man's work' and that anything else was 'cissy'. It is interesting to compare the evidence from Willis' book with that from Liam Hudson's book *Contrary Imaginations (1966),* which was a study of English public schoolboys. The study was not specifically about masculinity or femininity, but it showed nevertheless that certain forms of intellectual activity tended to be seen as more masculine than others, especially science. It did not, however, reveal any contempt by the boys for mental labour as such, as opposed to manual labour. One of the commonest candidates for a typically male theme in philosophy has been what is seen as a stress on abstract reason at the expense of experience or feeling. But such a conception of 'typical' maleness has difficulty in doing justice to the sorts of differences highlighted by the studies of Willis and Hudson. Ideals of masculinity are variable and contested things, and although at certain times and among certain social groups specific and relatively homogeneous ideals can be identified, these are not historically constant.

There is plenty of evidence of historical variability, and here I will simply give an example from Plato. It is from his dialogue, the *Symposium*. In this dialogue, guests at a dinner party, including Socrates, are discussing the nature of love. It becomes clear that the love of women is regarded as a second-rate thing. One of the guests, Pausanias, talks of the 'earthly Aphrodite' who governs the passions of the vulgar who are attracted by women as much as by boys. Sex itself is seen as a vulgar and dangerous distraction from the pursuit of truth and heavenly love. Aristophanes tells a mythical story about the origin of the two sexes; it is that there were originally three – male, female and hermaphrodite. Zeus decided that they were all troublesome creatures, so he cut them all in half, and this left each half yearning for its other half. But, Aristophanes says, those who are the most virile and masculine are those who are slices of the original male sex. They take delight in the company of boys and men; they show the greatest manliness in public life, and they only marry as a duty to society in order to beget children. It is difficult to imagine a greater contrast than this to those modern conceptions of masculinity which stress an aggressive heterosexuality, lay stress on sexual prowess with women and regard a man's desire for women as one of the most fundamental defining features of his masculinity.

But it is not simply that Plato has an ideal of masculinity which differs from most contemporary ones. The sort of detailed interest that we now tend to have in the differentiation between male and female psychological characteristics, the idea of a clear *contrast* or *polarisation* between masculine and feminine qualities, or the idea that they are *complementary,* is foreign to the work of both Plato and Aristotle. They held, indeed, strong views about what a man should be like, but they were basically very uninterested in women. They discuss their function, remark on their inferiority and make asides about such things as 'womanish' behaviour in men, but there is no view of 'femininity' in their work, nor of a masculinity which is essentially defined in opposition to this. The idea of women as emotional nurturers of men, for example, or the idea that women have their own distinctively female forms of excellence, is quite foreign to their thinking.

It is not really until the time of Rousseau that an interest in the idea of contrasting or complementary psychologies of masculinity and femininity begins to develop. This interest was related to the Romantic movement in European thought. It was also related to changing conceptions of 'home' and 'family' and of the distinction and relationship between 'public' and 'private' life. To Plato and Aristotle, the life of the household was merely the means of enabling free males to live a public life in the *polis.* It had no value in itself. In the *Republic* Plato even proposed the abolition of private life altogether among the ruling class of his ideal state, because of his fears about the way in which it might disrupt the unity and harmony of the state. Rousseau, on the other hand, saw private life as the source of the most intense affections and emotions (though he saw it, too, as the means of containing or controlling the power of women, and as the means of educating future citizens). Rousseau displayed an intense and passionate interest in the psychology of men and women, and in the emotional relationships between them. He wrote an autobiography whose objective was to reveal to readers the innermost recesses of his own psyche;[9] a great deal of the book is devoted to describing the agonised longings and moments of bliss that were caused by sexual love. And he wrote one of the earliest European novels, *Julie,* or *La Nouvelle Héloïse.* This was based on the correspondence between Julie, the heroine, and her lover, Saint Preux, their ill-fated love affair and separation, and Julie's subsequent marriage to the upright and self-righteous Wolmar. Rousseau was often pessimistic about the outcomes of passionate relationships between men and women. In *Julie,* the heroine's lover is condemned first to a life of hopeless longing, and then to a restitution of a relationship with Julie that is a pale and oversublimated version of what had gone before; and Julie herself dies tragically by drowning. In *Emile,* the relationship between Emile and Sophie is 'corrupted' by the move to the city, away from the simplicities of country life, and by Sophie's adultery. Nevertheless, Rousseau saw relationships between the sexes as the source, as well, of the most profound human joy and the deepest human feelings. Like many philosophers after him, his view of sexual relationships was based on a view of the complementarity of male and female qualities, and on an intense interest in trying to define and understand what these qualities were.

From the time of Rousseau onwards, many philosophers displayed great interest in the characterisation of masculinity and femininity, and in the psychology of sexual relationships. Kant, Schopenhauer, Nietzsche, Hegel and

Kierkegaard, for example, wrote quite detailed accounts of their perceptions of the nature of women. And some of them wrote veritable diatribes on what they saw as distortions of femininity. The idea of woman as tender, receptive, emotional, as pleasing or delighting man by her feminine charms; of sexual relationships between men and women as providing some of the deepest human emotions and pleasures; of a polarity and complementarity between male and female qualities – these are historically relatively recent. And I think they account for the particularly vitriolic nature of some of the opinions about women expressed, for example, by Schopenhauer and Nietzsche. If woman is believed potentially to be the source of some of man's most intense emotions and pleasures (provided she stays within the limited frame of activity and responses allowed to her), then what is seen as the undermining or corruption of those pleasures is so much the more horrendous, and the woman who oversteps her prescribed limits so much more a monster. Nietzsche, for example, was most especially contemptuous of those women who became monstrosities if they forgot their 'natural' tasks and graces.

In general, then, there is no single or homogeneous 'Western' ideal of masculinity or femininity. The fact that a philosopher holds strong views about what sort of life a man should lead does not in itself imply that they hold any explicit beliefs about the nature of femininity or any explicit theory about the contrast or complementarity between the 'natures' of men and women. Such beliefs are related to changing conceptions of the relation between the 'private' and 'public' spheres of life and to changing notions of things such as 'home' and 'family', and they cannot always easily be mapped from one historical period onto another.

Problems in Talking about Philosophy

There are two main problems with the enterprise of trying to argue that particular themes or oppositions in philosophy are distinctively or typically male. The first is the extent to which such themes or oppositions can really be identified at all in the way assumed, for example, by the argument of Sheila Ruth. The second arises from the fact that whatever theme or opposition is identified as male, it is always possible to find male philosophers who have profoundly disagreed.

First, then, the problem of identification. One feature of some attempts to identify male themes in philosophy is the vagueness with which such themes are characterised. Ruth, for example, talks of 'faith in systems rather than responses'; but if one were asked to list those philosophers of whom such a description was true, it would be very difficult to do because of the vagueness of the description. But it is not just a problem of vagueness. Ruth writes as it if were possible to identify clear oppositions in philosophy, such as those between mind and body or reason and feeling, which are assumed to have a similar sense wherever they occur. It is this assumption that is problematic.

To assume, for example, that there is such a thing in philosophy as *the* mind/body split is to adopt a thoroughly ahistorical approach. In his book *Philosophy and the Mirror of Nature* (1980) Richard Rorty writes:

Discussions in the philosophy of mind usually start off by assuming that everybody has always known how to divide the world into the mental and the physical – that this distinction is commonsensical and intuitive, even if that between two sorts of 'stuff', material and immaterial, is philosophical and baffling (p.17)

But he argues this is not the case. The sorts of distinctions between what is seen as 'mental' and what is seen as 'physical', which stem from the work of Descartes and which have set the agenda for much modern discussion in the philosophy of mind would have been foreign to the Greeks. In fact, Rorty argues, in Greek there is no way of dividing 'conscious states' – events in an inner life – from events in an external world. Descartes, by comparison, used 'thought' or 'thinking' to cover processes of perceiving and feeling, as well as doubting, understanding, affirming, denying, willing, and so forth.

And not only are Greek and Cartesian conceptions of 'mind' very different, it would also be a historical solecism to suppose that they served to answer the same questions or tackle the same sorts of problems. Conceptions of 'mind' and of 'consciousness' have been used to try and provide answers to very different sorts of questions – questions, for example, about what a human being is that is more than flesh and bone; about how it is possible to have knowledge about that which changes; about human freedom and responsibility; about the relationship between mental activity and states of the brain.

Similarly, there is not just *one* philosophical distinction between 'reason' and 'feeling'. There are, indeed, conceptions of reason which contrast it sharply with emotions or passions. Thus it has sometimes been supposed (by Hume, for example) that the ends or goals of human activity are unamenable to rational choice, and that reason of itself cannot move anyone to action. Reason can only decide on the means by which such ends or goals can be reached. But this 'cold' or instrumental conception of reason is one which would have been quite foreign to, say, Plato. Plato did not distinguish reason from feeling in anything like this sort of sense. It is true that he regarded many human passions with dislike and suspicion, especially those related to sexuality, and that one of his main concerns in his account of the ideal state and of the economy of the human soul was how they should be regulated. But it is not true that Plato's conception of reason was a cold or instrumental one, or that everything we would call emotion or feeling was foreign to it. Plato's descriptions of the quest for Beauty and Knowledge and the Form of the Good are often couched in metaphors of love and longing and sexual desire. Plato's philosopher is a *lover* of the Good, and, as Genevieve Lloyd (1984) shows, in much of his later work, the 'spirited' or emotional part of the soul is seen as a possible ally in the quest for truth.

It is wrong, therefore, to suppose that concepts or categories such as 'mental', 'physical', 'reason' or 'feeling' have always had the same sorts of meanings in philosophy, have always been contrasted with each other in the same sorts of ways or have always been used for the same purposes. And this in itself makes it difficult to line up maleness in philosophy, as it were, on one side of such supposed philosophical divides. The divides themselves are complex and shifting, and by no means always fall in the same sorts of places.

The second reason for the difficulty in identifying any characteristically male point of view in philosophy is that it is always possible to find male philosophers who have disagreed profoundly with any of the themes suggested as typically male ones. Jane Flax, for example, picks out a denial of the social and interactive character of human development and a fear of sexuality and the body as characteristically male themes. But what are we then to make of Hegel, Marx or Bradley? Or of Nietzsche? One of the main themes of Hegel's *Phenomenology of Mind* is the interdependence of human consciousness and social relationships. The same is true of Bradley's *Ethical Studies*. Bradley argued that if you abstracted the social you would not have a recognisably human self or person at all. Marx not only saw human beings as essentially embodied but also saw 'human nature' and human needs as produced by the forms of social and productive relationships into which human beings entered. The idea of a dislike of the body as such is as foreign to Marx's thought as Marx's own theory of human consciousness would have been to Plato's. Or consider Nietzsche. One of the things about classical and Christian philosophy that Nietzsche most disliked was its 'otherworldliness'; he rejected all distinctions between appearance and reality, and all moralities which denied the value of human passions and human bodily needs. Bodily health and vigour was in fact for Nietzsche a prerequisite for thought that was not anaemic or 'sick'. Nietzsche's thought was in many ways profoundly individualist, but to align his thinking with that of, say, Hobbes, and simply to see both of them as putting forward a typically male 'individualism' would be to distort the history of philosophy grotesquely.

Examples like these could be produced almost indefinitely. And they make Flax's method of argument seem very arbitrary and eclectic. It is possible to make her selection of male themes 'fit' aspects of the work of a large number of philosophers. But there are, as I have said, just as many philosophers whose work they do not 'fit' at all, or who exemplify some of the themes, but not others. In fact, what I think is most interesting about male attitudes to women in philosophy is not that they can be aligned with any particular sort of philosophical view or theory. Rather, it is the many *different* forms that misogyny or contempt for women can take, the many *differing* sorts of philosophical theories in which women are relegated to second place. Women have figured as second-class citizens, as inferior, as objects of the sort of idealisation which is associated with devaluation, in ways which are incompatible with each other and in theories which are inconsistent with each other.

Problems in Talking about Male Experience and Male Psychological Development

I will discuss these here quite briefly. The basic problem is similar to the problems involved in talking about 'Western' ideals of masculinity or in trying to pick out themes and oppositions which characterise philosophy; namely, the fact of historical variation and change.

Flax tries, as I have shown, to ground her account of the maleness of philosophy in a reading of Chodorow's account of differences between male and female experience which are ascribed to the fact that it is women who undertake the primary care of children. She writes that there may be factors which 'mitigate' the effects of mothering by women only, such as the increased participation of women in work outside the home, but that these mitigating factors were largely absent when the philosophers whom she is discussing lived.

But what is it exactly that such factors are seen as mitigating? Flax sometimes writes as if she is assuming some constant historical norm of 'mothering', which may or not at certain times be 'mitigated'. But even a cursory glance at history suggests that there is no such thing, and that patterns of infant care are extremely variable. Thus one might instance rural peasant households where the care of young infants often devolved on older siblings; households where children were brought up by slaves or wet-nurses; families during the earlier phases of Western industrialisation, where both parents often went to work in factories as a matter of course. In all of these situations, the sort of symbiosis

between mother and infant assumed by many versions of
object relations theory would have been impossible. And
even where mothers have themselves cared for their infants,
the modes and styles of care have varied enormously. The
mere fact of women's greater responsibility for child-care
cannot be abstracted from the different sorts of social
conditions and family nexus in which childrearing takes
place and regarded by itself as responsible for any particular
features of male psychological development. And this makes
it difficult enough to use object relations theory incautiously
as telling us anything about the actual psychological qualities
of males today, let alone throughout history from Plato to
the present.

Flax herself in fact acknowledges the importance of
variations in male psychological development and the
relationship of these to social conditions generally, and to
particular differences between individual families. She
suggests that object-relations theory ought to imply that
there is no static or fixed 'human nature'. If the nature of
human beings depends partly on the nature of early
relationships, then, if these differ radically, so ought human
nature to differ. But the general drift of her argument about
the maleness of philosophy loses sight of this and seems to
postulate a norm of mothering which has itself lost sight of
history.

I have argued that there are indeed important senses in
which philosophical theories can be seen as male. I have also
argued, however, that attempts to identify any sort of
characteristically male point of view in philosophy, a
typically or essentially male metaphysic, or male view of
human knowledge or human nature, founder on the rock of
historical complexity and difference. And if this is right, it
follows that there will be similar problems in trying to
identify any distinctive female point of view either. But at
this point I think there is more to say.

Most commonly in philosophy, whatever has been seen as
female has been devalued in one way or another.
Characteristics or qualities deemed to be female have been
regarded as inferior, or even if they have officially been

regarded as 'equal but different' to male ones, they have in practice usually been regarded as of secondary importance, or as less worthy of being included in some ideal of human excellence. Even more importantly, however, those *activities* deemed to be especially female have, in varying ways, been seen as less important than those deemed to be male.

In all societies known to us there has been a male/female division of labour. It has varied a lot; in some societies it has been very rigid, whereas in others, like our own, it has been more flexible and boundaries can be transcended by individuals with greater or lesser ease. Nevertheless in our own society there still exists a strong conception of what is 'men's work' and what is 'women's work'. Women have been regarded as having a 'sphere' of life that is particularly their own, even if at times they may also play a role in a sphere normally regarded as male.

The distinction between men's and women's spheres has been marked in different ways. Thus in social and political philosophy one can find a series of distinctions between 'public' and 'private' life which, as writers such as Jean Elshtain (1981) have pointed out, vary greatly. For example, from the time of Rousseau onwards one can find in the work of a number of philosophers an ideal of private life as a retreat, as an emotional centre, generating structures of intense love and affection between husband and wife. This would have been foreign to the Greeks. The Greek attitude to marriage, as expressed at least in the philosophy of Plato and Aristotle was very pragmatic. The household was the realm of necessity, whose role was that of reproducing future citizens and providing the economic basis for free men to associate with each other in the public life of the polis. *Plato* certainly did not see women as emotional companions for men; in his scheme of things, men's emotions were largely reserved for other men.

Now it would not be true to say that the sphere of life regarded as that of women has always been devalued or regarded as inferior in any simple or obvious sense. Sometimes it has been. But at other times, as in the work of Rousseau, it has been romanticised or idealised. And where it is idealised, it is not so much that it is regarded in an overt way as inferior; it is rather that, in a variety of ways, it is not regarded as so important. It may be charming, it may be necessary, it may be one's emotional stay, but *outside* it, however that is defined, is, as it were, where the action is. It is where one becomes fully human or achieves self-realisation; it is where heroic exploits and daring deeds are done; it is where 'culture' flourishes in the form of abstract ideas, intellectual achievements, or art; it is where Nature is mastered by science or 'technology'; it is where males run kingdoms and Empires, wage wars, conduct politics or manage businesses; it is where the lone soul faces the world in existentialist anguish. It is the realm of *important* things.

Now it is arguable that despite all historical variability, the lives of women can be seen in some respects as having had more in common than the lives of men. Women, more than men, have tended to be restricted to the microcosm, the smaller more intimate world of family, household, immediate community; and they have tended to be more closely involved than men in activities that involve the concrete day-by-day caring for of other human beings, including children. The macrocosm, the world beyond the confines and constraints of the immediate necessities of daily life, has been largely regarded as the world of men. And men, more than women, have tended to regard the concerns of the immediate or private sphere as inferior, less important, childish, mere Nature, something to be transcended or dismissed if they intrude on the worlds of culture, technology, politics or any of the other concerns which men have made particularly theirs. This suggests, I think, that it is crucially important to look at the ways in which the sexual division of labour has been characterised, and at the ways in which conceptions of masculinity and femininity have been related to differing conceptions of male and female activities.

But even if it is correct to say that the lives and activities of women have tended to have more in common than those of men, this does not imply that it is possible to identify any particular view of those activities which is, in a transhistorical sense, distinctively or uniquely female. The view that women have adopted, for example, even of the uniquely female activity of childbearing, has varied greatly; women have perceived childbearing both as the source of their greatest joy and as the root of their worst suffering and their subordination to men. There is no consensus among women about how their lives should be conceptualised. In philosophy there is a real danger of foreclosing philosophical debate, of assuming consensus where none exists, or of regarding women as having a vested interest, as it were, in accepting certain philosophical theories or assumptions and rejecting others.

There are danger, too, in an oversimple assertion of the value of what is feminine as against, or in addition to, what is masculine, and in the idea not merely of a 'woman's point of view' but of distinctively female strengths or excellences. The danger lies, as Genevieve Lloyd, for example, has pointed out, in the fact that 'femininity', in its varying forms, has been largely constituted through a process of exclusion and polarisation. What is female has been defined as what is excluded from maleness, what is in opposition to it, what is complementary to it, what 'fills the gaps' in male life or consciousness. And such definitions have usually existed in contexts where women were relatively powerless, dependent on and subordinate to men. Kant, for example, who incorporated both such things as sympathy and sensitivity and the 'virtues' of compliance and obedience in his conception of women, explicitly saw femininity as complementary to masculinity (the world would be a cold and dreary place without it), and the way in which he characterises it derives from that polarisation. As Lloyd (1984) says:

The idea that women have their own distinctive kind of intellectual or moral character has itself been partly formed within the philosophical tradition to which it may now appear to be a reaction. Unless the structural features of our concept of gender are understood, any emphasis on a supposedly distinctive style of thought or morality is liable to be caught up in a deeper, older structure of male norms and female complementation. The affirmation of the value and importance of the 'feminine' cannot of itself be expected to shake the underlying normative structures, for ironically it will occur in a space already prepared for it by the intellectual tradition it seeks to reject. [p.105]

It is problematic, therefore, for women to seek simple inclusion in many philosophical theories or ideals, since these are often defined in opposition to what is female. But it is also problematic simply to assert the value of the feminine or to characterise it in ways which simply recapitulate versions of old polarisations between masculine and feminine.

Finally, I would stress that I do not think that the enterprise of re-evaluating the feminine in philosophy simply concerns women. What a great deal of feminist argument has tried to show is that the devaluation of the feminine has not *only* worked against women, although of course it has done that, but that it has led to a distortion of values, concerns and priorities that is of quite general human concern. I shall disagree with some of the specific ways in which this has been argued, but with the general point I am wholly in agreement. The enterprise of considering the relationship between women and philosophy is not one that should just be the concern of women

3   Experience and Reality

THE DISCREPANCY BETWEEN EXPERIENCE AND THEORY

One of the central themes of feminism has been the importance of women's experience, and one of its central enterprises has been to show how a great deal of male theorising about women has tended to deny, invalidate or be unable to account for this experience. In her book *Woman's Consciousness, Man's World* (1973), Sheila Rowbotham describes her involvement in radical politics in the late 1960s and the increasing sense of alienation she and many other women felt from male perceptions of themselves. She writes: 'All theory, all connecting language and ideas which could make us see ourselves in relation to a continuum or as part of a whole were external to us. We lumbered around ungainly-like in borrowed concepts which did not fit the shape we felt ourselves to be' (p.30).

Many women have experienced this sense of discrepancy between some 'official' (and often male) definition of their identity (who they are supposed to be) and their feelings (or what they are supposed to feel). And two of the most common areas of women's lives where this discrepancy has been experienced are those of sexuality and motherhood. Consider sexuality, for example.[1] It is now common for feminist writers to point out the discrepancies that often exist between women's actual experience of sex and the theories of (mostly male) experts about what they are supposed to experience. The question of the vaginal orgasm is one of the most well known. Freud regarded the clitoris as

75

an inferior homologue of the penis, and women as not only anatomically deficient because they lacked a penis but as likely psychically to orientate much of their lives around the (unconscious) wish for a penis and the substitute satisfactions they sought, of which the most adequate was the birth of a baby boy.[2] Freud believed that a sign of 'maturity' in female sexuality was that the clitoris should relinquish its sensitivity to the vagina. And many psychoanalytic writers after Freud continued to stress the 'immaturity' of the clitoral orgasm and the necessity of vaginal orgasm, or of mutual climax during intercourse, to truly feminime sexuality.

Masters and Johnson, in their famous book *Human Sexual Response* (1966), demonstrated clearly that the idea of vaginal as *opposed* to clitoral orgasm was a myth, and that it was only clitoral stimulation which could lead to orgasm in women (which is not of course to say that women may not desire or enjoy intercourse). But the *Hite Report* (1981a) on female sexuality showed how many women were aware that they did *not* experience orgasm during intercourse, and that not doing so made them feel inferior and ashamed, so that they often faked orgasm to please their partners. Anne Koedt's paper, *The Myth of the Vaginal Orgasm* (1976) was widely read by women, although the *Hite Report* itself demonstrated the way in which ideas about vaginal orgasm persisted. But it is not merely theories about vaginal orgasm that have mystified the experience of women; it is arguable that much of the common language in which sex is described can be seen as more apt for describing male than female experience. Colloquially, for example, 'Did they have sex?' will normally be taken to mean 'Did intercourse take place?' And even theories of sexuality which recognise clitoral orgasm may still adopt a view of sexuality which is centred around the idea of 'penetration'. A good example is that of David Cooper, a one-time associate of the psychiatrist R.D.Laing. In his book *The Grammar of Living* (1976) he rejects the theory of the vaginal orgasm as representing sexual maturity in women. But the phallus and the notion of penetration are still used as norms with which to evaluate human sexual experience. So, writes Cooper:

The clitoris reigns supreme. But there is more to it than that. The principal erotic zone in women involves the labia minora and much more tissue around the clitoris that indirectly stimulates the clitoris when friction is applied. Compared to the penis and the undersurface of the glans of the penis, this means that *women have much bigger penises than men.* [p.45]

And he arrives by this route at the idea of the 'phallic woman'. 'Today we recognise the woman's clitoris and periclitoral zone as penetrating, also secondly, the woman's whole body may become experienced as a penis – this is the true sense of "the phallic woman"' (p.49). The degree of mystification for a woman in supposing that her whole body should be experienced as a penis is probably greater than that involved in supposing that she should have vaginal orgasms.

Another central area of female experience is that of childbirth and the care of infants and children. Ehrenreich and English (1979) have discussed the dominance of male 'experts' in theories of motherhood and childrearing. And many theories of motherhood have not merely been *prescriptive* – that is to say, told women what they should do – but have purported to be *descriptive:* that is, they have told women what it is they will feel or experience. Such description is, however, usually implicitly prescriptive too, in that these feelings are seen as essential to motherhood, and mothers will feel inadequate if they do not have them. A classic example is that of an influential book by the British psychoanalyst, D. W. Winnicott.[3] In this book, *The Child, the Family and the Outside World* (1964) Winnicott describes not only the methods of childrearing he thinks best but the *feelings* of the mother during the process. Despite apparently modest disclaimers ('I am a man, and so I can never really know what it is like to see wrapped up over there in the cot a bit of my own self, a bit of me living an independent life', p.15) Winnicott very confidently tells mothers what they will feel. The book is addressed to 'you', in an informal, intimate and confidently avuncular style, and it charts the progress of 'your' feelings during pregnancy and childcare. Here is Winnicott's description of 'your' experience on becoming pregnant:

A woman's life changes in many ways when she conceives a child. Up to
this point she may have been a person of wide interests, perhaps in
business, or a keen politician, or an enthusiastic tennis player, or one who
has always been ready for a dance or a 'do'...But sooner or later she
herself becomes pregnant...At first it may easily happen that she resents
this fact, because she can see only too clearly what a terrible interference
with her 'own' life it must mean...Experience shows, however, that a
change gradually takes place in the feelings as well as in the body of the
girl who has conceived...She slowly but surely comes to believe that the
centre of the world is in her own body. [p.19]

And when the baby is born, Winnicott depicts mother and
baby as living in a sort of symbiosis, with the mother
experiencing the baby as part of herself:

Properly protected by her man, the mother is saved from having to turn
outwards to deal with her surroundings at the time when she is wanting so
much to turn inwards, when she is longing to be concerned with the inside
of the circle which she can make with her arms, in the centre of which is
the baby. [p.25]

It is clear, I think, that women's experience of motherhood
is often very unlike that described by Winnicott. For one
thing, he totally ignores, for example, the experience of the
woman bringing up children on her own, the woman who is
obliged out of poverty to combine maternity with labour
outside the home, the woman with a large family who is
desperate at the thought of how she will cope with another
and wants an abortion. But even for those women who have
had economic security in the form of a male provider, and
for whom the birth of a child is an eagerly awaited event,
there is plenty of evidence of ways in which their experience
of motherhood is discrepant with Winnicott's picture.
Adrienne Rich (1977), for example, describes the way in
which, during years spent at home with three young sons,
she constantly experienced the tensions and contradictions
between the love and joy her children afforded her and the
isolation and frustration of fragmented and exhausting days
and years in which achieving anything 'for herself' was a
Herculean task, bordering often on impossibility. The sorts
of tensions experienced by Rich are reduced by Winnicott to

what he sees as the tensions produced by the conflict between a woman's previous 'autonomy', which Winnicott defines solely in terms of their freedom to establish their own domestic routines, and the demands of caring for a baby. The problem of a conflict between a woman's own needs and feelings and the responsibilities of child-care is reduced to that of how to negotiate domestic routines so that a compromise is effected between your right to organise your home as you wish and the child's right to have space and freedom of its own as well.

Sexuality and motherhood therefore provide two central examples of areas of women's lives where their experience is often radically discrepant with some perception of or theory about what it is or should be. Responses to these discrepancies vary, however. Sometimes it may be possible to try to 'block' the experience of discrepancy, scarcely to let it surface, to live with the contradictions it generates as best one can. Sometimes one might try very hard to reinterpret one's own experience in the light of some concept or theory. This is probably easiest if the concept is a very vague one. Thus one might imagine a woman trying to organise her experience around the concept of being a 'phallic woman' by modifying her sexual behaviour and trying hard to have whatever feelings she supposes to be appropriate. Most commonly, experiences of discrepancy have been occasions for shame, guilt, anxiety or fear. 'What is wrong with me?' is the question that most often underlies these fears. In some circumstances, however, such experiences can become a means of challenging a theory or conceptualisation of women's experience and coming to see it as distorted, inadequate or oppressive. Commonly, this has happened in the context of talking to other women, recognising the shared nature of these experiences and coming to reject the view that they simply demonstrate a personal failure or inadequacy.

Sandra Bartky (1977) has tried to give a phenomenological account of the sort of personal transformation that can happen; that is to say, to describe what it is like to experience radical changes in one's conception of oneself and one's experience. Social reality, she argues, can come to appear *deceptive* – things are not what they once seemed to be; what is really happening is different from what appears to be happening. Thus, for example, a remark which might once have been seen as complimentary or flattering is now seen as patronising or demeaning. Commonly, an apprehension of sexism in one place may lead to an apprehension of it in virtually all aspects of one's life; it is all-pervasive and can never be escaped from. Once one starts to notice the existence of sexism in language, for example – such things as the implications of using the term 'man' supposedly to mean 'human', or the way in which words associated with females tend to have a derogatory usage – this sexism begins to appear endemic and endless. Once a woman starts to experience such things as wolf whistles as demeaning and offensive, she may start to 'read' a great deal of male behaviour differently, including much that would not once have been seen as offensive.

Such changed perceptions can, however, lead to great inner uncertainty and confusion, about how to interpret someone else's behaviour, for example, or about one's own motives and reasons for acting as one does. Bartky describes this uncertainty as somewhat akin to 'paranoia'. An apprehension of the all-pervasiveness of sexism means that whole tracts of experience are seen differently, and the difference may be very difficult to communicate. Perception of it may depend on noting previously unremarked nuances of behaviour, the tone of a voice or of an article, the implications of a remark. This, Bartky suggests, leads to a problem of distinguishing between valid and invalid 'paranoia'; the problem of knowing or deciding when one is really justified in 'reading' peoples behaviour differently, and the problem of coping with denial ('What do you mean, "patronising" or "aggressive". I'm not being patronising or aggressive').

There are two features of Bartky's account which I want to note particularly here. First, it is premised on the notion of *truth;* that is to say, on the assumption that it is possible to perceive social reality more or less accurately, to make valid or invalid claims about the nature of social relationships. Second, it stresses the existence of radical doubt, uncertainty and confusion. And the reason I want to stress these things is that in a considerable amount of feminist writing, a way of talking about 'women's experience' has been adopted which explicitly or implicitly denies these things.

Feminists have wanted to 'step back' at times from looking at the specific ways in which many theories have distorted women's experience and to give a more general philosophical account of the way in which concepts such as 'experience', 'theory' or 'reality' should enter into women's thinking. In the course of so doing, a cluster of views has emerged, which it is the objective of the rest of this chapter to discuss. First, it has sometimes been suggested that there are quite distinct male and female 'realities' or 'world-views'. Allied with this has sometimes been a belief that the whole of language is man-made and therefore constructs a sexist reality, and that the task for women is to 'name' their own experiences, which have not so far been expressible in male language. Finally, there has been an insistence on the 'validity' of women's experience, linked often to a radical distrust of theory. I want now to show how these views underpin a considerable amount of feminist discourse, to indicate some of their philosophical sources, and to discuss the problems I think that they raise.

I will quote again here a passage from an article by Sheila Ruth (1981) to which I have already referred.

Men and women express their consciousness not only in *what* they think, but *how* they think. Men think, perceive, select, argue, justify malely. *What* they have thought, *how* they have thought, world-views and *Lebenswelten* imbedded necessarily in a male consciousness, become manifest in their intellectual constructions, their philosophies. That is perhaps as it should be. What should not be is the raising of these male constructs to the status of universals – the identification of male constructs with all allowable constructs, so that women cannot 'legitimately' think, perceive, select, argue from their unique stance. [p.47]

I have already discussed the belief that it is possible to identify typical and transhistorical male points of view in philosophy. Here I want to concentrate on the idea of the distinctiveness and separability of male and female 'consciousnesses', and on the belief that male and female experience generate alternative 'world-views'.

What Ruth says in this passage implies two things. First, it implies that male and female views of the world are discrepant and mutually exclusive. Second, it implies that they are incommensurable. Ruth here sees the male point of view as 'allowable', and the female one as simply an alternative to it, which takes a different 'stance' or point of view. A similar view has been expressed by Liz Stanley and Sue Wise (1983). They argue that 'women's experiences constitute a different view of reality, an entirely different ontology or way of going about making sense of the world...Women sometimes construct and inhabit what is in effect an entirely different social reality' (p.117). And they suggest that while we live our everyday lives around the assumption that an objective social reality exists 'out there', what feminism shows is that this 'real' reality isn't *the, one* real reality at all. It is merely one 'reality' which co-exists with others. So, they say:

we find the idea that there is *one* true objective social reality existing for all people quite unacceptable. We are perfectly ready to accept that all people operate on the *assumption* that there is an objective social reality...What we reject is that this 'reality' is the same for everybody – or should be the same for everybody if only they weren't falsely conscious [p.119]

Different states of consciousness aren't just different ways of *interpreting* the social world. We don't accept that there is something *really* there for these to be interpretations of. Our differing states of consciousness lead us into constructing different social worlds [p.130]

Dale Spender (1980) links a similar denial of the notion of 'objectivity' to a view of the relationship between language and thought:

One of the tantalising questions which has confronted everyone from philosophers to politicians is the extent to which human beings can 'grasp things as they really are'; yet in many ways this is an absurd question that could arise only in a mono-dimensional reality which subscribed to the concept of there being only *one* way that things can be. Even if there were only one way, it is unlikely that as human beings we would be able to grasp that 'pure' objective form, for all we have available is symbols which have their own inherent limitations, and these symbols are already circumscribed by the limitations of our own language [p.139]

Language, Spender argues, is not neutral; it is itself a shaper of ideas. Human beings cannot be impartial or objective recorders of their world, for they themselves, or some of them, have constructed that world. And those who have constructed the world are men. In the process, 'women's reality' has been omitted. Women have not been allowed to construct their own meanings or to name their own experiences. The task for women, therefore, it to construct a 'female reality' and to give expression to women's meanings via the development of language which does not, like male language, render these meanings inexpressible.

There are a number of concerns which lie behind this denial of 'objectivity' which are of fundamental importance and are central to feminism. Commonly, women's perceptions of social reality have indeed been denied, suppressed or invalidated, and women have been labelled 'deviant' or 'sick' if they refused to accept some dominant definition of their situation. Commonly, too, theories have been put forward in the name of 'science' or 'objectivity' which have not only denied or distorted female experience but have also served to rationalise and legitimate male control over women. Thus Ehrenreich and English (1979), for example, discuss the ways in which the advent of 'scientific' medicine in the nineteenth century may be seen at least partly as the means by which white middle-class males gained control of the medical profession and have since ousted from it not only women but black or working-class men as well. A further concern, especially of Stanley and Wise, is that of the way in which, in the name of 'objectivity', theories and research methodologies, especially in the social sciences, have 'objectified' human beings as objects of study and have assumed it possible to explain social phenomena and the 'structure' of society without reference to the *consciousness* of the human beings who are the object of study. It has not always been regarded as important to take into account the meanings that human beings themselves ascribe to social situations.

It is of fundamental importance to recognise the discrepancies between female experience and theories which distort this, and often to validate female perceptions where these may differ from dominant or male-controlled ones. The question I now want to ask, however, is this. In order to achieve this recognition and validation, and to do justice to the concerns I have outlined, is it either necessary or even possible to assume any of the following?

I shall argue that these three beliefs are not only unnecessary to the task of discussing the discrepancies between women's experience and many theories, but are actually in conflict with it.

1. A radical or total disjuncture between male and female 'realities'.
2. The denial of 'objectivity' and the view that since 'reality' is socially constructed, there are simply different 'realities', so that we cannot talk about 'how things really are'.
3. That female experience simply needs 'naming', and that it is always 'valid' – a final court of appeal – and that experience should be contrasted not just with particular theories but with the notion of theory in general.

I shall argue that these three beliefs are not only unnecessary to the task of discussing the discrepancies between women's experience and many theories, but are actually in conflict with it.

MALE AND FEMALE REALITIES

The experience of gender, of being a man or a woman, inflects much if not all of people's lives. Marilyn Frye (1983) has pointed out vividly the ubiquitousness of sex-marking and 'sex-announcing' distinctions, demeanour and behaviour in everyday life, and many feminist writers have stressed the importance of charting and understanding the processes by which gender differentiation is learned. Frye also points out the extreme importance it has to us that we know definitely whether the person we are dealing with is male or female, and the disorientation that may result from not knowing this.

But even if one is always a man or a woman, one is never

just a man or a woman. One is young or old, sick or healthy, married or unmarried, a parent or not a parent, employed or unemployed, middle class or working class, rich or poor, black or white, and so forth. Gender of course inflects one's experiences of these things, so the experience of any of them may well be radically different according to whether one is a man or a woman. But it may also be radically different according to whether one is, say, black or white or working class or middle class. The relationship between male and female experience is a very complex one. Thus there may in some respects be more similarities between the experience of a working-class woman and a working-class man – the experience of factory labour for example, or of poverty and unemployment – than between a working-class woman and a middle-class woman. But in other respects there may be greater similarities between the middle-class woman and the working-class woman – experiences of domestic labour and childcare, of the constraints and requirement that one be 'attractive' or 'feminine', for example.

Experience does not come neatly in segments, such that it is always possible to abstract what in one's experience is due to 'being a woman' from that which is due to 'being married', 'being middle class' and so forth. In certain contexts, such as that of rape or sexual harassment or unwanted sexual attentions, there are aspects of female experience in which one's femaleness may be experienced as a relatively isolable thing; this is happening to me because I am a woman. Nevertheless, the motivations behind such things as rape may be very different; rape may, for example, be perpetrated as an act of contempt for a particular ethnic group. Black women, and other groups such as Hispanic women in the United States, have often expressed the difficulty they have in understanding their oppression as women in relation to racism, and of understanding their feeling of solidarity with their own oppressed culture in relation to an awareness that they may also be oppressed by the men in this culture. They have also quite often expressed resentment and anger at the feeling that white middle-class feminists are presuming to speak for them or theorise about them in a voice that is not their own.[4]

It might be argued nevertheless that there are certain experiences which are so uniquely and distinctively female that men cannot understand or know what it is to experience these things. Two obvious examples are the uniquely female experiences of pregnancy and childbirth. And it is of course true that there is a sense in which men cannot 'know' what it is like to have a child (any more than a woman 'knows' in advance what the experience will be like). But experience of an event such as childbirth is always mediated by concepts and ways of understanding that event which are socially derived and which can be applied to events other than the particular one in question. Consider, for example, critiques of the medical handling of childbirth. Women have often experienced hospital procedures as infantilising, and they have felt deprived of any feeling of control over or active participation in the birth process. But such ways of describing the experience of childbirth derive their force precisely from the fact that notions of agency, control or infantilisation have a more general meaning and can be applied to situations other than childbirth. Men cannot have children, but a man *may* be able to understand from his own experience in other contexts (including perhaps that of being in hospital himself) what it is like to be infantilised, to be deprived of a sense of agency, to confront impersonal technology with a sense of being 'depersonalised' oneself.

However, it is true, I think, that there are ways of perceiving women or of relating to them which may be 'second nature' to many men – so deeply engrained that they are *in practice* impossible to transcend. And these ways of perceiving may make it immensely difficult for men to understand how women feel or what they are 'on about'. Many women have had the experience of trying to explain something to a man, and giving up because they *cannot* make him see, for example, why certain forms of sexual innuendo are found coercive or offensive, or why on earth a woman could be dissatisfied when she has a nice home and the apparent freedom to do what she likes all day. It is often this sort of experience, I think, that makes talk of a 'female reality' seem most apt. But in fact such experiences do not warrant the assumption of a 'woman's point of view' which is in principle in all respects inaccessible to men.

Aspects of the feminist debate about language are relevant here. Many feminist writers have discussed the ways in which language is often loaded against women. Dale Spender (1980), for example, has pointed to the frequent 'semantic derogation of women' – the ways in which words which apply to women often have derogatory connotations; to the ubiquitous assumption of the 'male-as-norm' via such things as the supposedly 'generic' use of 'man' to mean simply 'human being'; to the way in which the concepts used to refer to something such as sexuality may adopt a male frame of reference. In all these senses and more, language can be seen to be 'male'. But there is nevertheless a *way* of conceptualising the idea of language as 'male' which is very problematic and is closely linked to the idea of separate and discrete male and female 'realities'.

This way is evident in some discussions of the idea of 'naming' female experiences in a way that 'male language' cannot do. Dale Spender discusses the significance of the relatively new term 'sexual harassment' to refer to a range of experiences encountered by women. The introduction of the term has a political force; it not only makes it easier to conceptualise these experiences, it also makes it easier to oppose and resist them. But the force of the term derives, again, from the fact that the word 'harassment' is *not* used to refer simply to these experiences or simply to female ones. Sexual harassment is indeed usually a female experience. But the introduction of the term 'sexual harassment' constituted what can be seen as a *proposal;* namely, that certain sorts of sexual attention should be seen (like other things) as an unpleasant, intrusive and coercive imposition. The term 'harassment' is not itself used just to describe female experience, and were that so, it could not possess the force that it does.

The 'renaming' of female experience often involves a double process. The concept of 'work' provides a good example. Commonly, women's domestic labour is not merely seen as having low status, but is not even seen as 'work' at all. The insistence that it *is* work performs a double function. It points out that domestic labour is both necessary and arduous, and that it radically misrepresents female experience to see it as 'not work' or as done just out of love. But it *also* points to a critique of dominant conceptions of work which see this simply as wage-labour. The concept of 'sexual harassment' similarly performs a double function. It points out that certain experiences are indeed intrusive and coercive. But it also suggests a realignment of the concept of 'harassment' – a reorganised perception of *what sorts of things* are intrusive or coercive. And it draws new analogies between different forms of human experience – between, for example, the experience of black young people of police harassment and the experience of a secretary in her office.

This double function would be unintelligible on any assumption of discrete or separate male and female 'realities', or on the assumption that language was so irredeemably male that it could not describe women's experience at all. Without the possibility of a language shared between men and women, the political force of such a conceptual critique could not exist, and without shared forms of experience, there could not be such a shared language.

In an article about the language used in discussions of the 1984–85 miners' strike, Raymond Williams (1985) points out the way in which debate about the strike was often informed by dominant definitions of particular concepts. An example he discusses is that of 'management'. Dominant definitions of 'management' usually see this as necessarily involving such things as hierarchical forms of control, sharp demarcations between the functions of those who labour and those who manage, and assumptions that the aims of management have to be orientated around notions of rationalised efficiency and profit. Williams points out that of course many human enterprises need 'managing' in the sense that they need such things as planning, forethought, ways of setting and achieving goals. But he sees it as a politically urgent task to, as it were *reclaim* the concept of 'management'; that is to say, to unpick the sort of 'logic' behind the concept which sees it as intrinsically tied to hierarchy, and so on, to refuse to accept arguments which contrast dominant conceptions of management with simple anarchy, chaos or breakdown, and to struggle for new forms of social organisation in which such conceptions of management would be rejected.

Women have similarly wanted to 'reclaim' concepts, such as that of 'work'. They have also wanted to *extend* their use – to 'collect' aspects of human experience together in a new way, as with the concept of 'sexual harassment'. They have wanted, too, to *reject* concepts; an example might be that of 'frigidity', which it has been suggested might often be better named 'reluctance'. There are countless possible examples of concepts which need such extension, reclamation or rejection in order to do justice to women's experience and to break the links which their current associations make with forms of social relationships which are oppressive to women.

Mary Daly's book *Gyn/Ecology* (1979) is, among other things, an exercise in the imaginative reclamation of concepts from meanings and associations which are derogatory to women. Thus words like 'hag' and 'spinster', which are normally derogatory, are used in new and celebratory ways, linked often with explorations into their etymology to discover different or older meanings or associations for such words. But insofar as techniques like this are effective, they depend on the *possibility* of meanings and associations that are *not* sexist or demeaning to women. At times, however, Daly seems to slide into a view that the task is impossible, that 'male' language is almost intrinsically polluting and damaging and constitutes a sort of 'mind-rape' of women, and that the recourse is a sort of metaphysical silence, a wordless communication that can alone transcend sexism. But if this were really so, the attempt to 'rename' experiences would be quite self-defeating, and the attempt to communicate such renamings to men even more so. It is, as I have said, in practice impossible to explain to many men the nature of the experiences that underlie the critique of language, and it is often very difficult to articulate such a critique, since the habituation to 'common' ways of speaking and the social patterns that underlie these is so strong. But it is not impossible in principle. The assumption that language is irredeemably 'male' and that women and men are locked into separate 'realities' cannot explain the importance of 'the politics of naming', and can logically only lead to political defeatism. Spender and others whose work I have discussed are not at all political defeatists; but I do not think their politics can follow from the sorts of views of language and 'women's reality' that they adopt.

THE CRITIQUE OF 'OBJECTIVITY'

A number of strands of philosophical debate have tended to coalesce in the feminist critique of 'objectivity'. Three in particular seem to have been the most influential, and I want now to outline them briefly. They are:

1. The debate about the idea of 'value-free' knowledge.
2. The debate in the philosophy of science about the notion of a 'paradigm'.
3. The debate about the 'social construction of reality'.

The Debate about the Idea of 'Value-Free' Knowledge.

One of the main concerns of Liz Stanley and Sue Wise (1983) is to reject any approach to understanding human behaviour which assumes the possibility of a detached objective stance and the possibility of discovering 'the truth'. Such an approach they call 'positivism'. The term 'positivism' has a long history in philosophy, which I do not have space to elaborate here, but Stanley and Wise define it as follows:

Positivism sees social reality, social 'objects' and events as 'like' physical reality. Positivism also accepts the existence of an 'objective' social reality. It argues that just as there is a real, kickable, irrefutable physical reality, so there is one, equally real and irrefutable social reality. When examining social events of various kinds, if we use the right methods, the most appropriate techniques, develop the best possible set of hypotheses/ explanations, carry out this research without fear or favour and remain objective in doing so, then we shall eventually arrive at 'the truth' about it [p.108]

Instead, they suggest that there isn't one 'true' social reality, there are different ones, which are competently negotiated and managed by members of society.

There are two particular ideas which Stanley and Wise want to reject. First, they want to reject the idea that there are 'laws' governing social reality which are much the same as the 'laws' governing physical reality, and that human behaviour can be studied without reference to the purposes, meanings and intentions of those who are the object of study. A classic example of a theory of this sort is behaviourist psychology, which attempts to understand human behaviour as a result of processes of 'conditioning' which are to be explained without reference to human consciousness. Second, they want to reject the idea that it is possible for knowledge (including science) to be 'value-free', in the sense that there is a realm of facts which can be studied in a way that is quite detached from any particular human interests and concerns.

Now, I think Stanley and Wise are right to reject such ideas. Theories are not value-free. They arise in social contexts and out of particular human interests and concerns, and cannot be understood in isolation from these. They also imply conceptions of social and political relationships. A theory like behaviourism, for example, implies that human beings and human behaviour can be thought of as material to be 'modified', and the term 'behaviour modification' is often given to programmes which offer to apply behaviourist theory in order to effect changes in human behaviour. Such programmes not only imply the irrelevance of the consciousness of those being 'modified', they imply also a sharp distinction between 'controllers' and 'controlled' and are intrinsically and profoundly anti-democratic.[5]

Nor can human behaviour be studied or understood without reference to the social context and the meaning that behaviour has to the participant. An example of an approach which tries to deny this meaning is an approach to the study of the relationship between TV and violence which is, again, underpinned by behaviourist theory. It is supposed that 'violent' behaviour can be identified and understood as provoked by the 'desensitisation' resulting from the watching of TV violence.[6] No attention is paid to the very *different* meanings that violent behaviour may have in different contexts, or the problem of lumping together such

things as 'mugging', riots or football violence as if these
could all be understood as having the same sorts of causes.

The problem, however, I think, with Stanley and Wise's
argument is that they see their form of what I shall call
'radical subjectivism' as entailed by the rejection of
positivism; as the only alternative to the beliefs they
criticise. In the last section of this chapter, I shall argue that
it is not. First, however, I want to say something about the
remaining two strands of philosophical debate that I
mentioned earlier.

The Debate in the Philosophy of Science about the Notion of a 'Paradigm'

Spender and Stanley and Wise both refer to this debate. The
notion of a 'paradigm' is central to the work of the
philosopher of science Thomas Kuhn. In his book *The
Structure of Scientific Revolutions* (1970) he uses this concept
to give an account of the development of science, and
scientific theories. A common conception of science, he
argues, is that theories are progressively improved, so that
they come to give a better or truer account of reality. An
older theory will be disconfirmed by the discovery of new
evidence, and a new theory will be developed that fits the
evidence better. Thus Newton's theory of gravitation would
be seen as improving on existing theories.

Kuhn argues that this conception of science and scientific
development is inadequate. Scientists operate, he argues,
within a 'paradigm'; that is to say, a network of assumptions
and perspectives that define the nature of the problems
scientists face and the evidence that is relevant to these.
When working *within* a particular paradigm, a scientist is
doing what Kuhn calls 'normal science', and here, notions of
testing hypotheses, confirming or disconfirming theories,
can get a grip. Kuhn argues, however, that if we look at
'scientific revolutions' – that is to say, major shifts in ways of
conceiving of the nature of the physical world, such as the
shift from the Copernican to the Newtonian theory – notions
of 'fitting reality better', of confirmation or disconfirmation
of hypotheses, are no longer useful. A 'scientific revolution'
involves a shift of paradigm, and, Kuhn says, paradigms are

incommensurable with each other; that is to say, they cannot be compared in the sense of saying that either corresponds to or fits reality better. They simply 'construct' reality differently.

Quite a large number of feminist writers have used Kuhn's notion of a paradigm to express the idea that there are radically different male and female realities. Thus Ruth Hubbard (1983), in a discussion of Darwin's theory of evolution, argues as follows:

Every theory is a self-fulfilling prophecy that orders experience into the framework it provides...The mythology of science holds that scientific theories lead to the truth because they operate by consensus; they can be tested by different scientists, making their own hypotheses and designing independent experiments to test them...But things do not work that way. Scientists do not think and work independently. Their 'own' hypotheses ordinarily are formulated within a context of theory, so that their interpretations by and large are sub-sets within the prevailing orthodoxy. Agreement therefore is built into the process and need tell us little or nothing about reality [p.47]

Hubbard suggests that what we perceive or see as relevant when constructing theories depends to a great extent on our histories, roles and expectations. Since feminists are no different from other people in this, it would seem therefore that feminist theory must itself be a self-fulfilling prophecy, and if there is a feminist orthodoxy that much theory is a male construction, then agreement among feminists that this is so will tell us nothing about truth or reality. Feminist theory is, in fact, in a dilemma. Either it is doing 'normal science', in which case it is working within a paradigm that is male, or it is developing a new paradigm, in which case it is incommensurable with previous theories and cannot be used to challenge them.

The substance of Hubbard's article, however, is not really compatible with this Kuhnian analysis. Thus when she discusses Darwin's theory of sexual selection, she argues that his perception of male and female behaviour in animals was influenced by assumptions about male and female roles which *distort* the evidence. In other words, she supposes it possible to give a *better* account than Darwin; and she writes of the need to *overcome* our biases, so that our picture of the world can be more than just a reflection of our social arrangements. The fact that there is this discrepancy indicates in a preliminary way that it may be difficult to conceptualise feminist theory or criticism in the sort of way suggested by Kuhn's theory of paradigms.[7]

Kuhn's theory of paradigms is not always easy to interpret. He allows, for example, that there can be improvement in what he calls the 'puzzle-solving' ability of theories. But he also says: 'A scientific theory is usually felt to be better than its predecessors not only in the sense that it is a better instrument for discovering and solving puzzles but also because it is somehow a better representation of what nature is really like' (1970, p.206). And it is this notion of a 'better representation of reality' that he chiefly wishes to contest. I argue both in this chapter and in chapter 8 that the notion of 'reality' is indeed problematic, and that a concept of 'objectivity' which supposes that there is some true description of reality available which transcends all human questions, interests and concerns should be questioned. Nevertheless it is difficult to make sense of much feminist criticism of male-biased theories without supposing that the latter have in some way *misdescribed* reality, *misrepresented* how things are.

The Debate about the 'Social Construction of Reality'

Finally, the views of Spender and of Stanley and Wise about 'reality' have strong affinities to the work of two sociologists, Peter Berger and Thomas Luckmann. In *The Social Construction of Reality* (1971) Berger and Luckmann argue that we inhabit what they call 'social worlds'. A 'social world' is seen as a more or less coherent set of institutions, roles and social identities, with an associated pattern of beliefs which they see as forming a 'world-view'. To be on the 'inside' of a world-view is to accept it as 'real'; that is to say, to take it for granted or see it as natural, to believe that it offers a true account of reality. 'Social worlds' validate and confirm their members in these beliefs by processes of what Berger and Luckmann call 'reality maintenance' procedures, including those of day-by-day social interaction, that tend to validate beliefs which confirm those of the group and undermine beliefs discrepant with it.

But in another sense of 'real', Berger and Luckmann deny that *any* social world is real; all are precariously fabricated social constructions which shelter their members from the recognition that there is no such thing as 'objective reality'. In this scheme of things, different world-views are simply alternatives; the task of the sociologist is to decipher or see through the processes of illusion on which they are all based. Berger and Luckmann argue that most people naively assume that there *is* some shared reality, a common world which we simply interpret differently. And what Stanley and Wise do is, as it were, stand Berger's theory on its head. Instead of claiming that all 'world-views' are based on illusion, they argue that all are equally 'valid'. The reason for this inversion is their concern to validate the experience of women. But like Berger, they do not want to allow that any view of the world can be more adequate than any other; they are simply different.

EXPERIENCE AND THEORY

The concerns that underlie the feminist stress on experience, and the conceptualisation of this stress in terms of the idea of male and female 'realities' and the denial of objectivity, are exceedingly important and often intractable ones, and they have led to tensions in feminist thinking. On the one hand, as I have already argued, women have frequently had the experience of discrepancy between theories and their own experience; the feeling that 'this is not how things are'. And the notion that this is not how things are implies a notion of truth and falsity, of misinterpretation, of the inadequacy of theories. On the other hand, there is no consensus among women as to how things are. Many women reject feminism and oppose feminist campaigns; the anti-feminist 'backlash' in America, which has opposed things such as abortion and the campaign for the Equal Rights Amendment, has been strongly supported and sometimes organised by women.[8] Furthermore, some women have expressed concern, resentment or anger at the ways in which some feminists have at times appeared dismissive or contemptuous of other women, and at the ways in which some feminist theories have appeared to claim to speak for all women in a way that can sometimes appear as coercive as the male-orientated theories which were themselves the centre of attack. The notion of a single 'female reality' (or of a 'woman's point of view') is itself often a normative one; that is to say, it can be used to suggest that there is a 'correct' viewpoint which all women would (or should) adopt if only they were more enlightened or more courageous.

I think it is these sorts of problems that make the idea not simply of one female 'reality' but of multiple female 'realities' and the denial of objectivity so potentially attractive. Stanley and Wise for example, stress the importance of learning how other women, as they put it, 'do' their truth, negotiate and make sense of their lives. And this, they rightly argue, should apply not just to women who see themselves as feminist but also to women who oppose feminism or who reject it as having any relevance for themselves.

There is a further cluster, too, of concerns about the notion of 'theory'. One of the most important themes of contemporary feminism has always been the importance of the personal and the experiential. Yet feminists have also produced theories which have talked of 'going beyond' or of 'transcending' the personal. What is meant by such a 'going beyond', and how can the stress on the personal, on women *listening* to each other, survive in the face of such theory? There has been concern, too, about the 'élitism' of theories written in academic language and presupposing academic knowledge which is accessible only to a few, and about the 'imperialism' of white feminist theorising which has failed to take seriously the very different experiences of women of colour.

The only notion of 'theory' Stanley and Wise want to allow is one based on an approach derived from ethnomethodology. The ethnomethodological approach is one which sees the task of, say, the sociologist as that of *explicating* how people construct and describe reality, and 'do' everyday life. That is to say, researchers should aim to understand everyday life in the terms in which people themselves understand it and to attempt to 'go beyond' such understandings or see them as in any way inadequate is illegitimate.

The stress on the idea of 'doing' everyday life supposes a unity of thought and action. Thus, Stanley and Wise (1983) say, 'In a sense, ethnomethodology rejects the distinction between "beliefs and values", on the one hand, and "behaviours", on the other. It argues that there is a symbiotic relationship between the two. We know what we believe because we do it or don't do it, not because it exists purely in our heads' (p.141). They depict us as competently 'doing' or 'managing' reality, as making sense of it in ways that seem 'valid' to us, and as integrating our behaviour and our actions in ways that allow us to cope with or handle everyday living.

Now I think that Stanley and Wise are entirely right to suggest that any theory which either discounts or cannot account for large tracts of women's experience must be inadequate. They are rightly critical, for example, of theories which see 'the family' as the basic site of women's oppression but which take no account of the fact that for many women the family seems not so much a site of oppression as the seat of all that is most valuable in human life and the focus of their life's labours. There are plenty of examples of analyses of women's oppression which similarly set up such targets as 'motherhood' or 'childbearing'. Shulamith Firestone (1970), for example, argued that the basic cause of women's oppression was their childbearing and childrearing function. Pregnancy, she argued, was 'barbaric', and women's biology a trap; the only escape was via artificial reproduction and the abolition of the nuclear family in favour of experimental forms of communal living. Jeffner Allen (1984) has argued that motherhood oppresses women, and that entering into it under any conditions will turn a woman into little more than a 'creature' of patriarchy. Theories of women's oppression which disregard crucial aspects of much female experience of motherhood in this cavalier sort of way do indeed, I think, have to be rejected.

But consider again the notion of 'experience' which is

implied by the idea of 'multiple realities'. Stanley and Wise
assume, as I have said, both the *coherence* of 'normal'
conceptions of reality, and the *unity* of behaviour and
action. I think that these assumptions themselves
misrepresent much of human experience.

While it is true that in some sense the majority of people
competently 'manage' everyday life, it is not true that this
competence is always based on a feeling of being able to
make coherent sense of the world. Social reality can often
appear mystifying and confusing. And while it is true that
human behaviour cannot be understood without reference
to things like human purposes and intentions, it does not
follow from this that there may not be discrepancies between
thought and action, an incoherence in the relationship
between what one says and what one does.

In her book *Woman's Consciousness, Man's World,*
(1973), Sheila Rowbotham describes how, in the early
1960s:

I acquired an implicit way of thinking which made it impossible for me to
see my own situation in terms of social and historical change. Things just
happened in and for themselves. I picked up an insistence on direct
experience and feeling. I was inordinately suspicious of reason and
analysis. All removed ways of thinking appeared to me as necessarily
suspect [p.14]

At the same time, she says, in complete contradiction to
herself, she kept wanting to get back to the beginning and
find out how things happened and why. The difficulty she
encountered was that of finding a politics that could help to
illuminate and connect her own personal experience. She
describes a 'sense of dislocation between my sense of self
inside and my behaviour outside' (p.20). She describes how
she reacted to reading Karen Horney's book *Feminine
Psychology* (1967):

I was fascinated by it because she described areas of experience I had
never seen written down, but I hooked a lifetime of experiences suddenly
onto her clear statement of male cultural hegemony. Just as Marxism had
made sense because it made the experience of class suddenly something
you could understand and describe historically, so my sexual situation
became socially comprehensible (p.23)

She describes, too, how unaware she was, despite her feeling of being 'independent', of the extent to which her own behaviour was often designed to please men, and the way in which she would often identify with men (for example, with the male heroes of Kerouac's novel *On the Road* (1958) without realising that she was doing so.

The Italian Marxist philosopher Antonio Gramsci (1971) wrote of the contradictions that may exist between one's intellectual choice and one's mode of conduct; of the way in which there may be discrepancies between the conceptions of the world that are displayed in words and those that are displayed in action. Sometimes, he argued, individual self-deception might be an adequate explanation. But when the discrepancy occurred in the lives of large numbers of people, it was to be explained, rather, by the fact that subordinate or oppressed social groups may 'borrow' conceptions from the dominant group to explain their own lives. Slaves, for example, can come to see themselves, as it were, partially through the eyes of their masters, and women can come to see themselves partially through the eyes of men. At the same time, the hegemony of these dominant conceptions is never complete. People do not experience themselves wholly in terms of dominant ideologies, partly because these ideologies may themselves be contradictory, and partly because what Gramsci called 'good sense' may recognise, in however embryonic a way, discrepancies between ideologies and lived experience. The problem, as Gramsci saw it, was how to move *towards* a greater unity of thought and action; how to 'make sense' of one's life in a more critical and coherent way, and thereby develop a politics of coherent resistance to dominant ideologies and oppressive social relationships.

This highlights what is perhaps the most central problem of all in the theory of 'multiple realities', all of which are equally 'valid'. Theories, ideas and ideologies are not *only* ways of 'making sense' of the world. They may also be means by which one group of people may dominate or exercise control over another. And the fact that one group has power over or exploits another, cannot be reduced to anyone's belief that this is so; nor does the fact that someone does not understand their own experience in terms of oppression or exploitation necessarily mean that they are *not* oppressed or exploited.

Consider, for example, the relationship that women have to food, and to the question of their weight and shape. To many women, food has different and often contradictory meanings and associations. Preparing food is often presented as at the centre of a woman's care for others, and associated with love – the warmth of the family, and so forth. On the other hand, food is also something which women shun, become obsessive about, refuse to eat, or eat in uncontrolled excess. It is associated with guilt, fear, shame, it becomes a matter for morbid self-blame and stringent resolution. But large corporations make vast profits out of this obsession. Every year, millions of pounds of profit are made out of diet aids, slimming magazines, slimming classes and the like. It is in the *interests* of such corporations to maintain women's obsession with food. And the knowledge that this is so is not just a 'way of making sense of reality', it is an objective fact about the structure of capitalism. Recognition of this fact indeed may not in itself change a woman's attitude to food; it may nevertheless be very important to women to recognise it, and such a recognition cannot be conceptualised by a theory of 'multiple realities'.

The concept of 'interests' is a central one here. And the notion of 'interests' is a central feature of Marx's concept of 'ideology'. Roughly, an ideology, according to Marx, is a set of ideas which are used to *legitimate* the interests of a dominant group or class and subordinate other social groups to those interests (though they are not necessarily held by all members of a dominant group with that explicit intent). But ideologies are not merely *ideas;* they are *lived,* in the sense that they help to structure not merely social relationships in general but also people's motives and beliefs about themselves. In that sense they are not wholly false. Marx himself did not pay a great deal of attention to ideologies of masculinity and femininity; the question of the relationship between class and sex oppression is one that has never been adequately resolved in Marxist theory and is much debated among feminists. But the concept of ideology can nevertheless usefully be applied to gender. Consider, for instance, some Victorian conceptions of female nature, which saw the female brain as likely to come into conflict with the female uterus (it was believed by some that if a woman used her brain, her uterus would atrophy). Such beliefs about women helped to structure social relationships between men and women – sometimes infamously, as in the case of the so-called 'rest-cure', where a woman, for the sake of her 'health', would be subjected to a regime of lying in bed in isolation and darkness, or virtual sensory deprivation, under the authoritarian control of a male physician. Women themselves might accept such theories as to what was wrong with them (though they did also at times resist). But such theories were not *simply* a matter of beliefs about women, they were also a means of ensuring male control over women, of legitimating female dependence.

The questions 'Whose interests are served by these beliefs?' or 'What *difference* does the holding of these beliefs make to the social situation of women?' are ones, therefore, which require that it be possible, in some sense, to talk about what is 'objectively true' about the situation of women. But this is not a notion of objectivity which implies a sharp split between 'facts' and 'values', or the possibility of a totally detached theoretical stance. It is a notion of objectivity, rather, which assumes the necessary interconnectedness of analyses of the situation of women, and proposals or strategies for changing that situation. The concept of 'interests' itself is one that involves both factual and evaluative elements. To discuss what is in the interests of women (as opposed, for example, to the interests of multinational corporations) involves both an attempt to understand women's situation, their feelings and experience, the nature of the oppression from which they suffer, and involves, too, a conception of what potentialities women tend to be debarred from, that it is desirable they should be able to exercise. There is no consensus about what is in fact in women's interests. But such a discourse about their interests has to assume something about what is *not* in women's interests and what is foisted on to them in exploitative ways, and an analysis of such exploitation cannot always be worked out by the explication of everyday experience alone. The activities of things such as multinational corporations are usually extremely remote from everyday experience, yet they have profound effects on women's lives. And these effects do not depend for their existence on the recognition accorded to them.

I've argued that an assumption of separate male and female 'realities' is not a tenable one and does not do justice either to the extremely variegated nature of female experience or to the way in which this intersects with male experience. I have also argued that the assumption of multiple female 'realities', all of which are 'valid' and none of which have any claim to be regarded as more adequate than any other, cannot provide a way of conceptualising things such as oppression, exploitation, the domination of one social group by another.

That does not of course dispose of the problem of the politics of theorising. One cannot do without notions such as *improved* understanding, a *more adequate* theory, a *more illuminating* perspective. In fact,writers such as Spender or Stanley and Wise who in principle reject such notions in the name of the denial of objectivity, usually assume them in the details of their writing. Thus Spender frequently writes of the *falsity* of male accounts of women's experience and Stanley and Wise clearly believe some theories to be *wrong*. But none of this of itself solves the problem of how to develop an understanding of women's situation which does not presume falsely to speak for all women, or of how to develop theories and strategies which are not simply the preserve of a few. Above all, the rejection of the idea that experience simply speaks for itself, or that all ways of 'making sense' of the world are equally valid, should not be taken to deny the importance of *listening*. Maria Lugones, an Argentinian living and teaching in the USA, in an article written with Elizabeth Spelman (1983), says of the task facing white Anglo-women in understanding Hispanic women:

You will need to learn to become unintrusive, unimportant, patient to the point of tears, while at the same time open to learning any possible lessons. You will also have to come to terms with the sense of alienation, of not belonging, of having your world thoroughly disrupted, having it criticized and scrutinized from the point of view of those who have been harmed by it, having important concepts central to it dismissed, being viewed with mistrust, being seen as of no consequence except as an object of mistrust [p.580]

Lugones nevertheless envisages the possibility of a mutual dialogue, based on friendship and not on intellectually or culturally imperialistic notions of 'enlightening' or 'helping', which aims not to reduce each participant to an abstraction called 'woman', but to try to develop common ways of understanding women's lives that both respect those lives and illuminate them.

4 Human Nature and Women's Nature

Theories of human nature have had a central importance in philosophy. Their importance arises out of the frequent concern, in moral and political philosophy, to try and spell out a conception of a form of life for human beings, a mode of political and social arrangements, an ideal of human development, which is both possible and desirable.

The question of *possibility* is raised by asking whether there are limits or constraints set by 'human nature' on the sorts of social arrangements which can be seen as feasible. It is this sort of question which commonly underpins commonsense or colloquial remarks about human nature; thus phrases such as 'It's natural...' or 'It's only human nature' are often used to express a conviction that some feature of human life is inevitable or at least very deep-rooted ('It's only human nature to look after yourself first'; 'It's natural for a woman to do the housework'; and so forth).

The *sort* of appeal to 'nature' involved in such remarks is, however, quite complex. In particular, it does not always imply that human *behaviour* is unchangeable or that motives seen as fundamental to human nature always lead to the same sorts of behaviour. Consider, for example, the commonsense view that 'It's only human nature to look after yourself first'. Those who express such a view are not necessarily discomfited by being shown examples of behaviour which is apparently self-sacrificing or altruistic. What they are likely to claim, rather, is that behaviour which appears on the face of it to be altruistic is in fact motivated by self-interest or can be explained by reference to this.

Thus the behaviour of a mother in putting her child's welfare before her own might be explained by her desire that her child will 'repay' her care by looking after her in her old age. In some recent sociobiological theories, the altruism of a mother is given an explanation derived from an interpretation of evolutionary biology.[1] This claims, very roughly, that an organism will seek to maximise the chances of the survival and reproduction of its own genes, and that, given the different relations of the sexes to the act of reproduction, females have a greater 'investment' than males in the nurture and care of their offspring.

No theory of human nature claims, so far as I am aware, that any aspect of human behaviour is totally unalterable. It is important to grasp this, since the debate about 'human nature' is not usually one in which a belief in the complete fixity of human behaviour is starkly opposed to a belief in its plasticity or flexibility. It is usually, rather, a debate about what *underlies* human behaviour, about how it is to be explained, and about the social consequences that are seen as following from such explanations. Sociobiological theory, for example, which claims that females are 'naturally' more inclined than males to invest more energy in the care of their offspring, does not claim that all women actually want to invest their energy in this way, nor does it deny that social experiments in shared child-care can be undertaken. What is commonly argued is that such experiments in changing human behaviour are 'against nature', that they 'deny nature', and that they are 'unnatural' (and hence will be ineffective in the long run). And the idea of 'nature' here involves a claim that it is possible in some way to identify some sort of basic or fundamental human motives, drives, desires, which are universal in the sense that they can be thought of as the same in all historical circumstances. Human culture has to negotiate them, and their behavioural expression may vary; but they nevertheless underlie all cultures.

The concept of 'un-natural' behaviour is clearly not compatible with a belief in the absolute fixity of human behaviour; 'nature' is not something which dictates or determines everything that humans do. What does it mean, then, to claim that behaviour is 'unnatural'? Commonly, the idea of 'unnatural' behaviour suggests several things. First, it suggests that there is some sort of *hierarchy* of human drives or motives. For example, it might be argued that while some women may want and seek equality with men in the short term, in the long run the need of women to care for their offspring under male protection is a more 'fundamental' aspect of female nature and will defeat efforts to seek equality. Second, it allows that there may indeed be *conflicts* between different human desires or motives, or conflicts between different groups. But third, it suggests that these conflicts should be resolved in a way that is *compatible* with 'human nature'; attempts to organise a society along lines that are incompatible with human nature will not only in the long run be self-defeating, they may also lead to problems of social order and social control.

Notions of 'natural' and 'unnatural' behaviour clearly have a normative force here. It has often been pointed out that the concept of 'unnatural' behaviour has been used to justify or legitimate various forms of social oppression. Beliefs about the 'nature' of women, for example, have been used to justify the view that they should be dominated by and dependent on men. Beliefs about 'human nature' have been used to justify racism and racial inequality and oppression. But it is important to note that beliefs in a fundamental or essential 'human nature' have not *only* been used in these sorts of ways; they have sometimes been used, too, in the context of trying to spell out some ideal of human liberation, and of specifying ways in which human potentialities have been stunted or thwarted by certain social arrangements.

In the history of philosophy, the notion of 'human nature' has often been a normative one; being fully or truly 'human' is seen as a goal to be achieved. Notions of 'human-ness' have often been linked to a conception of characteristics that are seen as distinctively or typically human, which differentiate human beings from other species. The enterprise of trying to identify what is truly or distinctively human, and of using this as a way of conceptualising unrealised human potential and evaluating social arrangements is one that has constantly recurred in philosophical and social thought. Commonly, this enterprise has been associated with either or both of two beliefs: first, the belief that distinctively 'human' nature can be seen to reside only in those human activities and characteristics for which there is no analogy in other species, and second, that it is possible to identify human needs or motives or characteristics which are universal and can be understood as the same across all cultures.

Some analyses of human nature have relied on a notion of a common 'human condition' or 'human situation'. The psychoanalyst, Erich Fromm,[2] for example, argued that the *absence* of instincts in humans, the lack of forms of determination of human life and behaviour that were present in other species, led to certain specifically human needs for which all cultures had to provide some sort of resolution. Thus he identified, for instance, a need for a sense of 'identity', or of individuality. Fromm also argued that in certain cultures these needs could only find expression in dangerous or distorted ways; thus he thought that in a 'mass' culture, the need for identity might only be able to find expression in such things as group conformity and materialistic forms of consumerism. The underlying concern of Fromm's work was not only to spell out the nature of these basic human needs, but to develop an understanding of why it was that certain social arrangements did not adequately meet them.

The concepts of human nature and human needs are used normatively in what has become known as 'humanistic' psychology. Abraham Maslow, for example, whose thinking has influenced a number of feminist writers, argued that human needs could be understood as forming a hierarchy.[3] Only when the ones he saw as 'lower' (namely, biological needs and basic psychological needs such as those for affection) had been satisfied, could the 'higher' or fully human needs for self-actualisation come into play. The goal of psychology, he thought, was to understand the nature and conditions of realisation of these 'higher' human needs and the way in which human development was blocked by fixation at less than fully human motivational levels. Many theories of human nature use the concept of 'human nature' not just to give an account of limits and constraints on the possibilities of human social organisation but to give an account of human potentialities and the ways in which these have been frustrated or have failed to develop.

SOME PROBLEMS IN ARGUING ABOUT HUMAN NATURE

I want now to consider some general problems that arise when discussing the concept of 'human nature', before moving on to look at questions about gender and human nature, and at the ways in which conceptions of human nature and of male and female nature have figured in some important feminist arguments.

In some sense, it would be absurd to deny that there is such a thing as 'human nature'. By this I mean that it cannot sensibly be denied that human life is constrained in some ways by such things as the biological characteristics of the human species, by such things as birth, death, sickness and ageing, and by the need for human beings to work in order to produce their own means of subsistence. There is room for a great deal of disagreement about what these constraints actually are, and the constraints may change historically. Thus, for example, the advent of more reliable contraception and the possibility of different technological means of reproduction changes the nature of the constraints pregnancy and birth lay on human life. Nevertheless, questions about the limits laid on possible forms of social organisation by the nature of the human species should not be seen as questions about whether there are any limits or constraints at all, but rather as questions about the nature and form of these constraints. What has usually been seen as most contentious is the claim that human nature dictates the inevitability or necessity of certain very specific sorts of social roles (male and female ones, for example); that it determines certain very specific psychological characteristics of human beings, or of males and females; and that it dictates the necessity for certain sorts of social controls.

Arguments that human nature dictates these things have

taken very different forms. Some arguments, such as that of the philosopher Hobbes, have proceeded by what is basically an exercise in abstraction; that is to say, trying to 'think away' social controls and asking what would be likely to happen if they were not present. Hobbes argued that in a 'state of nature' – that is to say, a condition of human life without the coercion and authority of the state – life would be 'nasty, brutish and short'. He assumed an egoism of motivation – that human beings could only be motivated to act in their own individual interests. This assumption was based partly on a sort of conceptual legislation – that, for example, the concept of 'one's own interests' can only be *understood* in an egoistic or individualistic sense – and partly on arguments which appealed to commonsense considerations such as the fact that people take care to lock their houses and do not trust other people.

William Golding's novel, *Lord of the Flies,* is, rather similarly, an attempt to 'think away' normal social controls by the fictional device of supposing a group of schoolboys stranded without adults on a desert island. The picture Golding draws is of a reversion to savagery, in which deep human propensities for violence, domination, tribalism and various forms of superstition and primitivism erupt, with the declining influence of the taboos instilled by social controls.

Many accounts of human nature (including those which have often most exercised feminist thinking) have appealed directly to biology. The appeal to biology has recently most commonly been made in the context of an appeal to evolutionary theory, and to the idea that certain motivational and behavioural patterns or propensities have been genetically 'coded' into human beings as they have proved in the past to be evolutionarily advantageous.

Now one common response to theories which argue, either via an exercise in abstraction or via an appeal to biology and evolution, that certain behavioural propensities or patterns are 'natural', is that far from being 'natural' in the sense of endemic or universal in human beings, such patterns are the result of specific forms of human socialisation and social relationships. Thus it might be argued that even if William Golding's novel were to be 'tested', in the sense that something like the events described did actually take place, that would not show us anything about a universal human nature. It would show us, rather, something about the character structure and particular forms of socialisation of public schoolboys. This creates a necessary complexity in many arguments about human nature, since they appeal not simply to what people actually do or are like, but to what they *would or might* do in other circumstances, or to ways in which they might be different if human societies were different. And it is not always easy to see what sorts of evidence would be relevant to such claims.

Now the idea that the 'nature' of human beings (the sorts of psychological characteristics and motives they have and the sorts of behaviour they display) is a product of particular forms of socialisation and social conditions is one that *seems* to be incompatible with talk of a universal human nature. It is therefore one that has a particular appeal to anyone who wants to deny the idea of a universal human nature, and thereby deny that certain patterns of behaviour or human motivations are endemic or inevitable. But it is also one that raises its own problems. The first problem is that under some interpretations it seems to suggest that the nature of human beings is fundamentally malleable; that is to say, it can be shaped in very different ways according to the nature and norms of any particular society (subject perhaps to the general constraints governing human existence such as the need to produce, and so forth). But if this is so, then it may appear to be difficult to conceptualise the idea that a society does not meet human needs. If human needs and human nature are shaped by society, how can we give expression to the idea that there are needs that society does *not* meet, or that there are human potentialities which are unrecognised in a way that amounts to a *distortion* or a *stunting* of human personality?

It is considerations like this which have led many people towards normative theories of human nature or basic human needs which are derived from 'the human condition' as such, rather than from any particular set of social circumstances. Many theories of self similarly suppose that it is only possible to criticise social norms or institutions for stunting the growth of self if an 'inner self' or a 'real self' can be postulated, which is something conceptually distinct from the 'social self', which may be seen merely as the product of processes of 'conditioning' and the like.

Some of the fundamental problems, then, with which discussions about human nature have to engage, are these. Is it possible to identify characteristics of 'human nature', human motives, desires, drives, behaviour patterns which are universal, common to all known cultures, and bound to be endemic in all possible ones? If such a view is rejected, how can one do justice to the constraints laid on human life by things such as biology and the need to support material life? And if it is argued that such desires, behaviour patterns, and so forth, are in some way the product of particular cultural patterns or ways of socialisation, how can human *resistance* to these patterns be conceptualised, and how can we give expression to the idea of the blocking or stunting of fundamental human potentialities? Is it necessary to postulate a conception of basic and universal human needs or of a 'real' self distinct from the socialised self in order to do so?

FEMINISM AND HUMAN NATURE

One of the central concerns of feminism has been to argue, in different ways, that women's potentialities have been thwarted or blocked by oppressive social relationships, and that theories of human nature in general, but more especially of the nature of women, which see this as intrinsically tied to specific social roles or gender characteristics, have been instrumental in this thwarting. A centrally important philosophical task for feminism, therefore, is to consider such conceptions of human nature, and of male and female nature. It is important because such conceptions may provide a rationale or impetus for particular social or political strategies or goals.[4] This is as true within feminism as it is for anti-feminist views. Arguments about women's nature have been used to support or legitimate various forms of exclusion and oppression of women (just as arguments about human nature have been used to legitimate racist social policies). But there is substantial disagreement within feminist thinking on questions about male and female nature. What feminists share, I think, is a *concern* about the thwarting of women's potentialities and about theories of women's nature which consign women to subordinate roles. But feminists differ greatly in their political strategies and proposals, and some of these strategies and proposals have a close relationship to views about male and female nature. I want now, therefore, to map out what I think are some of the central themes and conflicts in feminist accounts of this nature, and to discuss the ways in which feminist argument has tried to negotiate the problems I referred to in the previous paragraph.

Conceptions of human nature have been gendered, or had implications for gender, in what I think are two main ways. First, as I have already argued in a previous chapter, ideals of human potentiality have often been masculine in the sense that they have excluded those qualities or characteristics seen as characteristically female or have believed women to be incapable of fully or truly 'human' excellence or self-realisation. But second, some theories of human nature have suggested that the *constraints* operating on men and women are different, and that these constraints account both for differences in the social roles and psychological characteristics of men and women, and for quite general features of human social relationships.

The single most important thing that has been seen as determining these differences is the fact that women, and not men bear children. The ways in which this fact is seen as constraining women's lives have varied. Thus in Freud's theories it is supposed that the desire for a (male) baby becomes the fundamental one around which a woman's life is orientated; it is a substitute for the penis she does not possess, and if a woman devotes her life to other things, these will be interpreted as a psychic *substitute,* a sublimation of the wish for a baby, which can never adequately replace actually having one. A great deal of psychoanalytic theorising has assumed, with Freud, that a woman's fulfilment can only come through children. Other theories, however, do not stress a woman's *desire* for a child so much as the different 'investment' by males and females in the care of children, which is seen as the evolutionary consequence of their different relationship to conception. In one way or another, however, the biological differences between men and women, especially those related to reproduction, are seen as determining, not necessarily how all women will actually behave, but what their deepest feelings and motivations will be and what forms of relationships between men and women will ultimately be viable. 'Biology' is often seen as the rock on which feminism will inevitably founder.[5]

The relationship of feminist thinking to questions about biology and reproduction has been a complex one. I want first to outline some central features of two sorts of arguments which, in different, though related ways, argue that 'biology' does not determine anything about human life or about women's fundamental nature or social role.

Sex and Gender

One of the most common distinctions made in feminist writing is that between sex and gender. And one of the clearest statements of it was made by Ann Oakley in her book *Sex, Gender and Society* (1972). Thus, she says:

On the whole, Western society is organised around the assumption that the differences between the sexes are more important than any qualities they have in common. When people try to justify this assumption in terms of 'natural' differences, two separate processes become confused; the tendency to differentiate by sex, and the tendency to differentiate in a particular way by sex. The first is genuinely a constant feature of human society, but the second is not, and its inconstancy marks the division between 'sex' and 'gender': sex differences may be 'natural' but gender differences have their source in culture, not nature [p.189]

Oakley produces a great deal of evidence from anthropology, studies of different socialisation patterns and the like, to show the immense variability of gender distinctions. She argues that the supposition that any particular version of these gender differences is 'natural'

argued that the supposition that women were not rational ignored the ways in which they had not been allowed the opportunities to *develop* their reason.[6] And while he and other liberals have expressed an official agnosticism about what women might achieve if given equal opportunities with men, they have thought that gendered characteristics might well disappear with the full flowering of 'human' potential and the capacity to reason. Sex would be a biological 'accident' which, while it would continue to have certain inevitable social consequences, would be irrelevant to the full development of human nature.

The sorts of normative conceptions of human nature that I have sketched here therefore rest on a distinction between sex and gender and between the 'biological' or 'physical' aspects of human life which are not seen as constituting specifically human nature. And this human nature itself is not seen as gendered; it is something which is the same in men and women.

Seeing the reproductive capacities and domestic labour of women as not fully 'human' has, of course, the consequence that these things are often seen merely as a trap for women, or a burden. In *The Second Sex* de Beauvoir often seems to see women's biology as a burden, and despite her recognition that attitudes to things like menstruation and pregnancy are socially formed, she nevertheless often strongly conveys the impression that she sees them as *intrinsically* making it more difficult for women to achieve human transcendence. (In this she seems to have been following closely the views of her life-long companion and philosophical mentor, Jean-Paul Sartre.) Her conception of life for a woman who has transcended her femininity is of one in which sex becomes an isolable question of mere physical pleasure, and in which domestic labour or the bearing and rearing of children seem to play no part at all. In *The Dialectic of Sex* (1975) Shulamith Firestone argued, as I have mentioned, that women's childbearing function was itself the basic cause of women's oppression, and the solution she envisaged to the problem of 'biology' was to consign reproduction to technology. While women bear children, they cannot be free or equal to men. Firestone's proposal to abolish female childbearing has not been accepted by many. Nevertheless, it has been common in feminist thinking for some appeal to be made to a universal 'human' nature which is contrasted in some way with the biological or the physical.

There are other strands in feminist thinking about human nature, however, which have taken a very different course. And I think there are reasons why they have had a strong appeal. Many women have felt not only anger at the ways in which women have been treated by men, but an extreme scepticism about the possibilities of changing men's attitudes to women. But this scepticism has sometimes been allied with a strong belief in the greater potentialities of women for change, and a desire, often in tension with the stress on woman as victim, to stress what are seen as female strengths and values. Further, there has been a dislike among some women of any theory which appears to denigrate women by consigning large areas of female experience to the realm of the purely 'biological' or not fully human. (Does not this, it is asked, simply *recapitulate* the devaluation of women which has been so endemic in male philosophy?)

Some feminist writers have given accounts of male and female nature which imply a radical asymmetry between these. Maleness and femaleness are seen as 'ultimates', irreducibly different dimensions of human existence. In this, of course, such feminist accounts have a lot in common with theories commonly seen as anti-feminist. And I shall now look at some ways in which ideas of an 'essential' male and female nature have figured in feminist argument.

MALE NATURE

Sometimes it is argued that males have a nature that is simply to be ascribed to their biology. A clear example of this is the work of Susan Brownmiller on rape. Brownmiller (1975) documents the ways in which rape and violence against women have indeed been endemic in human history. But she sees the fundamental explanation as lying in male biology: 'What it all boils down to is that the human male can rape. When men discovered that they could rape, they proceeded to do it' (p.4). The biological ability to rape leads, she suggests, directly and inevitable to the desire to rape. And rape is a conscious process of intimidation by which *all* men keep *all* women in a state of fear. All men benefit from rape, even if they do not themselves rape. Brownmiller is, I think, really suggesting that in some sense all men are really rapists 'deep down', and presumably are only kept from rape by fear of the consequences to themselves or by a precarious 'veneer' of socialisation which suggests that rape is wrong. The result is that she sees relations between the sexes as necessarily taking the form of a power struggle. Men will always rape if they can get away with it, and the only answer is for women to take power themselves. Hence her political solution to the question of rape proposes what is in effect an army of armed female vigilantes.

Not all accounts of an essential male nature are as explicitly biological as that of Brownmiller, and they may have an appearance of history. Sometimes this is achieved by using the concept of 'patriarchy'. 'Patriarchy' sometimes functions as what can be called a 'pseudo-historical' notion. It appears to refer to a specific form of social organisation. Often, however, it is used in an undifferentiated way to cover the whole of human history. In *Gyn/Ecology* (1979) for example, Mary Daly writes:

Patriarchy is itself the prevailing religion of the entire planet and its essential message is necrophilia. All of the so-called religions legitimating patriarchy are mere sects subsumed under its vast umbrella/canopy. They are essentially similar, despite the variations. All – from buddhism and hinduism to islam, judaism, christianity – to secular derivatives such as freudianism, jungianism, marxism and maoism – are infrastructures of the edifice of patriarchy. All are erected as part of the male's shelter against anomie. And the symbolic message of all the sects of the religion which is patriarchy is this; Women are the dreaded anomie. Consequently, women are the objects of male terror, the projected personifications of 'the Enemy', the real objects under attack in all the wars of patriarchy [p.39]

Daly is here postulating a universal and fundamental male need (shelter against anomie) and male fear (of women). What the origins of these are is not explained. They are just postulated as 'universals' which enter into all human societies and into all male actions and beliefs. They lead to a universal and basic male motivation, fundamental to all male enterprises, to attack women and see them as 'the Enemy'.

Rather similarly, in her book on pornography, Andrea Dworkin (1981) sees pornography as the quintessential expression of the 'unchanging faith' of men in their right to power and to the sexual objectification and domination of women. Terror, based on power, is the theme of male history and culture: 'Terror issues forth from the male, illuminates his essential nature and basic purpose' (p.16). Despite his power, the male is really a parasite on women, he drains their resources and their Being for his own purposes. As a child, Dworkin argues, the first female self he drains is that of his mother; then he transfers his parasitism of the mother to other females.

At times Dworkin denies that this male violence and desire to degrade women is inevitable or that it has biological roots. But it is all the same difficult to avoid concluding that she still sees it as endemic and fundamental in male nature:

In every realm of male experience and action, violence is experienced and articulated as love and freedom. Pacifist men are only apparent exceptions; repelled by some forms of violence as nearly all men are, they remain impervious to sexual violence as nearly all men do. [p.52]

Daly, similarly, is unwilling to allow that there could be 'exceptions' – males whose aim was *not* to terrorise or degrade women. Seeing some men as exceptions is, she suggests, female self-deception, cowardice or bad faith: 'Some feel a fake need to draw distinctions; for example, "I am anti-patriarchal, but not anti-male". The courage to be logical – the courage to name – would require that we admit to ourselves that males and males only are the originators, planners, controllers and legitimators of patriarchy', (1979, p.28).

What Dworkin and Daly both seem to propose is that there are universal male needs or desires which are an essential aspect of male nature and are the same throughout human history. Neither of them see these needs or desires as related specifically to biology. Mary O'Brien (1981), however, whose work has the aim of giving a feminist philosophical account of birth and reproduction, does seem to suggest that there are universal male psychic needs which arise from the particular relationship that males have to the reproductive act. Again, O'Brien's account apparently stresses the importance of history, and she mentions in particular the historical importance of such things as the discovery of male physiological paternity and the recent possibility of more or less efficient contraception. And far from seeing 'biology' as something which is blind or merely 'animal', O'Brien stresses the way in which human biology can never be abstracted from human consciousness – a point to which I shall return later. Nevertheless, she suggests that, given the discovery of male paternity, there is a common need or desire that men experience to compensate, as it were, for their distance from reproduction – the fact that after the moment of conception they are 'alienated' from the process of birth and the continuity of the species. At the root of male supremacy and the subordination of women is the male need or desire to assure himself of his paternity of a particular child, to deny or minimise the true importance of the female role in reproduction, to develop alternative principles of 'continuity' in culture or politics as a substitute for those he is denied by his distance from the process of birth. So, argues O'Brien (1981), 'The male theoretical attitude towards birth is neither natural, accidental, nor conspiratorial. It has a material base, and that base lies in the philosophically neglected and generically differentiated process of human reproduction itself' (p.21). But although it is not 'natural' (in the sense of 'merely' biological), it is nevertheless postulated as an attitude which arises from biological facts, plus a little knowledge about these, and can be abstracted from history and then seen as entering into it.

A rather similar sort of account of universal male needs, desires or unconscious fears is in fact found in a considerable amount of feminist writing. Adrienne Rich (1977), for example, writes, 'There is much to suggest that the male mind has always been haunted by the force of the idea of *dependence on a woman for life itself,* the son's constant effort to assimilate, compensate for, or deny that he is "of woman born"' (p.11). It is the *idea* of dependence on a woman for life that is seen as the crucial thing here, not simply the 'mere' biological fact, but the nature and power of such an idea is seen as endemic in human life, as part of 'the human condition' (and, in this case, the male condition in particular.)

The notion of universal (though maybe unconscious) needs and desires and fears is one that owes a lot to psychoanalysis. Freud, while believing that human biology could not be abstracted from human consciousness, also believed that psychic life followed certain universal patterns, which were part of human entry into culture. And while feminist writers have dissociated themselves from many of Freud's particular theories (e.g. the theory of female penis envy), they have nevertheless often explicitly or implicitly subscribed to a view that certain features of human life lead inevitably to the predominance of certain psychic needs, fears and desires which are gender differentiated. Dinnerstein, in *The Mermaid and the Minotaur* (1977) suggests that the human experience of initial symbiosis with the mother and subsequent separation from her leads necessarily to a psychic conflict in human beings, fraught with many dangers, between the desire to 'regress' and recapture the earliest experiences of relatedness, and the desire to reject that experience and develop as an autonomous and separate self. She argues that because men have been mothered by women only, their 'human' conflict between regression and autonomy is mapped onto a psychic need to reject and devalue women, and onto a fear of women as the object of the unconsciously desired regression. Dinnerstein argues that shared parenting between men and women, whilst not *abolishing* these psychic conflicts, since they are part of what it is to be human, might prevent them being projected by men onto women in the way they have been, she suggests, throughout human history to date. The trouble is that is is never clear what she takes 'mothering' to consist of; of course, men could and sometimes do participate in child-care, but that does not abolish the early relation to the body of a woman and the asymmetry involved in the fact that women and not men can give birth and nurse. Dinnerstein's supposition that shared parenting can solve the problem is not really consistent with some crucial aspects of her own analysis, and on this, the prospects for any change in those features of the male psyche which she sees as underlying not merely the devaluation of women but militarism and other forms of destruction look very dim.

The most common form of belief then in a universal male nature is, I think, one which holds there to be male beliefs, needs, fears and so forth, which are seen as a result of certain features of 'the human condition' (such as women giving birth), that results in a genderically differectiated male and female consciousness.

FEMALE NATURE

It is useful to see a number of feminist accounts of female nature as orientated around two central and related themes: first that of woman as victim and second, that of a 'true' or 'essential' nature of woman.

Women are seen as victimised in two ways: by the physical brutality and coercion of a great deal of male treatment of women, and also by the force of male ideology, by which they are conditioned or indoctrinated. The result of this brutality and indoctrination is that the *humanity* of women has been destroyed. Andrea Dworkin (1981) sees pornography as the quintessential symptom of, and as part of the process of, this destruction of women's humanity:

Woman is not born, she is made. In the making her humanity is destroyed. She becomes symbol of this, symbol of that, mother of the earth, slut of the universe; but she never becomes herself because it is forbidden for her to do so. No act of hers can overturn the way in which she is consistently perceived as some sort of thing. No sense of her own purpose can supercede, finally, the male's sense of her purpose; to be that thing that enables them to experience raw phallic power. [p.28]

In *Gyn/Ecology* Mary Daly presents a vivid picture of

what she sees as the state of women under patriarchy. A great deal of the book is devoted to an indictment of the brutalities such as suttee, clitoridectomy and footbinding which have been inflicted on women; but Daly does not see this brutality as merely physical. Patriarchy, she argues, has led as well to spiritual death, to the rape and brutalising of the minds of women, not just of their bodies. Women have been spiritually possessed and invaded. They have become domesticated, controlled, docile, submissive, dull, insipid, serving the purposes of others. They have become what Daly calls 'fembots': robotised, moronised, lobotomised. They are, she writes, like *mutants:* the 'puppets of Papa'. The power of the Fathers prevents women even realising the depths of the degradation to which they have sunk. And Daly's view of male nature is revealed in the way in which she uses semen itself as a symbol or metaphor for pollution. When talking of 'male' language, she writes: 'Exorcism requires naming this environment of spirit/mind rape, refusing to be receptacles for semantic semen' (1979, p.324). Women she says, are led into 'unwholesome alliance with alienating intercourse…Having lost touch with their selves, they are impregnated by the holy spirit of alienation, the discouraging, dispiriting sperm that expels the self' (p.345). Daly is here aligning herself with the line of feminist thinking which sees men as 'the Enemy' and all forms of collaboration with them, sexual, or otherwise, as leading to the danger of selling one's soul.

Something like this sense of the total destruction of women's selves and humanity comes across too in some of the work of Marilyn Frye. In an essay in *The Politics of Reality* (1983) Frye uses the example of girls or young women who are abducted and brutalised and then forcibly introduced to a life of prostitution and slavery as one that can provide an understanding of the mechanisms by which all women are enslaved. Women, she says, are *processed* by mechanisms of exploitation and enslavement, and the goal of this, for men, is the acquisition of their service. Since physical containment or coercion is too difficult to maintain, women are subjected to psychic bondage; they have to be 'broken', rather like animals, and remodelled to suit the interests of their exploiters. Left to themselves, she argues, women would not want to serve men. As it is, their existence is totally *mediated* by men.

The exploiter has to bring about the partial disintegration and re(mis)integration of the others' matter, parts and properties so that as organised systems the exploited are oriented to some degree by habits, skills, schedules, values and tastes to the exploiters ends, rather than, as they would otherwise be, to ends of their own [p.60]

And here, in this picture of the total degradation of women brought about by brutalisation and conditioning, there begins to be an asymmetry between conceptions of male and female nature. Male behaviour, especially if it is barbaric or brutal, is taken as evidence of what male nature is like – and even if men are *not* brutal, they are sometimes credited with a fundamental desire so to be. But the behaviour of women, on the other hand, does not tell us what women are 'really' like. If they submit to brutality, adhere to patriarchal norms, that simply shows the extent of their victimisation and conditioning. And what is postulated is some sort of 'essential' female nature which is totally distinguishable from these. Women are, as it were, the 'pure in heart', they are at bottom innocent of the corruption and brutality of patriarchy.

Daly's language of 'mutants' seems to imply that behind the mutant form there is some real or true shape which has become perverted or distorted. And, indeed, Daly does suppose that behind the robotised facade there is a true female nature. Daly's descriptions of this are couched in religious metaphors of salvation and rebirth. The genuine self (which corresponds to true female nature) has to be reborn by a process that is variously described, for example, as cleansing, exorcising, depolluting, unveiling or unwinding, dispossessing the internalised possessor.

The true or authentic female nature that will be unveiled by the removal of the 'shrouds' of patriarchy bears little relation to the historical lives and activities of women. Daly's history of patriarchy is one which so emphasises degradation and brutalisation (as does Dworkin's account of pornography) that it is difficult to see how the 'fembots' of her analysis could provide any source or resource for women to turn to. Frye, rather similarly, is sceptical about accounts of the past achievements of women; most of them, she suggests, really lived under the shadow of a man, and cannot provide us with any real intimations of what it might be like to lead a life that was *not* totally mediated by men.

But there are other accounts of female nature which have wanted to reverse this emphasis, and which, while not at all denying or minimising male power and brutality, have suggested that there is a 'womanculture' which is a source for an understanding of authentic and autonomous female values. Or they have suggested that there are forms of female experience which, if stripped of their patriarchal meanings, can reveal something about the nature of woman.

Adrienne Rich (1977) distinguished between motherhood as experience and motherhood as institution. There is no question that motherhood has been institutionalised in ways that have been oppressive and damaging to women. But in her account of 'experience', Rich seems to posit an essential female nature, related to female biology, which has been suppressed by patriarchy:

I have come to believe, as will be clear throughout this book, that female biology – the diffuse, intense sensuality radiating out from clitoris, breasts, uterus, vagina; the lunar cycles of menstruation; the gestation and fruition of the life which can take place in the female body – has far more radical implications than we have yet come to appreciate. Patriarchal thought has limited female biology to its own narrow specifications...In order to live a fully human life we require not only *control* of our bodies (though control is a prerequisite); we must touch the unity and resonance of our physicality, our bond with the natural order, the corporeal ground of our intelligence [p.11]

Rich is here suggesting, I think, that the biology of women of itself, if divested of the trappings of patriarchy, gives rise to a distinctively female nature and to a distinctively female bond *with* nature.

The concept of 'nature' is central, too, to the work of Susan Griffin. Fear of knowledge of the body, she argues, has created a dualism between culture and nature, intellect and emotion, spirit and nature. But Griffin's (1982) response to this is to restate the dichotomy between nature and culture:

In this ideology the denied self, projected onto the other, embodies all that is part of the natural, sensate, life of the body and all of the natural emotions which so often cause one to feel out of control, even frightened of oneself...The desire to hide from nature is the secret *raison d'etre* of this ideology...The mind would control natural life by denying natural power and by keeping a knowledge of that power apart from itself. Yet knowledge of natural power and the life of natural feeling cannot die; this knowledge, this life persists even with our own hunger, our own breathing [p.164]

In her prose and poetry, Griffin aims to explore the experience of women, and the horrors of such things as racism and pornography, through this conception of a natural realm of life and feeling, and a closeness to the rest of nature, which has been denied by patriarchy and to which, I think, she believes women to have an easier potential access.

RETHINKING BIOLOGY

Biology, then is often conceived of in various ways as a sort of *substratum* of human life; a *base* which is that which is most fundamental about human nature; a realm of 'nature' which *confronts* human culture and socialisation. And this sort of view of biology (or of the desires and needs which are seen as flowing directly from biology), underpins views of male and female nature which are, on the face of it, very different. It underpins conceptions of social arrangements which see these as limited or determined, at least in the long run, by the inevitability of male dominance and of the female childrearing role. It underpins views of male and female nature which see a radical asymmetry between male and female psychology as resulting directly from biological difference, or which posit a realm of 'natural' power, feeling or sensation, a 'natural life' of women, which flows from the female organism if 'untainted' by patriarchal culture or conditioning. But it also lies at the root of sharp distinctions between 'sex' and 'gender', in which 'sex' is seen as 'biological' and 'gender' as 'cultural'.

It is arguable that the view of biology as substratum has become part of 'commonsense' about human nature. It is given its power partly by the difficulties inherent in some views which can seem to be denying the importance of biology, or suggesting that such things as the bodily constitution of human beings, the differences in reproductive biology, are of minimal importance in either determining or explaining the patterns taken by human culture and social arrangements. Surely, it is felt, the fact that women and not men bear children is of *fundamental* importance in human life, and not something that can be dismissed as 'mere' biology, as a sort of 'accident' with few necessary social consequences. Or it is felt that there is a *givenness*, an ineluctable quality, about the biological aspects of human life, and that these have to be negotiated by human social relations and cannot be reduced to them.

Within Marxism, there has been a debate about biology and human nature which is of central relevance to feminism. In the *Theses on Feuerbach* (McLellan, 1977) Marx argued that there was no 'human essence', no fixed human nature, but that the self was the ensemble of social relations. What it means to say this, however, needs making clear. And some interpretations of Marxism, in the attempt to suggest directions for a Marxist psychology which did not assume any theory of fixed biological instincts or drives, have appeared to *reduce* the biological aspects of human existence to social relations. Lucien Seve (1978) for example, argued that all needs are always 'social' – including needs such as eating. The problem with a view like that of Seve was, again, that it seemed to ignore the way in which human biology can appear to *impose* constraints and requirements on social arrangements, and can enter into individual lives in the form of brute and inevitable contingency. The socialist philosopher Sebastian Timpanaro (1980) argued, on the other hand, that biology could *not* be reduced to social relations, and he stressed the way in which things such as sickness, ageing and death may block and resist human efforts at social change and have to be taken into account by any political programme for change. But again, in the work of Timpanaro, biology figures as the realm of the given, as a substratum with which all politics has to contend – and it appears as a realm of human passivity, that with which socialism has to contend, but cannot change.

It sometimes seems, therefore, that we are faced with a choice. We can submerge biology in social relations; but we may then seem to be denying what may appear as the intractability and inevitability of biological processes such as birth, reproduction and death. Or we see biology as a sort of substratum; in which case the constraints it lays on human life may appear as things which are passively experienced and allow no scope for change.

In fact, I think this choice should be rejected; it does not exhaust the options. And the first step in such a rejection is to think again about the concept of the 'biological'. The 'biological' is thought of in a number of ways. It is thought of as the realm of that which is genetically inherited (and is therefore often assumed to be unchangeable). It is thought of more generally as the realm of the 'bodily' – and biology is conceived of as the science which tells us about human bodies. And it is thought of, as I have said, as that which lays specific constraints on human existence and sets absolute limits to the possibilities of human social arrangements. In all of these ways, the notion of biology as a substratum is often a powerful one – and it is *that* which has, I think to be questioned. The central argument against the idea of biology as a substratum is that it is not possible to identify an absolutely clear, non-social sense of 'biology'; the biological is not a realm or sphere which can be isolated as a cause of any feature of human life. But neither is it possible to identify a clear non-biological sense of the 'the social'. The biological and social are not entirely distinct and separable things which can simply be seen as 'interacting', nor can one be seen as in any way more fundamental than the other.

The point is put like this by Alison Jaggar (1983):

A historical and dialectical conception of human biology sees human nature and the forms of human social organisation as determined not by our biology alone, but rather by a complex interplay between our forms of social organisation, including our type of technological development, between our biological constitution and the physical environment that we inhabit. It is impossible to isolate or quantify the relative influence of any one of these factors, because each is continually being affected by as well as affecting all the others [p.110]

As Jaggar points out, it may well be true that, in some environments, social survival may depend on infant care by women, but it does not follow that this is necessary for all environments.

We may say, if we wish, that the human biological constitution requires a certain form of social organisation *within certain material circumstances.* But we cannot universalise from this to what is required in other circumstances. And we should note that this way of putting it focuses on human biology in a way that is quite arbitrary. It would be equally true to say that the material circumstances determine a certain form of social organisation, given certain features of the human biological constitution. [p.109]

Human biological differences, and the human biological constitution, are themselves partly the product of human social evolution, including not merely such things as general physical structure but also things such as hormonal differences. The human body should not be thought of as an entity which can be understood by a 'biology' which is abstracted from the consideration of social phenomena. It is itself a site of the interplay between biology and culture – not only in terms of the more general evolution of the human species but also in terms of the way in which the psychic and emotional history of individuals (related to the social circumstances in which they live) may influence their bodily being. Central to Freud's early work, for example, was his view of the physical symptoms of 'hysteria' in women as inexplicable by purely physiological causes. Wilhelm Reich argued that the affective histories of individuals could be traced in the muscular structures and dispositions of their bodies.

If this view of the dialectical and historical relationship between human biology and human culture is accepted, it has a number of consequences for feminist argument. It leads to the rejection of biological determinism; that is to say, of any view that sees particular aspects of human behaviour or particular social roles as the inevitable outcome of a biology considered as a substratum. It leads also to the view that no sort of human behaviour is more 'natural' than any other; there is not, in human life, a viable distinction between those activities or behaviours which are 'natural' as opposed to those which are social. But this implies that the distinction made in some forms of feminist argument between those activities which are fully or distinctively human and those which are more natural or animal or biological is also not a viable one. 'Humanness' is not a property reserved for those activities which can be seen in some way as more remote from the biological contingencies of human life. It has been quite common in philosophy for human reproduction, for example, to be seen as 'natural' or 'biological'; in fact, as Mary O'Brien (1981) points out, the biological aspects of human conception and birth cannot be isolated or abstracted from human consciousness of these.

But if there is a dialectical relationship between human biology and human culture, it follows also that the biological dimension of human life cannot be dismissed as of relatively little importance, as has tended to happen with some versions of the distinction between sex and gender. Human life is always embodied. Marx argued that humans produced their own humanity and their relationships with each other in the course of producing their own material means of subsistence. Without the need to produce there would be no recognisably human life. Marx did not pay a great deal of attention to the process of human reproduction, but human life is conditioned as much by the biological dimensions of birth and sex as by the need to produce the means of subsistence. Unlike production, reproduction is a sexually differentiated process. This I think has consequences for the idea of an 'androgynous' human personality, which is 'merely' differentiated by sex but not by gender.

Sexual difference itself is not something which is simply given; it is something which can change historically and is conditioned by culture. But neither is sexual difference or reproductive difference simply reducible to culture; and insofar as it is not, there seem to me to be good reasons for supposing it likely that it will always lead, for example, to some sorts of psychological differences between males and females – a difference, perhaps, in such things as feelings about children or about sex. The 'meaning' of sexual differentiation may perhaps never be identical for the different sexes.

Neither, however, should one suppose that the 'meaning' of such events, and the significance they have for human beings, cannot change. There is plenty of evidence that it does. Thus it is certain that the significance of pregnancy and childbirth is different since the advent of lower infant mortality rates and the relatively easy availability of contraception from what it was in times when a woman might expect to bear a very large number of children, few of whom would live to maturity. And the meaning or significance of different male and female relations to birth and conception is not given; writers such as Adrienne Rich, Mary O'Brien and Susan Griffin have, I think, sometimes made the mistake of supposing that the different relationship of men and women to sex and reproduction by itself determines differences between the male and the female psyche. But though it seems to me to be likely that there will always be some difference, it does not follow from this that any particular difference is determined. In just the same way, it does not follow from the fact that conceptions of work in an advanced technological society will be different from those in a feudal agrarian one, that any particular conception of work is inevitable. Nor does it follow from the fact that all human beings die that any particular attitude towards death, or any particular way of coping with death, is inevitable. The question of the nature of gender differences under a form of social organisation which was not oppressive to women seems to me to be one which is not predictable in advance. But that of course does not mean that it is not possible to identify forms of gender differentiation which *are* oppressive and which can be seen as related to social structures within which women are devalued and in which their activities are often seen as less important than those of men.

SECOND NATURE AND THE HUMAN SELF

Marx argued, as I have said, that the human self was the ensemble of social relations, but what it means to say this is not immediately clear. What is clearest is what Marx meant to deny; namely, that there is an 'essential' human nature, thought of as a set of attributes or characteristics which are constitutive of human nature for all time. Marx indeed wrote frequently of the 'inhumanity' of capitalism, and of the way in which what he called the 'species being' of human beings was unrealised under conditions of alienated and exploitative labour. But this 'species-being' is not to be thought of as a set of specific characteristics or attributes; the 'species-being' of human beings was denied when the products of their own *human* labour came to appear to be set against them as alien 'inhuman' forces. In a rather similar way, the human character of reproduction is denied when it is conceived of as a merely biological event which simply 'happens' to human beings.

There are, however, some possible interpretations of a view that the self is constituted by social relationships which are problematic. First, as I have already argued, there are problems with any view which tries to *reduce* the biological dimension of human existence to social relations. But second, there are problems with any type of theory which sees the human self as in some way simply *reflecting* any particular set of social arrangements – or which sees human needs as determined, without remainder, by prevailing cultural forms or patterns. Just as the appeal to biology as a substratum has sometimes appeared as the only alternative to a view of human nature which appears to deny the importance of biology, so a view of 'basic' or 'universal' human needs or of an 'essential' human nature has sometimes appeared as the only alternative to an 'oversocialised' view of human beings which seems to make it impossible to understand how people can experience certain social forms as failing to meet their needs. Within feminist thinking, this opposition has sometimes appeared in the form of a contrast between a conception of women as totally victimised, conditioned or indoctrinated, and the free, pure or authentic woman who can emerge if patriarchal indoctrination is smashed or rejected, or who can re-establish contact with an essential femaleness that is buried under the layers of conditioning.

If one rejects such an opposition, it has consequences for one's understanding of the lives and needs of women. It is, I think, indeed often true that women may internalise damaging and oppressive conceptions of themselves. They may, for example, construct a sense of their own identity around a precarious conception of 'attractiveness' to men, or around a sense of a life devoted to serving others in which any desire for things for oneself is seen as 'selfish'. (And, of course, men may construct *their* identity around conceptions of masculinity which see this as centred on such things as an aggressive sexual style, or domination of women.)

But a critique of such internalised conceptions should not be carried out in the name of a 'real self' or a 'real nature' which is seen as 'underlying' the socially produced self (in rather the same sort of way as biology is often seen as underlying socialisation). Marilyn Frye argued that 'left to themselves' women would not want to serve men, and would pursue their own interests. But to put it like this supposes a 'real' or 'natural' self which, if simply 'left alone', would spontaneously or autonomously produce its 'real' needs or desires. It ignores the way in which *all* needs and desires are socially mediated.

Furthermore, to say that women, for instance, are not 'naturally' subservient, or men 'naturally' aggressive or dominant, that it is not 'human nature' that these things should be so, should not at all be taken to imply that such characteristics are necessarily superficial ones. It is sometimes assumed that to say that human beings are not 'naturally' aggressive or competitive or subservient, and so forth, is necessarily to propound a facile optimism or utopianism – against which is to be set the 'hardheadedness' and common sense of those who pay due attention to the apparently endemic nastier features of human behaviour. And there are theories of human nature and the self which *do* engage in such a facile optimism. A great deal of the theory of humanistic psychology, for example, and the therapeutic techniques with which it has been associated, uses the language of 'roles', 'masks', 'facades', and so forth, as if these were relatively superficial things which could simply be peeled away, given the help, perhaps, of the odd encounter group, to reveal the 'real person' within (who is assumed to be basically 'good' and desirous of 'growth'). But the denial of an essential human nature should not be taken to imply such a view. It may not be 'human nature' for men, say, to be aggressive or dominant, but in particular people in particular social circumstances, these characteristics may be so deeply rooted, and so constitutive of a person's sense of their own identity, that they can be said to constitute the 'nature' of that person. The concept of 'second nature' is a useful one here; 'second nature' is that which is so deeply rooted in a person's psyche or sense of themselves that it may in some circumstances be impossible, or exceedingly difficult, to change.

This 'second nature' has to be understood historically; it is, so to speak, sedimented history, both the broader history of the network of social relationships in which people are located and the more particular history of their own personal and affective biographies. Gramsci (1971) argued that the process of understanding oneself was intrinsically a historical one: 'The starting point of critical elaboration is the consciousness of what one really is, and is 'knowing thyself' as a product of the historical process to date which has deposited in you an infinity of traces, without leaving an inventory' (p.324). But this history is one of contradictions and conflicts, both in material and in ideological terms. And the nature of these conflicts changes over time.

Women's lives have been lived under many of these contradictions and conflicts. Women have, for example, often been faced with trying to make sense of contradictory conceptions of themselves. They are human beings and participate with men in human tasks – yet they have been seen by philosophical theories as not capable of full humanity. They have often been powerless – yet they have also been seen as too powerful, by virtue of the sexual power they hold over men. They have been dependent – yet seen as having an enviable 'freedom' to amuse themselves or do as they like within the confines of their own home. They have been seen as asexual – yet the illnesses and disorders from which they have suffered have been seen as having sexual causes. Notoriously, they have been seen both as madonna and whore, as virgin and slut, and they have had to try to reconcile contradictory imperatives, such as those of being *both* chaste and modest, yet *also* sexually available.[7]

Women have also experienced often barely articulated contradictions between thought and action. They have, perhaps, been fully aware of their own competence, yet publicly declared themselves to be weak and helpless, so as not to deflate the ego of a man. Or they have *believed* in their own lack of competence (or not defined the skills they *did* possess as constituting 'competence'.) Such contrasts between thought and action, if they are widespread, are, Gramsci argued, indications of profounder socio-historical contrasts – they are more than just an indication of discrepancy in the life of an individual. They signify, he argued, that the social group in question:

has, for reasons of submission and intellectual subordination, adopted a conception which is not its own but is borrowed from another group; and it affirms this conception verbally and believes itself to be following it, because this is the conception which it follows in 'normal times' – that is when its conduct is not independent and autonomous, but submissive and subordinate [p.327]

But to develop one's 'own' conception, to become autonomous, is not a matter of discovering a spontaneously authentic or 'real' self, and that which is seen as autonomous or independent should not be thought of in any way as 'less social'. Gramsci contrasted what he called a disjointed and episodic conception of the world with a critical and coherent one. A disjointed and episodic conception is one in which the contradictions and conflicts in dominant and commonsense conceptions of the world are simply lived with, negotiated in everyday life perhaps, but not questioned. A critical conception of the world is one which questions them. But this questioning necessitates not merely intellectual questioning, but new forms of social practice.

Gramsci did not much consider the situation of women.

But I think that many of his ideas can illuminatingly be applied to their lives. Consider, for example, the question of power. Women have often been in the power of men; at the same time, they have sometimes also had power over men. But the associations of 'power' in each case have tended to be different. The power of men over women has often been a matter of authority, of force and of violence. The power of women over men has often depended on wiles and cunning and on devious strategies to conceal that power. But women have wanted to 'empower' themselves to act in new ways and reject old definitions of themselves; yet the old associations of 'power' may seem inadequate for this. The meeting of women in feminism has sometimes suggested new ways to think about 'power'; about the 'empowering' of women in ways that do not recapitulate the dominant institutionalised forms of hierarchy, violence or cunning. Conceptions of unrealised potentialities, of new social forms and patterns, and of the development of self, go hand in hand. And these new conceptions arise in the space left, as it were, by old contrasts or contradictions, and by the way in which the latter are inadequate to conceptualise new social forms or more coherently articulated personal goals.

Thus insofar as the notion of the 'real self' or 'authentic nature' of a person is a useful one, it should be used, I think, to express the idea of a more coherent, less fragmented conception of oneself, more critically aware of those things which have deposited in oneself the 'traces' of which Gramsci wrote, of the contradictions one may have been living in one's life, and of potential ways in which these might be resolved. In this sense, it is best represented as an achievement rather than a discovery of something that was 'already there'. It can be represented as the possibility of transcending, in certain circumstances, what had been 'second nature'.

5 Women and Autonomy

In *Women and Writing,* Virginia Woolf (1979) described her battle with the apparition that appeared over her shoulder, and whom she had to 'kill' before she could write. Woolf named her 'The Angel in the House', and described her like this:

I will describe her as shortly as I can. She was intensely sympathetic. She was immensely charming. She excelled in the difficult arts of family life. She sacrificed herself daily. If there was chicken, she took the leg, if there was a draught she sat in it — in short, she was so constituted that she never had a mind or wish of her own, but preferred to sympathise always with the minds and wishes of others. [p.59]

This sort of view of women has been endemic in philosophy, as elsewhere.[1] I have already mentioned the ways in which Rousseau and Kant saw the rationale of women's lives as being that of being charming, compliant and obedient to men. I will give one more example here. Kierkegaard wrote that woman was essentially 'being for another'; that is to say, she had, he thought, no existence or purposes that had any value in their own right:

This being of woman (for the word *existence* is too rich in meaning, since woman does not persist in and through herself), is rightly described as charm, an expression which suggests plant life; she is a flower, the poets like to say, and even the spiritual in her is present in a vegetative manner. [in Mahowald, 1978, p.178]

In *The Feminine Mystique* (1965), Betty Friedan documented the profound dissatisfaction, sometimes desperation, of American suburban housewives who had

been sold the ideology of feminine fulfilment through
marriage, home and children. Here is a typical quotation
from one of her interviews:

All I wanted was to get married and have four children. I love the kids and
Bob and my house. There's no problem you can ever put a name to. But
I'm desperate. I begin to feel I have no personality. I'm a server of food
and a putter-on of pants and a bedmaker, somebody who can be called on
when you want something. But who am I? [p.19]

It is not surprising that one of the most consistent themes
of feminism has been the need of women for autonomy and
independence, and their need to pursue their own interests
and say for themselves what it is that they want or need. But
in tension with this stress on autonomy there has been
another influential strand in feminist thinking which has
wanted to stress what it sees as a particularly female capacity
for caring and relatedness and connectedness to others. This
has led to a critique of 'individualistic' conceptions of self,
and sometimes to a view that these are typically male.

I shall look at this critique of individualism in the next
chapter. It has largely, I think, been a response to the
implications of certain uses of the notion of 'autonomy' in
feminist thinking, and to the ways in which these are
anchored in a particular view of self. This view of self is not
only influential in the work of many feminist writers, it also
underlies some popular conceptions of feminism. This is
what I want to discuss in this chapter.

One of the central features of this account of self is a sharp
distinction between the true and the false self. The false self
is equated in some way with what other people tell one to
be, condition one to being, or define one as. The real self is
presented in one of two ways. Either it is that which lies
behind the false self and needs to be revealed or discovered,
or it is that which one *defines oneself* as being in a process
that originates from oneself alone and is not influenced by
the opinions or judgements of others.

Mary Daly's work provides a clear example of this
conception of true and false self. In an earlier book, *Beyond
God the Father* (1973), she wrote of the alienation of women
from their own deepest identity or authentic selves, and of

the way in which they had accepted 'limited and undifferentiated identities' (p.23) as a substitute. In *Gyn/Ecology* (1979), as I have already shown, she draws a picture of women as almost zomboid, as invaded and possessed by the brainwashing of 'the Fathers' such that they scarcely seem to be human at all. And Daly alternates between the language of choice or self-definition and the language of discovery. In *Beyond God the Father* she writes mainly of self-definition. In *Gyn/Ecology* the language of discovery predominates, and women's discovery of their authentic selves is seen as akin to a spiritual rebirth, as unveiling or unwinding the 'shrouds' of patriarchy to reveal the true spirit self underneath.

Sometimes, the true self is contrasted with 'roles'. Thus Angela Hamblin writes;

When we accept our role and lose touch with the vital core of ourselves we are sick...It is a sickness that doesn't noticeably affect our bodies. It doesn't impair our capacity to function. It doesn't prevent us from acting out our role. We are just dead inside...This is because in our sick role-playing society this inner core of self is never accorded recognition or legitimated. It is never acknowledged that such a thing exists, so how can it be lost? (in Rowan, 1976, p.114)

Here, the 'inner core' of self seems to be *contrasted* in some way with what is social. The process of discovering one's real self is seen as one of undoing or unwinding the layers of socialisation which conceal the inner core. This sort of view of self has implications for ways of thinking about needs and interests and about the relationship between self and others which I now want to explore.

NEEDS AND INTERESTS

This view of self presupposes an individualism of interests; that is to say, that my own interests can be sharply distinguished from those of other people. A clear statement of this is made by Marilyn Frye (1983)

The health and integrity of an organism is a matter of its being organised largely towards its own interests and welfare. *She* is healthy and 'working right' when her substance is organised primarily on principles which align it to *her* interests and welfare. Co-operation is essential of course, but it will not do that I arrange everything so that *you* get enough exercise; for me to be healthy, I must get enough exercise. My being adequately exercised is logically independent of your being so. [p.70]

This may be true of being adequately exercised. But the notion that *all* the interests of a person are logically independent of those of other people is one that I shall return to in the next chapter. It is a notion which follows from that of the 'real self' which I outlined above. If the real self is an 'inner core' which is distinct from the social self, then its interests are necessarily distinct from those of other people.

In the work of Daly, there are also two further assumptions. The first is that once the false self is destroyed, the real self will be integrated and harmonious. The second is that the needs and interests of all real selves will harmonise with each other. Daly sees splits and tensions in the psyche, and barriers between selves, as the result of patriarchy. She writes of:

the deep agreement that is present within the self and among the selves who are increasingly in harmony with an environment that is beyond, beneath, and all around the non-environment of patriarchal splits and barriers. [1973, p.159].

SELF AND OTHERS

There are two main themes which emerge here very clearly; first, an ideal of emotional self-sufficiency, of not needing others, and second, a co-operative or contractual model of relationships.

Daly's work constantly stresses the rejection of dependence and the need she sees for women to be able to 'stand alone'. Women, she says, should 'cease to play the role of complement and struggle to stand alone as free human beings' (1973, p.26). They should be able to 'love independently'. What this means is brought out more clearly in *Gyn/Ecology*. Here, she distinguishes 'binding' from 'bonding'. 'Binding' is done from need, and all friendships or relationships that are built on need victimise the other person. Dependence, Daly says, contaminates or pollutes words like 'sister', 'friend' or 'lover'. Even mothers and daughters should not demand sacrifices from each other; all of us should resist the temptation to lean on friends or lovers out of weakness or frustration. We need the ability to be radically alone: 'Spinsters too, learn to be at home on the road. Our ability to make our spirits our moving shelters will enable us to dispense with patriarchal shelters, the various homes that house the domesticated, the mentally sick, the destitute' (1979, p.395).

This rejection of dependence is common in feminist thinking. In *The Second Sex* (1972), de Beauvoir argued that the problem for women has been that she *needed* man to complete her being, whereas man, she thought, had been socially independent and 'complete' in himself. But she moved from a critique of this sexual asymmetry to arguing that the ideal relationship would not be based on need at all: 'The ideal, on the contrary, would be for entirely self-sufficient human beings to form unions with one another only in accordance with the untrammelled dictates of their mutual love' (p.490). Love is seen ideally as a matter of mere pleasure or choice, unrelated to need or dependency: 'The woman who achieves virile independence has the great privilege of carrying on her sexual life with individuals who are themselves autonomous and effective in action, who will not enchain her through their weakness and the exigency of their needs' (p.704). De Beauvoir sees it as a problem, a fault in women, especially in 'independent' ones, that they may continue to care about another person's welfare or success as much as about their own.

Now, there is at least one sort of relationship which it is clearly not easy to fit into this picture of entirely voluntary relationships between self-sufficient people, and that is relationships with children. The implication of much of what de Beauvoir writes is that 'independence' would be incompatible with having children at all. And relationships with children rarely figure in Daly's work. She talks of the grief and pain that children caused their mothers, and presents an idealised vision of mother-daughter relationships, but it is not at all clear how the care of children is to fit into her vision of free-spirited spinsters 'on the road'. I am irresistibly reminded here of the male 'beat' life-style described by Jack Kerouac in *On the Road* (1958), and tempted to suggest that children and their needs seem to be about as incompatible with Daly's vision as they are with Kerouac's. The difference is that whereas Kerouac clearly assumes that women will look after the children, it is not clear who Daly thinks will do it at all. It is difficult to see how the care of children, or of others who are needy or dependent, could fit into a world where all relationships were 'voluntary' and where the exigency of needs never enchained anyone.

An interesting attempt to derive principles for the care of children from an ideal of voluntaristic non-dependent relationships was made by Shulamith Firestone in *The Dialectic of Sex* (1979). Like Daly and de Beauvoir, in her ideal society, all relationships would be based on love alone, uncorrupted by dependencies. No one, in fact, should have a commitment to another person that cannot ultimately be opted out of if they wish. Firestone recognises, of course, that people will still want intimate relationships, but these are to be based entirely on choice. And this ideal is to apply to children too. Firestone uses the work of Philippe Aries (1962) to show that the concept of 'childhood' has not always been the same as it is now, but interprets Aries as showing that before the advent of the bourgeois nuclear family there was no real distinction between children and adults at all.[2] She regards the institution of the family based on genetic parenthood as one which oppresses children, and the concept of 'childhood' itself as one weapon in this oppression, in which parental authority (rationalised as 'love'), deprives children of their autonomy, their independence and their rights. Children, Firestone thinks, fare best when they are left alone. '"Raising" a child is tantamount to retarding his development. The best way to raise a child is to LAY OFF' (p.90). So Firestone envisages replacing the family with a system of loosely structured households, contracted to stay together for a number of years, with all members sharing responsibility for a certain number of children. If a child wishes to leave a household, he or she may do so at any time. (It is not clear whether anyone else has an obligation to take them in.) In this scheme of things, claims of duty or need almost seem to be ruled out of order. And the rationale of close relationships is either that of mere choice or of the mutual contracting of the partners to co-operate with each other in the furtherance of their interests.

What happens to notions of responsibilities or obligations to others in this picture? It is not so much, I think, that they disappear as that they become diffused. One has a generalised responsibility and obligation to help other people meet their needs, and in the work of Daly and Firestone (though not so much in de Beauvoir), images of 'community', in which everyone cares for everyone else, abound. Daly's sisterhood of 'Spinsters' and 'Hags' is such a community. So is Firestone's Utopia. Plato, in the *Republic,* saw the abolition of particular or private affections as leading to a greater love for the community; maybe Firestone is making a similar assumption. But in her community, one would not have permanent obligations to other people which could not be opted out of if they became uncongenial, and duties, unless specifically contracted to, are to the whole community rather than to specific others.

Now I think that one image of feminism that is quite widespread is that being a feminist should imply both emotional self-sufficiency and a willingness to ditch obligations or commitments to others without guilt or emotional ambivalence. In the *Guardian,* for example, on 6 September 1984, there was an article by Rachel Pennington explaining why she left her husband and children, and the guilt and ambivalence this had caused her, despite the fact that she was happy for the first time in years, and maintained a relationship with her children. But, she wrote:

I'm not a feminist, an independent woman. I rely very much on my new partner for his supportiveness. Perhaps if I *was* a feminist things might be easier – I could logically fit the idea of leaving one's children into the comforting philosophy of the Sisterhood. But no, I don't have the protective mantle of united womanhood to draw about me.

What is interesting is the way she equates being a feminist
with not needing other people, and with being able to leave
one's children without guilt feelings. And I think this sort of
image of feminism is quite widespread, and the one that is
most common in the media. The magazine *Cosmopolitan,*
for example, which in its British version has aspirations or
pretensions to feminism and sometimes carries features on
or by well-known feminist writers, frequently presents an
image of the 'independent' woman as assertive, pushy,
insistent on the right to enjoy herself here and now, and
leading a life-style free of much in the way of responsibilities
or obligations to other people.

FEMINISM, HUMAN POTENTIAL AND SELF-REALISATION

The view of self and autonomy which I have outlined is one
which is anchored in a number of philosophical sources,
some of which I shall discuss in the next chapter. But the
immediate inspiration for some of its more recent
manifestations in feminism (in the work of both Friedan and
Daly, for instance) is what has beome known as 'humanistic
psychology' or the 'human potential' movement.

The 'human potential' movement is a variegated and
diverse phenomenon which has led to a proliferation of
various sorts of 'therapy', most of which have the professed
aim of enabling a person to penetrate behind the 'masks',
'fronts' or 'facades' of everyday life and get in touch with the
real person behind these. Despite its varied manifestations,
however, it has a consistent theoretical core, whose
development is largely owed to the work of the major
theorists of humanistic psychology, Carl Rogers and,
especially, Abraham Maslow. Friedan used the work of
Maslow in giving her account of the needs of women, and
Daly, in *Beyond God the Father* (1973), quotes him as
expressing exactly the sort of conception of self-realisation
that she wanted to see as a goal for women.

The major concept in Maslow's theories is that of
'self-actualisation'. He saw human needs as existing in a

hierarchy; the 'lowest' were the needs for food and shelter; above these came needs for things like security and self-esteem, and once these were adequately gratified, the 'higher' needs for self-actualisation could come into play. Self-actualisation, according to Maslow, was the realising of one's unique inner potential, the flowering and development of one's 'highest' capacities.

Much of his work was devoted to a detailed discussion of what he thought to be the characteristics of self-actualising people. Two of the central characteristics that he identified were those of autonomy and of not needing others. Those who have not yet reached the 'highest' level of human motivation still need others. But, 'far from needing other people, growth-motivated people may actually be hampered by them' (1970, p.34). They like solitude and privacy and they can remain detached from other people. Maslow constantly contrasts those who are self-actualising with 'ordinary' people. So, he argues, their detachment may create problems in their relations with these ordinary people:

In social relations with most people, detachment creates certain troubles and problems. It is easily interpreted by normal people as coldness, snobbishness, lack of affection, unfriendliness or even hostility. By contrast, the ordinary person is more clinging, more demanding, more desirous of reassurance, compliment, support, warmth and exclusiveness. It is true that self-actualising people do not need others in this ordinary sense. But since this being needed is the usual earnest of friendship, it is evident that detachment will not easily be accepted by average people [1970, p.161.]

Relationships between self-actualising people are more like a disinterested appreciation of the other's qualities; self-actualising people love because of 'the objective, intrinsic qualities of the perceived person...He is loved because he is loveworthy rather than because he gives out love.' (1970, p.36).

So, according to Maslow, there are human beings who need others and those who do not. And there are also those who are autonomous or self-determined and those who are not. Self-actualising people are autonomous, and their actions and decisions, Maslow says, come from within:

My subjects make up their own minds, come to their own decisions, are responsible for themselves and their own destinies...They taught me to see as profoundly sick, abnormal or weak what I had always taken for granted as humanly normal: namely, that many people do not make up their own minds, but have their minds made up for them, by salesmen, advertisers, parents, propagandists, TV, newspapers and so on. They are pawns to be moved by others, rather than self-moving, self-determining individuals. Therefore they are apt to feel helpless, weak and totally determined; they are prey for predators, flabby whiners rather than self-determining responsible persons [1970, p.161]

Although the theories of Carl Rogers differ in some respects from those of Maslow, they share some basic presuppositions.[3] What Maslow calls 'self-actualisation' Rogers calls 'becoming a person', and, again, Rogers sees 'being a person' as involving emotional self-sufficiency and the determination to pursue one's own individually defined goals. And, like Maslow, Rogers draws a sharp distinction between those people whose focus of evaluation is external and those in whom it is internal; those who, as he puts it, are pawns rather than persons.

More than Maslow, Rogers, through the varieties of counselling and therapeutic work that he has undertaken, has spelled out the consequences of this sort of view of self for relationships between people. He has, for example, written extensively about what he calls 'open marriage'. This is an arrangement whereby a man and a woman choose to have a central relationship with each other but are so strong and emotionally self-sufficient that they can allow each other to have what Rogers calls 'satellite' relationships with other people, and are so autonomous that they are able, as Rogers sees it, to pursue a self-directed course without being influenced by the opinions of others. The old 'sin' of infidelity is, of course, out. But there are new sins; they are jealousy, possessiveness and guilt. To be 'jealous' is to be emotionally disturbed by the 'satellite' relationships of your partner. To be 'possessive' is to make demands of any form on them. And to be 'guilty' is to be unable to enter into other relationships without worrying about the effect it might have on your partner. Rogers sums up the whole thing as follows:

I think the ideal situation is when one can tell the partner: 'I need and I owe it to myself to experience this other relationship now. I'm hearing your hurt, your jealousy, your fear, your anger; I do not like to receive them, but they are a consequence of the choice I'm making, and I love you enough to want to be available to work through them with you. If I decide not to have this other experience, it is because I choose to do so and not because I let you stop me. In that way I won't feel resentful of you and I won't punish you for my lack of courage in making my choices and being responsible for the consequences.

This is a mature kind of striving for both independence and richness. [1978, pp.55-6]

Now, humanistic psychology owes its intellectual origins, I think to a number of sources. One of these is Existentialism. Both Maslow and Rogers say that they have gained 'insights' from Existentialism, and their stress on authenticity and on not being bound by 'roles' is a kind of derivation from the Existentialist concept of 'bad faith' as developed by Sartre. Another source is the sort of individualist theories of human nature that I have already mentioned, and shall return to in the next chapter. Maslow, in particular, has been seen by some critics as the arch-ideologue of liberal individualism, and humanistic psychology has been seen as preaching a doctrine of self-interest and personal autonomy at the expense of recognising the social origins of the self, the necessary interdependence of human beings and the profound social changes that are necessary before any substantial form of human liberation can come about.[4] They have been accused, as have liberal philosophers, of a false egalitarianism; that is, of supposing that a process of personal change or individual effort will lead all by itself to individual liberation and fulfilment, or to the abolition of things like poverty or racial and sexual oppression.

I think there is substance to all of these criticisms. The notion that working on one's feelings, individually or in groups, is the only route to personal or social change, is endemic in humanist psychology. (Rogers, for example, has supposed that the problems of Northern Ireland might be solved if only sufficient trained humanistic counsellors were to go there and hold encounter groups on every street corner.) The notion of the autonomy of the self and the autonomy of individual desires is a liberal individualist one.

The assumptions made by both Maslow and Rogers (and evident, as I have tried to show, in the work of Daly) that individuals have only to find their 'real' or authentic selves, and that there is a sort of pre-established harmony between the needs and interests of these selves such that there will never be any real conflict, are ones that are very reminiscent of the idea of the beneficent hand of the market forces which will ensure that if only individuals maximise their own self-interest, the whole of society will benefit.

But to see humanistic psychology simply as liberal individualist is to miss certain crucial aspects of it, especially of the work of Maslow; aspects which I think have had profound reverberations in the work of feminists who have used his or similar ideas. Maslow was a great admirer of Nietzsche, referring to him frequently in his *Journals* (1982), and despite the veneer of egalitarianism in Maslow's work, with its emphasis on the self-actualisation of every human individual, he was not really an egalitarian at all. In fact, after the manner of Nietzsche, he was frequently contemptuous of egalitarianism.

In his studies of self-actualisation, Maslow constantly uses the language not only of 'higher' levels of motivation or needs, but of 'superior' human beings. Thus, he asks, 'Could these self-actualising people be more human, more revealing of the original nature of the species, closer to the species in the taxonomical sense?...Ought a biological species to be judged by its crippled, warped, only partially developed specimens?' (1970, p.159). The study of 'superior specimens', he argued, could help us to develop what he called a 'normative biology', which would identify what would count as a 'good specimen' of humanity. He compared these 'superior specimens' to Olympic gold-medal winners. If we want to know how tall human beings can grow, we should study tall people, not average ones, and if we want to know how fast a human being can run, we should study medal winners. We will be misled if we look at 'an average of what amounts to indiscriminately sick and healthy, good and bad specimens, good and bad choosers, biologically sound and biologically unsound specimens' (1971, p.7).

Maslow believed that we have what he called an 'instinctoid' inner nature, unique individual capacities which can develop once our basic needs are satisfied, and that we can rely on the 'biological wisdom' of our organisms to set the direction for this. Now the use of the word 'instinctoid' and the constant references to biology might seem to suggest some form of biological determinism. Maslow denied on a number of occasions that he accepted any form of biological determinism, but in fact in much of his work he assumes that some people are just naturally superior to others. He coined a word 'Eupsychia', by which he meant the ideal society that he envisaged, and this society was to be designed so that 'superior' people would become its leaders. He even suggested that one day we might be able to select these people by a series of laboratory tests, impossible to fake, which would enable us to make predictions about the kind of people who would make better leaders, managers, supervisors and bosses in later life.

Maslow's vision of society was a hierarchical one, and he was consistently contemptuous of egalitarianism and democracy, and of what he saw as the failure of many people to recognise the excellence and superiority of the élite of self-actualisers, and to acknowledge the legitimacy of their leadership.

Thus, he said:

Under good conditions the superior person is totally freed, or anyway more freed, to enjoy himself completely, to express himself as he pleases, to pursue his own selfish ends without worrying about anybody else, or feeling any guilt or obligation to anybody else, in the full confidence that everybody will benefit by his being fully himself and pursuing his own selfish ends. [1965, p.105]

Consistently too, throughout his work, Maslow identifies self-actualisation or superiority with dominance, with success, with winning. Betty Friedan (1963), who used Maslow's theories as the basis for her analysis of the situation and needs of women, quotes with approval some early studies done by Maslow (Maslow, 1939 and 1942) on strength or 'dominance' in women. She does not question, however, the way in which he *equates* strength with dominance, and she does not notice, for example, that one of the things, according to Maslow, which characterises 'high dominance' women, is that they behave like men, prefer the company of men and are generally rather contemptuous of women. Nor does she notice that Maslow's high-dominance women need a man, he thinks, who is even *more* dominant to give them sexual satisfaction. More than other women, they especially want to be dominated, to be forced to submit and to be subordinate, and Maslow thought that they especially loved to pick fights in order that the male would become brutal.

Maslow's 'Eupsychia', or ideal society, was to be based throughout on notions of hierarchy, superiority, inferiority, dominance and submission. It was to be one in which an élite of self-actualisers would pursue their own interests ruthlessly (and in which women would be subordinate to men, since the essence of feminity, as Maslow saw it, was to want to submit to and be protected by a dominant male). He saw self-actualising people as almost like a *transmutation* of the human species:

The self-actualising person is, after all, very different from other people in thought, impulse, behaviour and emotion. When it comes down to it, in certain basic ways he is like an alien in a strange land. Very few really understand him, however much they may like him. He is often saddened, exasperated and even enraged by the shortcomings of the average person and while they are to him ordinarily no more than a nuisance, they sometimes become bitter tragedy. However far apart from them he is at times, he nevertheless feels a basic underlying kinship with these creatures whom he must regard with, if not condescension, at least the knowledge that he can do many things better than they can, that he can see things that they cannot see, that the 'truth' that is so clear to him is for most people veiled and hidden. [1970, pp.165-6]

The major themes in Maslow's work have a close affinity to those in the work of Nietzsche, including those of a 'higher' type of human being, and the dislike of any form of egalitarianism. And, given the sort of rejection of ideas of hierarchy, dominance and élitism that has characterised a great deal of feminist practice and thinking, it is perhaps surprising that the work of Maslow, in which these things are endemic, should have been seen as an inspiration. I think it is probably to be explained by the potential attractiveness to feminism of any theory of self which has a vigorous image of self-assertion, self-affirmation and independence, given the way in which these things have often been more or less totally denied to women. I suspect that neither Friedan nor Daly can have read Maslow in detail, and I certainly do not think that either of them would want to have anything to do with Maslow's near-fascist views on dominance and submission, or with ideas about 'superior' human beings. But the problem is whether it is possible to use a Maslovian (or Nietzschean) theory of self without implicitly accepting some aspects of their work which in many ways seem most antithetical to feminism.

In many respects the work of Daly is profoundly Nietzschean; she talks of Nietzsche, in fact, as a prophet whose prophecy was short-circuited by his own misogyny. Now the core of much of Nietzsche's work was an attack on Judaeo-Christian morality and, in fact, on the idea of 'morality' itself, insofar as this was based on ideas of duty. Thus he was contemptuous of the moral philosophy of Kant: 'Nothing works more profound ruin than any "impersonal" duty, any sacrifice to the Moloch of abstraction...What destroys more quickly than to work, to think, to feel, without inner necessity, without a deep personal choice, without joy?...as an automaton of duty? (1968, p.122). Nietzsche believed Christian morality, with its otherworldliness, its emphasis on the spiritual, on self-abnegation, altruism, duty, pity, meekness, humility and poverty, to be responsible for what he saw as the decadence of humanity in the nineteenth century – its degeneration, corruption and psychic near-death. He saw these as manifested in such things as humanitarianism, egalitarian ideas in politics and the decline of what was 'noble' in art and education.

Christianity, he thought, was hostile to everything that was life-affirming; it led to the degeneration of 'instincts'. Nietzsche's concept of 'instinct' is that of a physiologically based urge or desire for self-affirmation, which he called 'the will to power'. If this was not corrupted by an effete and

decadent culture, a few élite individuals might become what
Nietzsche saw as a 'higher' human type – strong, brave,
masterful and proud. This concept of a 'higher' human
nature was as far removed as possible from moral ideals of
'higher' human qualities to be striven for as a duty;
Nietzsche was contemptuous of such ideals. His 'higher' type
of human being acted not out of morality or duty, but out of
an urge for self-affirmation and self-aggrandisement, a sort
of wisdom of the organism that knew by instinct what was in
its interests. A culture was to be judged by its capacity to
produce such 'higher' types, and by the ability of the rest of
its people to be satisfied with the mundane labours of their
mediocrity, and not be corrupted by decadent ideas of
rights, of equality and, especially, of humanitarianism.
Nietzsche was particularly contemptuous of
humanitarianism: 'Here everyone helps everyone else, here
everyone is to a certain degree an invalid and everyone a
nurse. This is then called virtue...among men who knew a
different kind of life, a fuller, more prodigal, more
overflowing life, it would be called something else;
"cowardice", perhaps, "pitiableness", "old woman's
morality"'(1968, p.90). Liberal institutions were particularly
harmful, since 'they undermine the will to power, they are
the levelling of mountain and valley exalted to a moral
principle; they make small, cowardly, smug...The man who
has become free...spurns the contemptible sort of well being
dreamed of by shopkeepers, Christians, cows, women,
Englishmen and other democrats' (p.92).

Christian 'virtues' Nietzsche thought, did unutterably
more harm than any of those things normally called 'vices'.
They took the side of everything that was weak, base and
ill-constituted. They led to cowardice and self-deception.
Christian values were a reaction of the downtrodden and
ill-constituted against a morality of breeding, of race and of
privilege, and their universal legitimation meant the death of
the human spirit.

Nietzsche called for a 'revaluation of all values';
previously 'that which is most harmful to life is here called
"true"; that which enhances it, intensifies it, affirms it,
justifies it and causes it to triumph is called "false" (p.120).

Taming or domesticating people was called 'improving' them; decay of vitality was called 'virtue'. Nietzsche saw himself as a prophet, an innovator of the spirit, calling for a reversal of values, for rejection of ideals of pity, humility, and so forth, and an exposure of the ruin they had brought about.

Daly entitled Chapter 4 of her book *Beyond God the Father* (1973) 'Transvaluation of Values: The End of Phallic Morality'. She quotes Nietzsche as follows at the beginning of the chapter: '"A transvaluation of values can only be accomplished when there is a tension of new needs and a new set of needy people who feel all old values as painful – although they are not conscious of what is wrong"' (p.98). Nietzsche was profoundly and savagely misogynistic and contemptuous of women. But, as I have said, Daly sees him as a prophet. And the half-truth I think she saw in his work, the insight that could be gained from him, was that the Christian morality he so despised, the morality of humility, self-abnegation, service to others and so forth, was in fact the morality which had been thought especially appropriate to women. In his contemptuous dismissal of this as an 'old woman's morality', Nietzsche himself acknowledges this, in a distorted way.

In many places in her books, Daly discusses the hypocrisy and doublethink underlying the moral ideals of self-abnegation to which women in particular have been subject. Thus, she says, there has been a *theoretical* emphasis upon the virtues of charity, meekness, obedience, humility and self-sacrifice. But these qualities have often been foisted on women, hypocritically idealised and then used as a concealment or cover for power, ruthlessness, avarice, ambition and violence. Thus, for example, powerful, rapacious and ruthless prelates have preached the virtues of humility and self-sacrifice to women in particular, whilst leading lives that displayed the very antithesis of these qualities. Christian morality, she argues, has not only denied responsibility and self-actualisation to women. It has also stifled honesty in men.

I think there is no doubt of the frequent truth of this, and I think that the conclusion that Daly sometimes draws from it is right. She argues that we need a 'transvaluation' of values, not in the sense of a simple reversal, a decision to affirm or validate what was once denied, but in the sense of a breaking down of an initial polarisation. Thus, she says 'love cut off from power or justice is pseudo-love, power isolated from love and justice is inauthentic power of dominance, and justice is a meaningless facade of legalism split off from love and real power of being' (1973, p.217). Values, she argues, need forcing out of the mould of inane and impotent good, and self-destructive evil. Why should love be associated merely with self-abnegation or self-affirmation with domination? Larry Blum (1982) similarly asked why the virtues Kant saw as especially feminine, such as sympathy, sensitivity or compassion, should be seen as intrinsically associated with docility or obedience to men. The same question is asked by Jean Baker Miller in her book *Towards a New Psychology of Women* (1978). Miller suggests that some of what are sometimes seen as women's weaknesses can in fact often be seen as strengths, and that it is crucial for feminist thinking to avoid the sorts of polarisations which see *any* form of dependence on others, for example, as a threat to autonomy.

Now, precisely what neither Nietzsche nor Maslow do is to 'transvaluate' values in this sort of way. Nietzsche's philosophy is, I think based rather on simple reversal: what had previously been thought good was evil. It is true that Nietzsche talked of philosophy as moving 'beyond good and evil' (the title of one of his books), but by that phrase he meant to indicate his intention to reject any morality that thought in terms of duty or obligation. Nietzsche described his work as an 'anti-morality', or sometimes as a 'natural morality', one that flowed from the intrinsic nature of a human being uncorrupted by ideas of morality or duty. But this form of self-affirmation was *totally* inconsistent with things like pity or concern for others; it was a form of total individualism and egoism. Nietzsche rejected in their entirety all those Christian values that he despised, and would have seen any effort to reinterpret them as simply another nail in the coffin of the human spirit. It was *either* self-aggrandisement and life *or* self-abasement and death.

Maslow's work is similarly based on a series of sharp dichotomies: inner/outer, autonomy/dependence, needing others/not needing them. So is much of Daly's: life/death, binding/bonding, self-denial/self-affirmation. Her work is full of Nietzschean themes. One of the most prominent is that of the death and decay and decrepitude wrought by Christian (patriarchal) morality. As I pointed out earlier, Daly sees women as not merely brutalised by patriarchy, but as reduced to a state of near-robotitude. And while the overt target of her anger and contempt is patriarchal morality itself, the language she frequently uses to describe women veers very near to Nietzschean contempt for those who are subject to that morality. To describe women as 'fembots' or the 'puppets of Papa' seems to me to be perilously close to Nietzsche's contempt for cows, shopkeepers, Christians and women.

Furthermore, Daly (1973) uses a very Nietzschean concept of self-affirmation, of life-force as the opposite of the images of psychic death and decay: 'For men...life has meant feeding on the bodies and minds of women, sapping energy at the expense of female deaths...It is men who have sapped the life-force of women' (p.173). The task for women is to take back their own stolen power and being; to *come alive,* to unleash a new flow of energy from their innermost being: 'The source of the energy is women's participation in power of being as we hear and speak forth our own new word' (p.173). Similarly, 'Our revolution means life against death. It is not losing oneself for a cause, but living for oneself and therefore also living a cause' (p.144).

Daly has, in fact, a quasi-instinctual view of authentic being and self-affirmation which is very much like that of Nietzsche. And, like Nietzsche, her style of writing is often prophetic. She does not of course end up with a Nietzschean vision of a 'higher' type of human being, or a vision of a society (like Maslow's Eupsychia) whose rationale is to produce such a caste of beings (though her description of women as 'mutants' might seem to move in this direction). Nor does she end up with a vision of a society based on dominance and hierarchy. She talks instead of community and harmony: 'The power to regain our own life comes from

the discovery of the cosmic covenant, the deep harmony in
the community of being in which we participate' (p.177).
Her harmony is clearly intended to be based on equality and
on the recognition of the life in all women, not on the 'false
harmony' of patriarchal domination, which is the sort of
harmony envisaged by Nietzsche and Maslow. But I think
there is a gulf between Daly's conceptualisation of self-
affirmation and the harmony to which she thinks it may lead.
Nietzsche's philosophy of self-affirmation led to a pure
egoism, untainted by concern for others, and to a harmony
based on will and domination. It may be that in this he was
more consistent. Daly's leads to an idealised spiritual
harmony of equality, but it is not clear how this could come
about, or why it should be the consequence of the sort of
individual self-assertion, self-definition and quest for
authenticity of which she writes.

I stress again that I do not think Daly, or any other
feminist writer whose work I have quoted, would accept the
explicit élitism and contempt for 'ordinary' people that
appears in the work of Nietzsche or Maslow. Nevertheless, I
think that the sort of conception of self-affirmation that I
have discussed poses immense problems for feminist theory
and practice. In various ways it can be seen as
'individualistic'. Now 'individualism' is a concept that can
have a variety of different meanings, some of which I shall
discuss in the next chapter.[5] Here I want to note the way in
which the view of self I have discussed is premised on a
series of sharp oppositions between such things as
dependence and independence, serving others and affirming
oneself, needing others and not needing them, and between
what is variously seen as authentic selfhood, real self,
self-definition or determination, and a state in which one is a
mere pawn, a non-person, a puppet who is simply
manipulated by strings pulled by other people, or degraded
by subservience to others to an almost subhuman state.

Implicit in this is a derogatory or even contemptuous
attitude towards those women who do not fit whatever
precise model of self-affirmation or self-actualisation is in
question. This is most striking in the work of Daly. It is
linked with the more or less total absence, both from Daly's

analysis of patriarchy and from her vision of a feminist future, of any real discussion of the ways in which women have spent their lives, the activities that have been particularly theirs, the values and concerns that might be associated with these, or the particular strengths and capacities to which they might have given rise. And this absence is itself, I think, linked to the kind of distinction between those activities which are fully 'human' and those which are not, that I discussed in the last chapter. I pointed out there the way in which Betty Friedan and Simone de Beauvoir, for example, viewed the tasks of childbearing and rearing, or of domestic labour and caring for others, as 'infantilising', or as constituting a realm of 'immanence' in which truly human projects could not be undertaken. Views such as these, which see women's lives as spent in nothing but servitude or 'robotitude', and women's activities as intrinsically infantilising, are divisive and potentially threatening. They are divisive because they implicitly divide women into two camps: those who are liberated and have shaken the dust of service to others from the soles of their feet, and those who are still trapped in the old ways and not sufficiently enlightened even to perceive the depths of their own degradation and dehumanisation. They are threatening because they imply that those who *have* devoted their lives, say, to their homes and children, have done nothing of value, nothing which can be seen as fully 'human', and nothing which they would have chosen to do of their own free will. To be told this sort of thing can constitute an intolerable threat to one's identity or conception of oneself.

Now many feminists have been critical of this dismissive attitude towards women's lives and work. They have pointed out, for example, the way in which women's labour has (often invisibly) sustained the world of male achievement. Adrienne Rich, (1980) for example writes of:

the efforts of women in labour, giving birth to stillborn children, children who must die of plague or infanticide; the efforts of women to keep filth and decay at bay, children decently clean, to produce the clean shirt in which the man walks out daily into the common world of men, the efforts to raise children against the attritions of racist and sexist schooling, drugs, sexual exploitation, and brutalisation and killing of barely grown boys in war. There is still little but contempt and indifference for this kind of

6 The Critique of Individualism

In this chapter I shall discuss the feminist critique of 'individualism', and of the sorts of ideals of autonomy, self-realisation and self-sufficiency that I outlined in the last chapter. I want to start by looking in some detail at an article by Naomi Scheman (1983) since it seems to me to encapsulate aspects of this critique that have been influential in a considerable amount of recent feminist thinking.

Scheman's article is entitled *Individualism and the Objects of Psychology,* and her starting point is a critique of what she calls 'individualism' in the philosophy of mind. Individualism, she suggests, is the belief that psychological states can be assigned and theorised about on an individual basis. So, she says:

What I have in mind is the assumption that my pain, anger, beliefs, intentions and so on are particular (in theory) identifiable states that I am in, which enter as individuals into causal relationships. Some examples of individualistic states are being five feet tall, having pneumonia, missing three teeth, and having some immediate subjective experience (though how to describe the latter is by no means clear). Being the most popular girl in the class, or a major general, or divorced, are not individualistic states; nor, I want to argue, are being in love or angry or generous, believing that all eels hail from the Sargasso sea, knowing how to read, or expecting an explosion any minute now. [In Harding and Hintikka, 1983, p.226]

Now from this I think it is not at all clear what Scheman means by calling a mental state 'individualistic'. In fact, there are several aspects of her critique of individualism

162

which are not clearly distinguished from each other.

First, Scheman wants to argue that many psychological states can't be understood as being like simple twinges or pangs which either occur or not. So, she argues:

> We can, I think, maintain that our twinges and pangs and so on are particular events, no matter what our social situation, but it does not follow that the same is true for more complex psychological objects, such as emotions, beliefs, motives and capacities. What we need to know, in order to identify *them* is how to group together introspectible states and behaviour, and how to interpret it all. The question is one of meaning, not just at the level of what to call it, but at the level of there being an 'It' at all. And questions of meaning and interpretation cannot be answered in abstraction from a social setting. [p.229]

The philosophical point that Scheman wants to make here is that concepts such as 'pity' or 'remorse' or 'love' have an internal complexity. What 'remorse' refers to, for example, is not a 'particular' in the way in which a twinge of toothache is. It is true that we do sometimes speak of 'pangs' of remorse, and so forth, but the remorse is not identifiable with something that can be understood, in a quasi-physiological sense, as a pang or a twinge. This is because to feel something such as remorse involves such things as the concept of responsibility, beliefs about the situation of a person, about one's relationship to that person, and such beliefs and concepts are necessarily socially derived. So to identify oneself as 'in love' is to *interpret,* to see a *pattern* in a complex range of behaviour, impulses, feelings and thoughts. If we do not know what we really feel, it is usually because the pattern is not clear to us; because our thoughts and feelings and impulses do not 'fit' any pattern clearly enough for us to be able to say what it is that we feel.

This view of the complexity of psychological states and the way in which we learn to ascribe them relates to the second thing that Scheman wants to maintain. In general, it is that all concepts are necessarily socially acquired. More particularly, Scheman engages with a tradition in the philosophy of mind which argues that the way in which we learn concepts such as 'anger' or 'remorse' or 'pain' cannot be understood as arising merely from a sort of 'inner pointing' to some introspectible object.[1] The reason is that these are concepts in a language which is publicly used and shared, and therefore there must be *some* criteria for the use of a word which are not purely 'private' if it is to be intelligible at all. This is true just as much of concepts such as 'pain' as of those such as 'love'.

This debate in the philosophy of mind is a long and complex one, and raises questions which I do not have space to go into here. (It might, for example, be argued that there is still an important difference between concepts such as 'pain' and 'love', in that if a person does not have a *concept* of love available to them, they could not be said to love at all, whereas it makes perfectly good sense to ascribe pain to a person who lacks the ability to talk, communicate or name their experiences to themselves.) In general, though, despite all the further questions and complexities, I think there is broad agreement among most philosophers that concepts are socially acquired and that those which refer to psychological states must be anchored in some way by criteria for their use which are interpersonally shared. But there are times at which Scheman seems to be arguing not merely for the social learning thesis, or the view that many psychological states have an inner complexity, but for a third thesis, which is, I think, both unclear and problematic. She argues that mental states do not *'attach'* to us singly; and what seems to be implied is the view not only that psychological states cannot be *identified* on an individual basis (the social learning thesis) but that they cannot be *ascribed* to individuals either.

Now these two things are quite different. Because I cannot identify what I feel as 'anger' or 'love' without socially acquired capacities, it does not in the least follow that my anger is in some sense not mine, and cannot be ascribed just to me. The issue is confused by some of Scheman's examples. Of course, I cannot be divorced unless someone else is too, or be a major-general unless other people are soldiers. There are many states which cannot be ascribed to just one person or which depend on social institutions for their meaning. The latter is true of many actions as well; I cannot write a cheque or vote in a society in which there are no banks or elections. But this does not mean that *I* did not vote or write the cheque, or that the relevant actions did not 'attach' to me singly.

I have tried to bring out what is unclear in what Scheman says here, because I think it links with a view she expresses later in the article about the 'essential indistinctness of persons'. I shall return to that later; but first I want to look at the connections Scheman makes between her critique of individualism and feminism.

INDIVIDUALISM, LIBERALISM AND FEMINISM

Scheman links what she calls individualism in the philosophy of mind to a doctrine which is often known as 'abstract individualism', and which has been the foundation of some versions of political liberalism. Abstract individualism is a doctrine which assumes that it is possible to think of human nature as 'given', of human beings as possessing fundamental characteristics or desires which can be abstracted from particular social circumstances. Sometimes, as I mentioned in chapter 4, abstract individualism has been linked with the idea of a 'state of nature', a conception of human beings as existing before the foundations of society. Sometimes, as in the utilitarian philosophy of Jeremy Bentham, there is an explicit recognition that the *objects* of human desires are socially formed; but Bentham nevertheless saw human society as made up of millions of individuals, each of whom was under the governance of the 'sovereign masters', pleasure and pain, and each of whom pursued their own interests in seeking pleasure and avoiding pain.

Abstract individualism is often linked to some version of the doctrine of psychological egoism; the belief that at bottom all human beings pursue their own individual interests. Again Hobbes and Bentham are clear examples of philosophers who held egoistic doctrines. Hobbes held that the only thing which could move a person to action was the thought of their own good, and Bentham believed that all human actions were motivated by the desire to gain pleasure and avoid pain. Behaviourist psychology, in the twentieth

century, has subscribed to an egoistic doctrine very similar
to that of Bentham, in which the only thing seen capable of
motivating a person is what is called 'reinforcement' (which
is thought of in behaviourist theory as a quasi-physiological
event occurring within the individual organism). In his book
Beyond Freedom and Dignity (1972) the behaviourist
psychologist B.F. Skinner asked why anyone should be
concerned about the good of their own culture. The answer he
gave was that there was no good reason. Altruism is only
possible if your culture reinforces (roughly, rewards) you for it.

Abstract individualism has generated a political
philosophy – namely, liberalism – which has seen as its
central questions those of why I should obey the state, and
of the extent to which the state is justified in interfering with
the liberty of private individuals to conduct their lives as
they please. Analogously, it has generated a moral
philosophy which sees as its central problem that of egoism
and altruism, of why I should be 'moral', or why I should
respect the interests of others and behave altruistically
towards them. Not all versions of liberalism put forward a
doctrine of egoism after the manner of Hobbes or Bentham
or Skinner. The political philosophy of the liberal John
Rawls (1972), for example, certainly does not assume that
no one is capable of 'disinterested' concern for the welfare of
another, and his theory of justice is premised on the
possibility of an impartial consideration of the interests of
others as well as oneself. Nevertheless, the individuals
whom Rawls assumes to be planning the hypothetical society
that will best exemplify the principles of justice are
fundamentally concerned, according to Rawls, with
maximising their own individual share of the social goods
which might be on offer. In that sense, they are necessarily
all in competition with each other for such shares and are
primarily concerned with their own individual self-interest.
(Rawls' philosophy does not at all entertain the idea that
there might be some 'social goods' which cannot be
conceived of in terms of being 'shared out' among
individuals.)

Scheman describes what she sees as the ideology of liberal
individualism as follows:

It is supposed to be a natural fact about human beings, and hence a constraint on any possible social theory, that, no matter how social our development may be, we exist essentially as separate individuals – with wants, preferences, needs, abilities, pleasures and pains – and any social order has to begin by respecting these as attaching to us determinately and singly, as a way of respecting us...The societies thus envisioned aim at maximally respecting the separateness of their members by providing mechanisms for adjudicating the claims that one member may make against another, while leaving as intact as possible the rights of each to be self-defining [in Harding and Hintikka, 1983, p.231]

What is the relationship between liberal individualism and the view, as Scheman puts it, that psychological states 'attach' only to individuals. Well, she argues, it is only if psychological states 'attach' to us as individuals, in abstraction from their social setting, that we can appeal to them to justify certain forms of social organisation. So, she suggests:

A view of human beings as socially constituted, as having emotions, beliefs, abilities, and so on, only in so far as they are embedded in a social web of interpretation that serves to give meaning to the bare data of inner experience and behaviour, would in fact seem to be incompatible with a social and political theory that sees social groups as built on the independently existing characteristics of individuals. [p.232]

Liberals have, therefore, she argues, good reason to resist a view of the social construction of the objects of psychology.

What, then, is the connection between these views and feminism? Scheman takes as her starting point the account given by Chodorow and others (which I outlined in Ch. 2) of the development of boys and girls in the situation where early primary care is undertaken by women. She argues that the stress on separation and difference from others which Chodorow's theory sees as characterising the masculine psyche can be seen as connected to the doctrine of 'individualism' in psychology, and to political liberalism: 'It is through this emphasis that he comes to fit the picture underlying individualism in the philosophy of mind and in political theory; he is defined as a person by those properties that he senses as uniquely his and that somehow seem internal to him' (pp.236-7). On the other hand: 'A girl's sense of self is typically weaker than a boy's...her ego-boundaries are less strong. Who she is is much more closely bound up with intimate relationships and with how she is perceived by others; it is less natural for her to separate how others react to her and treat her from how she perceives herself to be' (pp.238-9).

Men, Scheman argues, who have traditionally had the power to define what it is to be human, to be adult, to be moral, have done so in response to their own experience of and need for separateness and distinctness. And although the lives of women, and the work they have done, have tacitly questioned these norms, women too have accepted this view of self (and felt a sense of failure if they did not live up to it). Scheman therefore sees a need for:

a radically different conception of the nature of persons and a deep suspicion of some of the underpinnings of philosophical psychology, metaphysics, epistemology, ethics, and political theory; the essential distinctness of persons and their psychological states, the importance of autonomy, the value of universal principles in morality, and the demand that a social theory be founded on an independent theory of persons, their natures, needs and desires. [p.241]

Now the first thing to note about the connections Scheman sees between individualism, liberalism and feminism is that it involves some major historical difficulties and conflations.[2] It looks as if Scheman is supposing that all men (or all those mothered by women) have a sort of natural affinity to abstract individualism or political liberalism, and that all women have had a tendency, at least tacitly, to question these. But, in fact, there have been many male critics of individualism, both in the form of abstract individualism and psychological egoism. The word 'individualism' itself has had different meanings and associations. Steven Lukes (1973) has pointed out that the *word* 'individualism' was first coined in the nineteenth century (like the words 'socialism' and 'communism'), and that, initally, it had mostly pejorative connotations. It was used in particular by conservative critics of the doctrines of the rights of the individual which were seen to have underlain the French Revolution. Critics such as Edmund Burke argued that doctrines of the power and autonomy of individual reason, the 'Rights of Man' and the sovereignty of the individual conscience would, if allowed to take hold, crumble the very foundations of the 'commonwealth' and lead to anarchy and the dissolution of all the bonds that hold a society together. Burke shared with a number of French thinkers a horror of social atomisation and the desire for a harmonious, stable and hierarchically organised social order.

Philosophers in the Hegelian and Marxist traditions have argued that the self is necessarily social. Hegel argued that to be aware of oneself as a person involved being *recognised* by others as such, and that human beings cannot either recognise or meet their needs in isolation from other people.[3] The English Hegelian philosopher Bradley, in *Ethical Studies* (1927), lucidly and forcefully criticised the doctrines of abstract individualism and psychological egoism. He wrote:

If we suppose the world of relations in which [a person] was born and bred, never to have been, then we suppose the very essence of him not to be; if we take that away, we have taken him away; and hence he is not now an individual, in the sense of owing nothing to the sphere of relations in which he finds himself, but does contain those relations within himself as belonging to his very being. [p.166]

Bradley gives a description of the infancy and growth of a child which is in many ways remarkably similar to that given by Chodorow. Bradley writes:

his earliest notions come mixed to him of things and persons, not distinct from one another, nor divided from the feeling of his own existence. The need that he cannot understand moves him to foolish, but not futile cries for what only another can give him; and the breast of his mother, and the soft warmth and touch and tones of his nurse are made one with the feelings of his own pleasure and pain; nor is he yet a moralist to beware of such illusion and to see in them mere means to an end without them in his separate self. For he does not even think of his separate self; he grows with his world, his mind fills and orders itself; and when he can separate himself from that world and know himself apart from it, then by that time his self, the object of his self-consciousness, is penetrated, infected, characterised by the existence of others. Its content implies in every fibre relations of community [p.172]

There have, therefore, been plenty of male critics of 'individualism'. And there are other historical complexities. 'Liberalism' itself is not easy to define, and most contemporary philosophers, I think, who would see themselves as political liberals would certainly not agree with abstract individualism, nor accept theories in the philosophy of mind which denied the importance of social learning or interpersonal criteria for the use of psychological concepts.[4] Furthermore, there have been plenty of women, since the time of Wollstonecraft onwards, who have expressed their feminist convictions and arguments in liberal terms.

I argued in Chapter 2 that there are immense difficulties in seeing any particular cluster of philosophical views as typically male, and those arguments are all relevant to what Scheman says. What I want now to discuss, however, is what seems to me to be a further conflation in her argument. She wants, I think, to defend several theses:

1. The view that relationships with others structure the human psyche, and that the self is social in that it cannot be conceived of as existing independently of social relationships; in other words, the view that abstract individualism is false.

2. The view that my needs and desires cannot be considered as entirely distinct from those of other people, and that my desires are not all for things for myself; in other words, the view that psychological egoism is false.

But there are intimations, in what Scheman writes, of two further theses:

3. The view that my psychological states are not just states of myself, and that they cannot be ascribed just to me.

4. The view that I cannot ultimately distinguish myself from you.

Now I think that Scheman is right to reject abstract individualism and psychological egoism. I have already argued, in Chapter 5, that abstract individualism is false, and I shall turn in a minute to discuss psychological egoism. But Scheman sees the rejection of these things as entailing a view of the 'indistinctness' of persons which I find both unclear and worrying. I think it *is* possible to give the idea of the 'indistinctness of persons' a sense, but in what follows I shall argue that acceptance of this should not be seen as following from the rejection of abstract individualism or psychological egoism, and that it is not an ideal which feminism should support.

PSYCHOLOGICAL EGOISM

I want now to bring out some of the problems with psychological egoism, the view that the interests of each person are separable from those of all other people, and that each of us is motivated solely by those interests. I shall try to do this by looking at some examples.

Take the case, first, of a mother who is anxious or distressed about the serious illness of her child. How could one map the notion of 'interests' onto her feelings or behaviour? The problem is that both the notion of 'self-interest' and that of 'disinterested altruism' may seem inadequate to describe the situation. The mother is clearly concerned with the child's welfare; she wants the child to flourish. Now, an egoistic interpretation of her feelings would be that her desire for the child's welfare is simply derivative from her desire for her own welfare. She may feel that she herself could not flourish if the child died; so, the egoist argues, she is *really* concerned basically for herself. The welfare of the child is simply instrumental to her own happiness.

It can be pointed out here that the egoist assumes that the welfare of the child only matters to the mother if she knows about it; whereas, in fact, the welfare of another person might matter to someone even if they knew for certain that they would never know about it. More importantly, though, one can argue that the concept of 'interests' is being illegitimately run together by the egoist with notions of 'self-interest' thought of in a narrow sense as something like selfishness.

The notion of altruism is commonly opposed to that of egoism. Altruism is sometimes thought of as implying disinterestedness; a desire to do good for its own sake or to help another person simply because it is the right thing to do, without regard to one's own inclinations or feelings or desires. A sharp opposition between egoism and altruism implies that *either* one acts out of self-interest, prudentially, helping others simply as a means, perhaps, of getting something oneself in return, *or* that one acts out of abstract duty towards other people. The egoist implies that only the former is possible. And the response should be, I think, to query the sharp distinction between egoism and altruism on which the egoistic view depends. We have 'interests' in the welfare of others if we care about them, and if our lives are intimately involved with theirs, or if we share common projects or goals. In these cases, neither the notion of abstract duty nor the idea that the interests of others may be merely a means to one's own ends can adequately characterise all human relationships or all the reasons why we might be concerned about the welfare of other people.

The 'contractual' model of human relationships, which I mentioned in the last chapter, raises these problems. They are nicely illustrated by an account given by the behaviourist psychologist H.J. Eysenck of a method of improving marriages which is supposed to be an application of behaviourist theory. Married couples, Eysenck (1977) says, expect to enjoy reciprocal relations with their partners. But he defines this reciprocity as follows:

These reciprocal relations are defined to mean that each party has rights and duties, and this in turn carries the behavioural implication that each party to such an interaction should dispense social reinforcement at an equitable rate...Whenever one partner to a reciprocal interaction unilaterally rewards the other, he does so with the confidence that he will be compensated in kind in the future. For example, if the husband agrees to entertain his wife's parents for a weekend, he does so with the expectation that his wife will accompany him on a weekend fishing trip at some time in the future [p.142]

Marriages, Eysenck argued, break down if there is insufficient reciprocal reinforcement. So a form of 'marriage therapy' was designed, on the following principles. Each partner lists three types of behaviour that she/he would like the other to display, and notes the 'pre-therapy' frequency of these. Tokens are then obtained by each partner for the performance of the desired act; thus I might earn a token by talking to you for an hour, in return for you earning one by making love to me tonight.

Now, Eysenck admits that this is 'crude', but I do not think he sees why. What he is supposing is that people are motivated by 'reinforcements', which can be defined as isolated stimuli (in this case, 'bits' of behaviour from other people) which can be dispensed as if they were like Smarties. This is really an updated version of Bentham's view of happiness. Steven Lukes (1973) quotes Thorstein Veblen's description of utilitarian 'man' as follows; he is:

a lightning calculator of pleasures and pains who oscillates like a homogeneous globule of desire and happiness under the impulse of stimuli that shift him about the area, but leave him intact...He is an isolated definitive human datum, in stable equilibrium except for the buffets of the impinging forces that displace him in one direction or another [p.139]

Utilitarian or behaviourist 'man' identifies the good life with a mere series or succession of isolated pleasures or reinforcements.

A central problem with this bizarre sort of technique of improving a relationship suggested by Eysenck is that it supposes the motivation or desires underlying the way people behave towards us to be unimportant. Provided I am talked to, or made love to, the reasons why another person does these do not matter. But in fact there is frequently nothing that undermines a relationship quicker than the feeling that someone is acting towards us *either* out of mere self-interest *or* merely out of a feeling of duty. If you visit me in hospital, and I know or sense that you have not the least desire to see me or be with me but are doing it because you feel you ought, it will destroy any pleasure I might have in your visit. Larry Blum (1980) argues, in a critique of the Kantian idea of morality which is just based on the idea of duty, that it is misleading to suppose that it is possible to separate the motive sharply from the act, and represent the action of visiting me in hospital as 'the same' regardless of your feelings or intentions. If the techniques described by Eysenck 'worked' at all, it could only be because they were a means to reinstituting some form of care for one person by the other.

It is essential to human welfare that one both care and be cared for, and the feeling that there is no one to whom one's welfare matters, or that there is no one who really matters to oneself, can be extremely destructive. My 'flourishing' is not something which is independent of the 'flourishing' of those I live with or care about or work with in common projects. To say this is not of course to deny there are some forms of emotional involvement with others or dependence on them which are themselves destructive. Nor is it to make an idealistic or sentimental point that everyone really cares for everyone else, or that care for others characterises all human relationships. It is to argue that a person who conceived of their own welfare as totally distinct from that of others, or who saw their relationships with others simply as a means to their own purely private ends would strike us as 'inhuman'.

Human beings are dependent on each other in many ways. They are materially dependent on each other and could not survive without the common labour that provides the means of material existence (something which is apparently forgotten by theorists like Maslow who claim that self-actualising people do not need others). Infants are dependent on care by adults not only for their physical survival but also for their psychical survival and well-being. Patterns of infant care vary a great deal of course, and women have been right to be sceptical, for example, about claims that a child will suffer if its mother is not in constant attendance twenty-four hours a day for about five years. Nevertheless, there is evidence that continuity and quality of care are essential to a child's well-being.

A child is born into a particular culture, and into a particular segment of that culture. The child's sense of self will develop in the context of the immediate style and quality of care of her parents or other primary caretakers. The psychoanalytic picture of the development of the child sees the period of infancy and early childhood as being the most crucial. Chodorow, for example, argues that aspects of relationships with others become 'internalised' in the sense that they become part of the psychic structure of the self. Thus, if early care was totally inconsistent and unreliable, it might lead not only to an inability to feel secure, but to a feeling that one was oneself 'bad'. The processes of 'introjection' and 'projection', she argues, lead to a sort of dialectic in which feelings about oneself are unconsciously projected onto the world or onto other people, or feelings about the world or other people are introjected so that they become part of oneself.

The classic Freudian psychoanalytic picture depicted the dynamics of family relationships in a very decontextualised way – an isolated triad of father, mother and child. Chodorow and others have recognised that families cannot be understood without taking into account the ways in which family relations are structured by wider social relationships – gender relationships, for example. But it has been argued by Peter Leonard (1984) that the account given by Chodorow still fails to give adequate recognition to the way in which things such as class relationships may enter into the construction of self. Leonard has also questioned the heavy stress laid in psycholanalytic theory on the period of infancy and early childhood. He suggests that the experience of being a member of a subordinate class, or of a class which thinks of itself as having a 'natural' superiority, and the experience of work, may deeply affect the conception of themselves that a person has.[5]

The human self is 'embedded' in a network of relationships with others, both at very immediate and intimate and at wider levels. Human needs and interests arise in a context of relationships with other people, and human needs *for* relationships with other people cannot be understood as merely instrumental to isolable individual ends. For all these reasons, it is right to reject an 'individualistic' account of the human self, if by that is meant that the doctrines of abstract individualism or psychological egoism, or the notion that the 'interests' of each human being are sharply separable from those of other people, are untenable.

176   *The Critique of Individualism*

The question I now want to raise, however, is whether a rejection of these doctrines should be taken to imply a belief in the 'essential indistinctness of persons'. As I have said, this is a very unclear idea; and I want to try to give it a sense by looking at the case studies of eleven young women who had been diagnosed as 'schizophrenic' which were presented by the psychiatrist R.D. Laing in his book *Sanity, Madness and the Family* (1970).[6]

THE IDEA OF THE ESSENTIAL INDISTINCTNESS OF PERSONS

Laing's book consists largely of transcripts of the interviews conducted both with the women themselves and with members of their families, especially their parents. The symptoms displayed by these young women, both before and during their frequent hospitalisation, included such things as catatonic and paranoid symptoms, autistic withdrawal, and hallucinations and delusions of various kinds. They also frequently involved a feeling of being unduly 'influenced', and the feeling that thoughts and actions were not really 'owned', were not really part of the self. As 'Maya' put it, 'I don't think, the voices think' (1970, p.45).In a previous book on schizophrenia, *The Divided Self* (1965), Laing had drawn attention to the experience of the schizophrenic in which the 'inner' self was felt as detached from the 'outer', such that everything done by the 'outer' self was felt as mechanical, as not really an *action,* as not involving the 'real self' at all. Such an experience also characterised some of the women in *Sanity, Madness and the Family*.

The typical situation of these women was as follows. Their mothers, in every case, described them as having been very 'good' children; with the onset of adolescence, they suddenly started to become 'bad', and progressed from there to being 'mad'. What really happened, Laing showed, was that absolutely any attempts to achieve any form of independence from parental control or wishes were interpreted as 'bad'; all attempts at autonomy were blocked.

The progression from 'badness' to 'madness' was a result of the *failure* to achieve any sort of autonomy. It was a desperate and self-defeating last-ditch attempt to break out. But the really crucial thing which lay behind this failure was not just the fact of parental control, but the ways (largely unconscious) by which this was achieved.

In another book, *The Politics of the Family* (1976) Laing talked of the ways in which a family phantasy (which he called 'the family', in inverted commas) is mapped onto the family by some or all of its members. It is clear that the parents, and especially the mothers of these women had a need (which Laing does not attempt to explain) to preserve 'the family', and in the course of so doing systematically denied or invalidated anything which did not fit in with this picture. Thus time and again their daughters were told, not simply that they must not do things of which their parents disapproved, but that *they did not want to,* or that insofar as they did want to, it was simply evidence of their 'illness', of their 'not being themselves'. Time and again they were told they could not, or did not, think, perceive, remember, do or want what they did; in fact, think, perceive, remember, do and want. This insistent denial of anything that contradicted a parental perception of the daughter was allied with other forms of mystification; thus an assertion that the parents *did* want the daughter to go out on her own, or *didn't* disapprove if she read on her own in her room, would be combined with the attempt to block absolutely any *particular* attempt to do these things (and often with a denial that she *really* wanted to do them).

Now no doubt some of these things happen some of the time in all families. But Laing's families were all very isolated (a constant theme of the interviews was how they kept themselves to themselves and didn't like 'crowds'); and the sorts of help or validation that might have come from outside the family were signally lacking. The result, in the daughters, was severe confusion and disorientation. This was cognitive, in the sense that they often felt unable to trust their own judgements in any way, or distinguish between appearance and reality. It also led to severe confusions about self, in the sense that they did not know sometimes whether they thought or wanted something or *if it was they* who thought or wanted it.

Now this sort of severe identity confusion could quite well be described, I think, by the notion that these women were not sure whether their thoughts and desires 'attached to them singly', or by the idea that they felt themselves to be 'essentially indistinct as persons'. They lacked almost any sense of 'who they were', in a radical way; not just at the level of being ordinarily confused or conflicted about their commitments or priorities, but at the level of being unsure whether there was a 'person' there to *have* such commitments or priorities. Laing often describes them as lacking a sense of 'agency', of being uncertain whether it was they who actually did or thought things.

This is the sort of sense that I can give to the idea of the 'indistinctness of persons'. It is a sense derived, as I have tried to show, from an analysis of the lives of some women who were in a situation of extreme powerlessness and mystification. And it would clearly be wrong to see this sort of 'indistinctness of persons' as something that feminism ought to applaud or to suppose that the rejection of certain individualistic and egoistic doctrines implies any such thing.

Now, I do not suppose for a minute that Scheman would be anything other than appalled at the situation of the women described in *Sanity, Madness and the Family,* or that she would want to give a Laingian meaning to the idea of the 'indistinctness of persons'. The reason that I have pointed out the difficulties and unclarities in her use of this term, however, is that it seems to me to echo an insistent theme in a great deal of recent feminist writing, which has been a response to the sorts of worries about an over-individualistic stress on female self-assertion and autonomy that Scheman herself expressed. The theme is that of a capacity for intimacy and empathy with others, for care and 'nurturing', that is seen as especially female.

Despite all the dangers of being ahistorical, of overgeneralisation, and so forth, I think it is true that women commonly see 'caring' relationships for others as having a more central role in their lives than men do. There has been, as I have shown, an influential strand in feminist thinking which has stressed the frequent oppressiveness of women's 'caring' role, and the need for female autonomy and independence. Against this, however, has been set a concern to criticise institutional forms, often male-dominated, that are built on an ethos of self-assertion, competitiveness and the achieving of individualistic goals. This concern has often been linked with the belief that the different concerns of women's lives, and the different psychic qualities or strengths that they may possess, offer a basis for a re-evaluation of this male ethos.

Now Chodorow's use of psychoanalytic theory seemed, I think, to offer a basis for understanding the psychic differences between men and women in a new way, and for understanding, too, the respects in which theories or institutions could be seen as 'male'. I have already discussed the problems in using Chodorow's theory to offer a general account of the psychological characteristics of males, or to give a general account of 'masculinity' in philosophy. Here, I want to focus again on Chodorow's theory, and on what I think is the unclearness of some of the language she uses; this lack of clarity seems to me to be similar to (and perhaps reflected in) Scheman's notion of the 'indistinctness of persons'.

Chodorow and others give the names of 'separation' and 'individuation' to the processes by which the child learns both that it is a separate self and what sort of self it is (a gendered one, for example). Chodorow argues that the different path taken by the girl in her relationships with her mother leads her sense of self to be typically different from that of a boy, and leads her to be more preoccupied with relationships with others and less concerned than the boy to assert or experience the separateness and distinctness of self. Chodrow (1978) says, for example, 'Girls emerge from the pre-oedipal period with a basis for 'empathy' built into their primary definition of self in a way that boys do not. Girls emerge with a stronger basis for experiencing another's needs or feelings as their own, (p.167). Further, she says:

from the retention of pre-oedipal attachments to their mother, growing girls come to experience themselves as continuous with others; their experience of self contains more flexible or permeable ego boundaries.

Boys come to define themselves as more separate and distinct, with a
greater sense of rigid ego-boundaries and differentiation. The basic
feminine sense of self is connected with the world; the basic masculine
sense of self is separate. [p.169]

I do not wish to question the idea that there may
commonly be some important psychological differences
between men and women; it would, I think, be surprising if
there were not, given the frequent major differences in the
life experiences of men and women. But there is a lack of
clarity and some important ambiguities in the language
Chodorow uses to give her account of these differences –
about terms such as 'separation', 'empathy', 'connection' or
'continuity with others'.

What does it mean, for example, to 'experience another's
needs and feelings as one's own'. It might mean that one is
capable of an imaginative understanding of what someone
else needs or feels, and has, too, the disposition to *try* to
understand them. I am a little loth to describe such a
capacity as 'empathy'. The word 'empathy' tends to convey
the idea of a rather mysterious capacity to 'enter into'
another person's feelings, which is reminiscent of ideas of
'female intuition'. The capacity to understand another
person's feelings is one that is learned, and if it is true that
women are commonly rather better than men at doing it, I
would see this as arising from the fact that the circumstances
of their lives give greater need and occasion for developing
this capacity.

But 'experiencing another's needs and feelings as one's
own' might also be taken to mean that I simply 'map'
another person's feelings and needs, as I understand them,
on to myself, and try to identify with them. Jean Baker
Miller (1978) has discussed the way in which some women,
for example, may feel themselves so 'connected' to their
husbands that they subordinate any life goals of their own to
those of their husbands and try to live through the latter.

Or what does it mean to 'experience oneself as continuous
with others'? Again, there is an ambiguity. It could mean
that the welfare of, say, loved others is so near and
important that it touches one's own very closely. It could
mean, on the other hand, that one has little conception of

one's own needs as being identifiably differentiated from those of other people. But a capacity for an imaginative understanding of other people, or for holding their welfare very close to one's own heart, does not at all entail that one cannot differentiate one's own needs from theirs, or that one defines all one's life goals as the same as theirs. This is brought out very clearly, I think by the relation to their mothers of the women in Laing's *Sanity, Madness and the Family*. They were indeed 'connected' to their mothers, and the mothers to them, and the mothers were scarcely able at all to perceive the daughters as 'separate'; but the result of this was that, far from being able to 'empathise' with their daughters, the mothers showed an almost total inability to understand what they were thinking and feeling, or even that they *had* separate thoughts and feelings. (One of the things that most worried 'Mrs Danzig' about her daugher 'Sara' was that 'Sara' was always *thinking,* and sometimes even doing it in her room all alone.)

Marilyn Frye (1983) has written of what she calls 'the arrogant eye':

The arrogant perceiver's expectation creates in the space about him a sort of vacuum mold into which the other is sucked and held...To the extent that she is not shaped to his will, does not fit the conformation he imposes, there is friction, anomaly or incoherence in his world. To the extent that he notices this incongruity, he can experience it in no other way than as something wrong with her. His perception is arrogating; his senses tell him that the world and everything in it (with the occasional exception of other men) is in the nature of things there *for* him...If a woman does not serve man, it can only be because he is not a sufficiently skilled master, or because there is something wrong with the woman. He may try to manage things better, but when that fails he can only conclude that she is defective: unnatural, flawed, broken, abnormal, damaged, sick. [p.69]

Frye is here talking of course about some male perceptions of women. But the interesting thing is how closely in many ways her description also fits the way in which the mothers in *Sanity, Madness and the Family* perceived their daughters. Chodorow and Scheman tend to write as if human relationships can be described in terms of two 'poles'. On the one hand, there is something called 'connectedness', which involves being in some way 'less distinct from' or 'more continuous with' other people; and this is seen as related to the capacity for 'empathy', or for the imaginative understanding of others. On the other hand, there is something called 'separateness', which involves a *lack* of this understanding. Now, the man described by Frye, who has an extremely egoistic conception of his own interests, is indeed unable to conceive of the 'separateness' of other people, in the sense of being unable to imagine that they might have purposes which are not orientated around service to him. The mothers described in *Sanity, Madness and the Family* are 'connected' to their daughters, in that they see them simply as a projection of a family 'phantasy' or of their own beliefs and desires. And they are also unable to imagine or conceive of the 'separateness' of their daughters. Certain forms of 'separation' and 'connection', in other words, turn out to have much the same effects.

Frye contrasts 'the arrogant eye' with 'the loving eye':

One who sees with a loving eye is separate from the other whom she sees. There are boundaries between them; she and the other are two; their interests are not identical; they are not blended in vital parasitic or symbiotic relations, not does she believe or try to pretend they are...What is required is that one know what are one's interests, desires and loathings, one's projects, hungers, fears and wishes, and that one know what is and what is not determined by these. In particular, it is a matter of being able to tell one's own interests from those of others and of knowing where one's self leaves off and another begins [p.75]

Now Frye moves from this, as I showed earlier, to a conception of an 'individualism of interests' that sees all the interests of each self as distinct from those of others, and suggests a merely co-operative or contractual model of human relationships, and I have already argued that this is inadequate. Nevertheless, what she says here seems to me to be extremely important. It is important not merely because certain forms of symbiosis or 'connection' with others can lead to damaging failures of personal development, but because care for others, understanding of them, are only possible if one can adequately distinguish oneself *from* others. If I see myself as 'indistinct' from you, or you as not having your own being that is not merged with mine, then I cannot preserve a real sense of your well-being as opposed to mine. Care and understanding require the sort of distance that is needed in order not to see the other as a projection of self, or self as a continuation of the other.

Now Chodorow does indeed talk about the *problems* women may have, for example, in achieving independence from their mothers; and others (such as Flax, 1978, and Baker Miller, 1978) have written about these problems. I do not think that Chodorow wants to present an idealised vision of female 'relatedness' or 'connectedness' that glosses over the problems some women may have in achieving any form of autonomy or independence. But Scheman does not mention these problems; she describes women, in fact, as having a 'weaker' sense of self, whereas Chodorow explicitly denies that her theories imply that women's sense of self is weaker than that of men.

What has happened is that a critique of certain sorts of individualistic doctrines has tended to be equated with unclear notions of women as less 'separate' from others than men, and this has in turn been equated with what is seen as women's greater capacity for care for or empathy with others. This seems to me to be a dangerous mix, for several reasons. First, as I have just pointed out, care and understanding of others seem, precisely, to require that one be well able to distinguish oneself from others. Second, on more than one occasion when I have discussed views of women's 'lack of distinction' from others, I have encountered a response which can be summed up as 'We've heard that one before'. We are back, in other words, if we are not careful, with Virginia Woolf's 'Angel in the House'. Third, it seems to me that an unclear or idealised vision of female relatedness and connectedness can lead both to unrealistic expectations of community or harmony among women, and sometimes to a sort of coerciveness, a denial of the needs of individual women to forge their own path and develop their own understanding and goals. To quote Marilyn Frye again:

We have correctly intuited that the making of meaning is social and requires a certain community of perception. We are also individually timid and want support. So it is only against a background of an imagined community of ultimate harmony and perfect agreement that we dare to think it possible to make meaning. This brings us into an arrogance of our own, for we make it a prerequisite for our construction of meaning that other women be what we need them to be to constitute the harmonious community of agreement we require. [p.81]

Some of the problems experienced by some women's groups can perhaps be seen in this light; a feeling, by some women, after the initial euphoria of connection to other women, that their own individual needs and problems might sometimes be lost in an ethos of community and connection.

Questions about autonomy and dependence are central to feminism. Given that the lives of women have so often been supposed to be devoted to serving others, and that they themselves have so often orientated their self-conceptions around such notions of service, the problems of staking out a claim for one's own interests and of negotiating the relationship between these and the needs and interests of others are both central and endemic. In the course of trying to conceptualise these problems women have drawn, as I have shown, on various philosophical theories and traditions of thinking. I have also tried to show some of the ways in which these are problematic. They are problematic not merely because they are sometimes theoretically inadequate, but because they can promote illusory expectations, or suggest ways of escaping from old forms of coercion and constraint, only to lapse into new ones.

Sue Cartledge (1983) describes how, in her childhood and early life, she was taught a morality of Duty as conflicting with Desire. When she first rejected this morality, however, she did so, she writes, in the naive expectation that if Duty was thrown out of the window and everyone acted on Desire, conflict would be eliminated and acting on desire would lead to an easy harmony. But the ways in which this proved to be an illusion showed her that while a morality of self-abnegation and self-sacrifice may be psychologically disastrous, to counterpose to it a Rogerian sort of ethos of 'duty to oneself' or of self-affirmation ignores the complexities of human needing. What is to happen when human desires conflict? How is one to cope with asymmetries of need or desire, when the need or desire of one person for another is not reciprocated? What is one to do when one's own projected well-being seems likely to lead to the unhappiness of someone else? What is to happen when one's own needs or desires seem to conflict with each other? If it is supposed that an imperative, say, to 'be one's own person' and reject the legitimacy of the emotional claims and demands of others can solve these problems, the result may well be that the 'liberation' of one person (as in the case of some of Rogers' so-called 'open marriages') will become an instrument of egoism, self-deception and the emotional coercion of others.

The emotional as well as the physical interdependence of human beings has to be recognised. But just as I think we cannot say clearly in advance what gender characteristics might be like under radically different social relationships, so we cannot know exactly how structures of need and dependency might change. They clearly can change; thus it is possible for a woman to cease to feel that her whole psychic well-being is dependent on the sexual admiration or approval of men, or from being unable to see concern for her own interests as anything other than 'selfish' to being able at times without guilt to say 'no' to the demands of others. If, however, people's needs, desires and emotions are deeply structured by the social relationships under which they live, then the task of rethinking questions about the relationship between dependence and autonomy has to go hand in hand with working for changes in those relationships. And that requires a continuing effort to understand the relationships between gender identity, the conceptions people have of themselves, the needs they experience and the immediate and wider circumstances of their lives. It requires, too, a continuing effort to break down the sorts of philosophical dichotomies which suggest, for example that to be 'autonomous' is *not* to need others.

I have raised questions about some aspects of Chodorow's work and some ways in which it has been used. But I think that the enterprise of trying to understand the relations between gender and psychological needs and characteristics is a centrally important one. In the last two chapters I have tried to point to tensions and define a problem rather than offer solutions. But in the attempt to see solutions I think it is important not to suppose that the problems can be solved by easy appeals either to self-affirmation or to a somewhat Utopian idea of female 'connectedness'. There is no possibility of ever eliminating *all* conflict between human needs and desires; the problem is rather how to identify and eliminate its most damaging and destructive forms.

7   The Idea of a Female Ethic

In a paper called *Some Psychical Consequences of the Anatomical Distinction between the Sexes*, (1977), Freud wrote as follows:

I cannot evade the notion (though I hesitate to give it expression) that for women the level of what is ethically normal is different from what it is in men. Their superego is never so inexorable, so impersonal, so independent of its emotional origins as we require it to be in men. Characteristics which critics of every epoch have brought up against women – that they show less sense of justice than men, that they are less ready to submit to the great exigencies of life, that they are more often influenced in their judgements by feelings of affection or hostility – all these would be amply accounted for by the modification in the formation of the superego which we have inferred above [p.342]

Freud is here suggesting two things: that women's approach to ethical problems is typically different from that of men, and that this difference is somehow related to more general differences in female psychic development.

This passage has caused anger among many women; here is yet another man saying that women are overemotional, implying that they are inferior to men. But a considerable amount of recent feminist work has argued, however, that Freud is *half* right. He is right to suggest that women typically approach ethical or moral problems in a way different from men, and he is right to see this as related to the different psychic development and experience of women (even if the particular account he gives of that development is problematic). But what is wrong is his assumption of the deficiency of women. Woman have been measured against male norms and found wanting, but what is needed is a critique of those very norms; and this for two reasons: not only because justice is not done to women if they are simply seen as deficient, but because the inexorable and impersonal nature of the male ethic of which Freud wrote leads to a dangerous and damaging sense of human priorities.

In this chapter and the next I want to look at the idea that women typically think differently about moral or ethical problems from men. First, I shall look at some claims that this is so, and at the sorts of evidence and arguments on which they are based. Second, I shall discuss some ways in which such differences have been described (one common way, for example, of characterising differences between male and female moral reasoning is to suggest that men tend to see ethical problems 'abstractly' in terms of rules and principles, whereas women think more concretely and contextually). Finally, I mentioned in Chapter 1 the importance of the question of women's mothering in much recent feminist theory; in a great deal of feminist writing in the late 1960s and early 1970s, women's mothering was often seen mainly as a problem and a burden. Since then, however, it has not only been recognised that motherhood is not *just* a burden; it has been argued that a distinctively female 'ethic' may arise from women's experience of mothering and of being mothered themselves by women. In some cases, female ethical thinking has been largely *identified* with what is seen as 'maternal thinking'. So I want to discuss the question (which is by no means a new one, but which has been given a new lease of life in some recent feminist theory) of the association of women with 'caring' values in general, and with the exemplification of these in the task of mothering in particular.

THE EVIDENCE

There is plenty of evidence that women are *believed* to be psychologically different from men. In Chapter 3, for example, I referred to the *Hite Report on Male Sexuality* (1981b). Most of the men who responded to the questionnaires on which the report was based saw masculinity as involving qualities such as being self-assured, in control, autonomous, and so forth, whereas they saw femininity as involving qualities such as being helpful, loving, sweet, nurturing, supportive. Some further interesting evidence was provided by an experiment done by Broverman *et al.* (1970). The experiment involved first constructing a list of bipolar items, such as 'not at all aggressive/very aggressive', on which a high agreement could be obtained as to which typically characterised men and women. Broverman and others then conducted an experiment in which they asked seventy-nine clinically trained psychologists, psychiatrists and social workers, both male and female, to judge, on a list of such bipolar items, which qualities they would consider evidence of 'mental health'. One group was asked to do this for 'adults' (gender unspecified). Another was asked to do it for males, and a third for females. The results were interesting: there was a significant correlation between the items thought to characterise *male* mental health, and those thought to characterise *adult* mental health (gender unspecified). But there was very little correlation between 'female' and 'adult' (in other words, you cannot be *both* a mentally healthy female *and* a mentally healthy adult!)

Broverman and others do not discuss in detail the particular items that are seen as masculine and feminine – they simply see the problem as one of 'sex-role stereotypes'. But there are some interesting features of the list of 'feminine' items. First, and perhaps unsurprisingly, women are seen as much less ambitious, competitive, independent, objective and so forth. Second, many of the feminine items are described in an implicitly *pejorative* way. Here are some examples, with the feminine side given first:

1. Very sneaky/very direct
2. Very uncomfortable about being aggressive/not at all uncomfortable about being aggressive
3. Unable to separate feelings from ideas/easily able to separate feelings from ideas
4. Very easily influenced/not very easily influenced.

In many of the items, females are made to appear confused, ambivalent, uncertain, dependent, *unable* to do things, uncomfortable and anxious, and so forth. Some female qualities are positively valued, but the dominant impression given by the list is that if a characteristic is ascribed to women, there is a tendency for it to be described in a pejorative way.

Now the sort of evidence provided by Hite and Broverman is evidence about *beliefs* about men and women, and it cannot be taken incautiously as evidence that men and women actually do differ in these ways. I have discussed before the problems that there are with hasty assertions about the psychology of masculinity or femininity. Attempts have been made, however, to ground ideas of male and female psychological differences in approach to ethical problems by empirical research that does not start out with any assumptions that females are inferior; and I want now to outline as example of such research.

In her book *In a Different Voice: Women's Conception of Self and Morality* (1982), Carol Gilligan argues that much developmental psychology, and many accounts of the development of moral reasoning, see the ways in which males typically develop as 'more developed', and the ways in which women develop as deviant or deficient. I have already noted the way in which this happens in Freud; Gilligan argues that the same is true of the work of others such as Piaget, Erikson and Kohlberg.[1] I will explain this by giving an example of the research she undertook.

A common method that has been used in studying the development of children is that of asking them questions or posing them problems, and trying to categorise the answers they give in a way that, it is hoped, will shed light on norms of development. Piaget used this sort of method in his studies of the nature of children's thinking and intellectual development, and proposed a theory of a sequence of *stages* of development. Kohlberg used a similar method to try and understand the way in which children developed a capacity to reason about moral problems. Similarly, one of Gilligan's methods was to interview children in depth and discuss with them the way in which they would try to resolve a moral dilemma.

One of the interviews she describes was with two children,

both eleven years old – pseudonyms Jake and Amy. Both Jake and Amy were presented with a problem that had been used by Kohlberg in his research. The problem is this: a man called Heinz has a wife who is dying, but he cannot afford the drug she needs. Should he steal the drug in order to save his wife's life?

Jake is clear that Heinz *should* steal the drug; his answer revolves around a resolution of the rules governing life and property. In the course of the interview, he describes the dilemma as a 'sort of math problem with humans', a problem which needs solving by a logical working out of the priorities that should be given to certain rules. Amy's answer can appear evasive. Here are two of her comments. Asked if Heinz should steal the drug, she says:

> Well, I don't think so. I think there might be other ways besides stealing it, like if he could borrow the money or make a loan or something, but he really shouldn't steal the drug – but his wife shouldn't die either... If he stole the drug, he might save his wife then, but if he did, he might have to go to jail, and then his wife might get sicker again, and he couldn't get more of the drug, and it might not be good. So they should really just talk it out and find some other way to make the money. [p.28]

Amy also suggests that Heinz should talk to the druggist – she finds the puzzle to lie in his failure to respond; and she suggests that if Heinz and the druggist talked it out long enough, they could find some solution other than stealing.

Amy, Gilligan argues, sees the actors in the dilemma 'arrayed not as opponents in a contest of rights, but as members of a network of relationships on whose continuation they all depend' (p.30). Both children, she says, 'recognise the need for agreement, but see it as mediated in different ways – he impersonally through systems of logic and law, she personally through communication in relationships' (p.29). Jake sees a conflict between life and property, Amy a failure or fracture of human relationships.

Gilligan also shows how the children responded to a question about the way to resolve conflicts between responsibility to others and responsibility to oneself. Jake immediately answers that 'you go about one-fourth to the others and three-fourths to yourself' (p.35). His answers show, Gilligan suggests, that he begins by taking for granted his responsibility for himself, but, recognising that you have to 'live with others', he looks for rules that will limit interference and minimise hurt. Amy, on the other hand, begins by taking for granted what Gilligan calls 'a premise of connection' – that relationships involve responsibility and care for others – and she then considers the extent to which care or responsibility for oneself can be fitted into this.

Kohlberg's account of the moral development of children, Gilligan argues, would see Jake as being at a 'higher' stage than Amy. Moral maturity is equated largely with the ability to bring logic to bear on moral dilemmas, to have a principled sense of justice, to be able to differentiate morality from law, and to be able to discuss and resolve a conflict of principles. But Amy sees things that Jake does not. She sees more clearly than Jake the *problems* that are created by *any* choice, the fracture of human relationships that may have led to a dilemma like that of Heinz, and the inadequacy of any solution that is not based on improved communication and understanding. Gilligan argues that Kohlberg's theory is partial; there is a need to 'restore the missing text of women's development', to include the perspectives of both the sexes. But Gilligan does not, I think conceive of this task as a purely *additive* one. Throughout the book she suggests that the differences of approach between men and women raise common or typical *problems* which are different for each sex. Women, she suggests, tend to be so orientated towards a conception of responsibility to others and the primacy of relationships with others in their lives, that they can have real problems in developing a conception of their *own* rights or needs, or of responsibilities towards themselves. She conducted a series of interviews with a number of young women who were considering having an abortion after an unplanned or unwanted pregnancy, and shows how difficult many of them found it to feel that it was 'legitimate' to consider their own desires and interests at all. Men, on the other hand, she argues, may feel threatened by intimacy with others; they may find it less easy to feel a sense of connection to others, less easy to understand or negotiate problems of communication in relationships. The problem, therefore, as Gilligan sees it, is how to resolve the dilemma of retaining a clear sense of one's own identity and interests and needs while at the same time seeing these as necessarily embedded in relationships with others.

The sort of evidence Gilligan offers clearly needs treating with caution (and she herself, I am sure, would be the first to agree). It doesn't, for example license inferences about particular individuals; it doesn't claim anything about 'all men' or 'all women'. It would be easy to find examples of children who responded differently to Jake and Amy, of women who have great difficulties in relating to other people, or of men who are self-effacing and have difficulty in asserting their own needs or rights. Gilligan is simply claiming that women *more commonly* have certain approaches to moral dilemmas than men do. Now, I think there may be some problems about how such differences are *described,* and I shall return to these later. But in any case, it is important to note that it is not simply a question of the characteristics of individuals. Gilligan's research was conducted at the individual level, but of course, she is not talking just about characteristics that individuals may or may not possess, but about *norms* as to how people should behave or how they should develop. Such norms may be written into institutions; people may be expected to behave in certain ways, or behave as if they thought or felt certain things, even if the relationship between these norms and how they do actually feel is tenuous. Soldiers, for example, may be expected in some circumstances to behave as if 'enemies' were not human beings, to suppress any emotional recognition of the human suffering they may be causing and any critical awareness of ideologies which see napalm, for example, as a legitimate means to 'freedom'. Business men may be expected to give total priority in their lives to a ruthless pursuit of personal advancement. But not all soldiers or business men are happy with these norms (the sorts of emotional anguish and personality disturbances experienced, for example, by many Vietnam war veterans, is evidence of that).

Gilligan does not discuss the way in which moral or behavioural norms may penetrate institutions, sometimes despite the ambivalence or even anguish of the individuals who are required to obey those norms; she sees them as leading primarily to problems in *personal* development.[2] What a number of feminist writers have argued, however, is that while male norms have indeed been personally damaging to women and men (and doubly so to women since what is female is so often regarded as inferior), it is not merely at the personal or interpersonal level that the damage has been done. It has been argued that male conceptions of morality have permeated human social life and institutions in a way that leads to a distorted and dangerous sense of human priorities; to a morality, in fact, that may be seen as underlying such things as militarism.

The idea of a 'female ethic', therefore, incorporates a number of strands. It incorporates a belief that there are common differences of approach between men and women towards moral problems and ethical reasoning. It offers certain ways of *describing* those differences. And it suggests not merely that women's ethical approaches and priorities are commonly *different* from those of men (and should not be devalued merely because they are different), but that male approaches and priorities are, as such, humanly damaging and dangerous. It is sometimes suggested that this amounts to seeing women as ethically 'superior' to men; but I think this misrepresents the issue. There are indeed some feminist accounts of men which see them as vicious or violent 'by nature', but those accounts of a female ethic that I shall look at do not all suppose this, nor do they suppose that women as individuals are inherently morally superior to or purer in heart than men. They suppose, rather, that female life and experience creates the possibility for women more easily than for men of perceiving the dangerous and ruinous and inhuman nature of ideologies and actions that have led to so much destruction.

PUBLIC AND PRIVATE MORALITY

Earlier I talked about the difficulties in supposing that there is a 'male point of view' in philosophy, and of the many different forms that 'masculinism' in philosophy has taken. There are similar problems with the idea that women as such have a point of view, or a distinctive approach to ethical problems or anything else. Nevertheless, it has been suggested that the idea of a 'female ethic' might be grounded in considerations such as the following.

Agnes Heller (1980) has argued that the very fact that women have been so largely *excluded* from broader sociopolitical activity, and restricted to the world of household or family, has meant that there are *more* similarities, historically, between the lives of women than between the lives of men. Women have tended to live, as it were, on a smaller scale, occupied not so much with bold deeds or great causes or 'world historical events', but with the dailiness of a life spent in the detailed tasks of managing a small community and meeting daily needs. So, suggests Heller, 'Within the framework of their small world, women had to learn how to manage a community. It was a painstaking but peaceful occupation which required enormous tact, a great ability to smooth away conflicts, as well as devotion and sympathy' (p.210). Women have of course often supported their men in the bold deeds and great causes, but it is arguable that they, more than men, have tended to have a profound scepticism and ambivalence about the sacrifice of human lives and loves and the daily fabric of human life to the causes in the name of which men have fought and despoiled and oppressed others.

The conditions of women's lives, and the conceptions they have had of the work that was theirs, have of course varied (and do vary) enormously; thus the idea, for example, of an intimate family life whose rationale was emotional rather than economic production postdates capitalism. And women's exclusion from 'public' life and dependence on men has worked to their disadvantage, to say the least. So too has their concern for 'emotional maintenance' and the preservation of relationships. Commonly, I think, women feel not only an imperative to maintain relationships, but that the whole responsibility for doing this lies on their shoulders. They are therefore especially prone to guilt, and to a form of concern for relationships with others which can lead, for example, to the feeling that 'not upsetting people' must always be given priority, and that it can *never* be right to do something which will fracture a relationship or break a connection. They are prone, too, to the feeling that they should never put their own needs or desires before those of others, or prone to the sort of self-sacrifice that can damage those who receive it as well as those who give it.

Despite the dangers of 'false universalism',and despite the frequent oppression that has resulted from the confining of women to a life often bound more than that of men by the practical details of daily care for human life, the idea of a 'female ethic' suggests, I think two things. It suggests that the priorities accorded to the concerns and demands of those spheres of life which have commonly been seen as especially female need re-evaluating. And it suggests that perhaps women's lives often provide a space for these questions about human priorities more readily than the lives of men. In particular, they provide space for questioning the sorts of priorities that see human lives as easily dispensable in the service of some abstract idea or great cause; that see care for others or a life devoted to serving others as relatively unimportant; or that see the tasks of maintaining human life and sustaining intimate connections as sharply distinct from and inferior to the concerns of the 'public' world.

The particular conception of the public/private split that is still influential today has its origins in the decline and eventual demise of economically productive labour in the home after the Industrial Revolution, and the consequent sharp demarcation between the world of home and family, and the world of work and public life. Ross Poole (1985) argues that a certain conception of rationality and of morality can be seen as related to the development of a capitalist market economy. In the ideology of such an economy, individuals are seen as pursuing their own separate ends and as motivated by the pursuit of private gains. The form of 'rationality' associated with this is the instrumental rationality of efficiency, of seeking efficient means of achieving given ends; and underlying this conception of rationality is the assumption of a pervasive self-interest. The morality associated with this form of rationality is that which seeks simply to contain individuals' self-seeking, to provide a framework of legal and moral rules which will ensure that the whole system does not break down through the untrammelled egoism of such self-seeking. Thus laws are instituted governing such things as property and contracts, imposing constraints on the liberty of one individual to 'interfere' with another, and protecting individual rights and freedoms against such encroachments.

As a consequence of individuals pursuing their own essentially self-directed goals, however, the wants of others will also supposedly be satisfied, by the way in which the market tends to maximise the quantity of goods produced by given amounts of human productive activity. This 'invisible hand' (the unintended consequences of the pursuit of individual self-interest) will be undermined unless individuals, in their public life, avoid certain kinds of altruistic behaviour. Thus:

> if participants in market transactions were moved by the circumstances of those with whom they were bargaining, they would not enforce the competitive price; if employers were moved by the plight of their unproductive employees, they would not introduce more efficient methods of production; if entrepreneurs were more sensitive to the feelings and aspirations of their debtors, they would not enforce bankruptcies, and so on. [p.18]

Furthermore, in public or productive life, relationships can only be conceptualised as means to pre-given ends. So, 'within these structures, it is impossible to conceive of activity which is genuinely other-directed, i.e. which takes the well-being of another as the goal of one's activity' (p.18).

Set against this conception of the public sphere is that of the private one of the intimacies of home and family. This is construed as the polar opposite of the world of impersonal instrumental rationality and self-interest. It is personal, particularistic, based on emotion and on care and nurturance for others. Each aspect of social life is defined by what it excludes. The public sphere thus excludes emotion, except insofar as this is transformed into rational self-interest. The private sphere of domestic life excludes reason, except insofar as this is represented by males who also figure in market relations.

And, as is already clear, this distinction between public and private also marks a distinction of gender. So the public sphere is seen as paradigmatically the province of males and the private one that of females. Hence:

If male individuality seeks ends which essentially pertain to self (and perhaps to those represented by self), women must take the interests of others as a sufficient basis for action. But not, of course, all others; only those within the same private sphere (husband, child). Even the structure of motivation is different. What moves men to action are emotions which have been transformed by the requirements of reason into channels of efficiency and consistency; feminine emotions, devoid of reason, are everywhere infected by excess and particularity, hence the lack of proper regard for what is due to impersonal and unknown others; the lack of a sense of justice, which has – notoriously – been supposed to be characteristic of women [p.22]

Now, as Poole acknowledges, the above is a highly schematic account of an ideology, and it is very important not to assume that it corresponds in any clear way to social reality. Thus, for example, this picture ignores the fact that women have always undertaken wage-labour in large numbers, that the particular account of the 'private' sphere that it gives may be class-based, and so on. Nevertheless, I think he is right that the conceptions he outlines are recognisable and influential. I want, however, to consider here the way in which this ideology may have affected feminist thinking.

THE IDEA OF FEMALE VIRTUE

These conceptions of the public and private generate conceptions of value and of morality which are in tension with each other. Usually, the private has been subordinated to the public; concerns seen as female have been regarded as inferior, as trivial or less important. In males, at least, private values or concerns were (and often still are) supposed to lose out in the case of a conflict. Not many male spheres of work look very kindly on the intrusion of 'personal' considerations into work efficiency. And women tend to be doubly caught; they are often criticised, for example, for taking time off work for looking after sick children; but they are *also* often criticised for being at work in the first place.

But the realm of the private was also necessary for refuge from the harshness of the public sphere. And along with the subordination has gone an idealisation of the private sphere and a sentimental account of the virtues of women which are its anchor. This is clearest in the Victorian middle-class ideal of the family. At the centre of the family was the saintly (and asexual) mother, who was both to be protected from the harsh and corrupt realities of the male public world and also to be the guardian of moral purity.

Now this ideal was very evident *both* in arguments for *and* against female suffrage. A common argument against giving women the vote was that they were too pure to be allowed to be contaminated by having anything to do with politics. Here is a typical anti-suffragist argument, quoted by Jean Elshtain (1981).

Man assumed the direction of government and war, women of the domestic and family affairs and the care and training of the child...It has been so from the beginning, and it will continue to be so to the end, because it is in conformity to nature and its laws, and is sustained and confirmed by the experience and reason of six thousand years...The domestic altar is a sacred flame where woman is the high and officiating priestess...To keep her in that condition of purity, it is necessary that she should be separated from the exercise of suffrage and from all those stern and contaminating and demoralizing duties that devolve upon the hardier sex – man. [p.232]

It is interesting, however, how often arguments *for* women's suffrage were couched in similar terms. They simply stood the anti-suffragist argument on its head. The purity of women, instead of being an argument *against* women having the vote, became an argument *for* them having it; since, it was suggested, it was only the purity of women that could purify politics. Here, for example, is what Elizabeth Cady Stanton said (again, quoted in Elshtain):

The male element is a destructive force, stern, selfish, aggrandizing, loving war, violence, conquest, acquisition, breeding in the material and moral world alike discord, disorder, disease and death. See what a record of blood and cruelty the pages of history reveal...The male element has held high carnival thus far, it has fairly run riot from the beginning, overpowering the feminine element everywhere...The need of this hour is not territory, gold mines, railroads or specie payments, but a new evangel of womanhood, to exalt purity, virtue, morality, true religion, to lift man up into the higher realms of thought and action. [p.232]

This supposes that an idealised feminine virtue can simply be mapped onto the public world and magically transform it. Elshtain writes that such arguments really seem to presuppose the end of politics; if virtue rules, then what is right will be unambiguous and clear and all dissension will disappear under its guidance.

Cady Stanton's view of feminine virtue and purity simply mirrors the sharp division between the harsh and immoral public world and the uncontaminated world of domesticity and its associated view of men as corrupt and females as pure. What it does not do is challenge these polarisations in any way. It supposes that women can remain quite unchanged, and it does not ask whether women's powerlessness and dependence might not have led to distortions in the idea of female virtue which both worked against women's interests and misrepresented any particular capacities or insights that they might have. It also supposes that men are 'naturally' corrupt; both the suffragist and the anti-suffragist argument see the role of women as saving the world from the corruption of men, although they differ as to how this is to be achieved.

It is possible to find echoes and reiterations of these sorts of arguments in a fair amount of feminist writing. The idea of 'natural' male propensities to violence is found, for example, in Susan Brownmiller's view (1975) that the basic reason men rape is because they have the biological capacity to do so. A belief in the intrinsic purity of women is often associated with a representation of woman as victim. Thus in the work of Mary Daly (1979), as I have already shown, a stress on what she sees as the utter degradation and 'robotitude' of women under patriarchy is linked with a belief in the intrinsic 'virtue' of women and harmony among women, if only the conditioning inflicted by patriarchy can be undone.

There are also echoes of these suffragist arguments in some anti-feminist writing and thinking. Robyn Rowlands (1984) has collected together a number of essays both by women who have an allegiance to feminism and by women who reject it. Among those who reject it there is often a striking similarity of theme. They feel that feminism has denigrated the importance of motherhood and the 'traditional' labour of women in the home, and that in so doing it has simply aped the aggressive and competitive strivings of men. They tend to see contemporary feminism as something invented by a clique of dissatisfied and frustrated women who have sought success outside the home in compensation for their failures in it, and have then tried to force their cold and 'lifeless' vision onto other women. The issue of 'life' is central, and all of them bitterly oppose abortion as symptomatic of what they see as the feminist denial of life. Valerie Riches, for example, says that feminists see a pregnant woman as a failure of technology rather than as a symbol of life and health. And she says, 'I could have given my heart to a feminist movement concerned with the cultural growth of the characteristics most deeply associated with womanhood; tenderness not aggression, people not things, love not hate, spirituality not materialism. But women's liberation fosters the aggressive values of men' (p.150). This is a view of women's values and women's purity which is very similar indeed to that of Cady Stanton. And Robyn Rowland also points out the existence of a strong feeling among many women who oppose feminism that men *are* naturally wilful and corrupt, and that only home and family, and the associated male responsibilities, can keep men on the rails. Sexual freedom, abortion, even equal rights will tend to undermine those very things that have kept male aggression or philandering under control.

I have suggested that it is reasonable to suppose that women commonly do tend to have concerns and priorities which differ from those of men, and that these may arise from the particular concern of women with the physical and emotional care of others in the intimate context of domestic life. I have also suggested that this may provide space, may make it easier for women to question in certain ways the common concerns and priorities of men. But ideas of a female ethic have also to be located, as Ross Poole points out, in the context of a conception of a sharp dichotomy between private and public worlds, and an associated sharp polarisation of male and female qualities. Male concerns are thus depicted as universal, general, impersonal; female ones as particular. Males are seen as egoistic, females as caring: males are seen as rational, females as emotional.

The conceptions of the idea of a female ethic that I shall discuss do not all assume a doctrine of intrinsic female virtue or purity. But I think that sometimes, in their description of what they see as the particular qualities of female ethical thinking, they may tend to lapse into a recapitulation of precisely those dichotomies and polarisations that I have just mentioned. And insofar as they do so, I believe there is also a danger of *misdescribing* what they set out to characterise.

Insofar as there are distinctively female concerns or priorities, they have been developed in a context of dependence and often associated with powerlessness. I believe it is wrong to present a conception of woman *merely* as victim; nevertheless I think it is crucial to recognise the way in which women are sometimes disabled and oppressed by the very qualities which are also in a way their strength. Furthermore, insofar as these female concerns have been associated particularly with intimate personal relations, questions have to be asked about how values or priorities associated with these concerns can be translated, as it were, into a wider context. Sometimes these questions are not asked. Thus, in an article proposing the struggle to establish a 'matriarchy', Shanklin and Love (1984) suggest that in a 'matriarchy' all relationships will be modelled on the nurturant relationship between mother and child. But quite apart from the problems in supposing that the maternal relationship forms a model for all others, to say that all relationships should be 'nurturant' simply raises the problem of how it is possible for care or nurturance to inform relationships that are not personal or intimate ones, and what it could mean to talk of 'nurturance' when one is faced with broad problems of social policy and organisation. Even if it is important that social policy or movements for social change should be informed in some way by ethical priorities that can be seen as anchored in the 'personal', such an informing is dependent on a *transforming*, and on a challenging of the sharp distinction between a public and a private ethic.

With these questions in mind, I now want to look in more detail at some particular characterisations of a 'female ethic'. Three main themes seem to me to recur constantly, in one form or another, in the discussions of this that I have encountered.

1. A critique of 'abstraction', and a belief that female thinking *is* (and moral thinking in general *should be*) more contextualised, less bound to abstract rules, more 'concrete'.
2. A stress on the values of empathy, nurturance or caring, which, again, are seen as qualities that women both value more and tend more commonly to display.
3. A critique of the idea that notions of *choice* or *will* are central to morality, and of a sharp distinction between fact and value; a stress, instead, on the idea of the *demands* of a situation, which are discovered through a process of *attention* to it and require an appropriate response.

In my discussion I shall refer to the work of a number of feminist writers. I shall not, however, aim to provide an exhaustive discussion of everything they say. I am trying, rather, to present an analysis of some important common themes and directions. Similarly, while I shall refer sometimes to the history of moral philosophy, I am not aiming at a comprehensive discussion even of those aspects which I shall mention. My aim is simply to locate feminist debate where relevant in the context of debates in moral philosophy from which it both derives inspiration and has and needs a critical relationship. Some of these debates are quite long-standing ones; discussion and critique of the fact/value split, for example, or debate about the notion that one's moral principles are fundamentally a matter for choice or decision. But some of the reasons for entering into these debates, or believing them to be important, are distinctively feminist. So I shall now look in detail at these three main themes, and show why they have been thought to be central to feminist thinking. In the remaining part of this chapter, I shall look at the critique of abstraction and at the notion of 'caring'. In the next chapter I shall discuss the idea of 'maternal thinking' as a paradigm of female moral thinking, and the relationship this has been seen to have to a critique of some conceptions of morality.

THE CRITIQUE OF ABSTRACTION

The word 'abstract' quite often has a pejorative sense in feminist writing, but it is a word which can mean many things. Sara Ruddick (1984) gives the following account of it: 'Abstraction refers to a cluster of interrelated dispositions to simplify, dissociate, generalise and sharply define. Its opposition, which I call 'concreteness', respects complexity, connection, particularity and ambiguity' (p.249). But this account is still extremely broad and vague. And I think, in fact, that the opposition between 'abstract' and 'concrete' has been used in two main ways, which it is useful to distinguish and discuss separately. These two uses are as follows.

1. To make an abstract moral judgement is to apply to a situation a rule or principle which is seen as applying to all other situations of that sort. To judge concretely, on the other hand, is to concentrate on the particularity or uniqueness of a situation and judge on that basis (and to be sceptical about the value of general rules). It is to judge contextually. To look at a person or situation abstractly is to 'abstract' – that is, discount or think away – the unique or particular features of that person or situation and see it as coming under some general concept or category. To judge concretely is to refuse to discount such unique or particular features.

2. To look at a situation abstractly is to make a judgement about a situation, or take a course of action on the basis of such a judgement, without considering the 'human consequences' of that course of action, the specific and detailed effects which that course of action might have on other human beings. Or it is to make a judgement which is 'distanced' in some way from the actual or potential experienced reality which would be the consequences of a course of action. Concreteness requires that one experience or vividly imagine such consequences, either to oneself or to others, and judge on the basis of that awareness.

Rules and Principles

A critique of the idea of a morality based on rules and principles is clearly expressed by Nel Noddings in her book *Caring: a Feminine approach to Ethics and Moral Education* (1984). Noddings argues two main things: first, that a morality based on rules and principles is in itself inadequate, and second, that it does not capture what is distinctive or typical about female moral thinking.

She points out that it has been supposed in a great deal of moral philosophy that to act morally is to apply a general rule or principle to a situation and act accordingly. The moral task is then, as it were, to abstract the 'local detail' from a situation and see it as falling under such a rule or principle. Beyond that, it is a question of deciding or choosing, in a case of conflict, how to order or rank one's principles in a hierarchy, in this particular situation, if not more generally. Moral dilemmas take the form of a clash of principles.

Noddings argues that this view of morality offers an inadequate account of women's moral reasoning. It is not, she says, that women *can't* order principles hierarchically. Rather, 'it is more likely that we see this process as peripheral to, or even alien to, many problems of moral action. Faced with a hypothetical dilemma, women often ask for more information. We want to know more, I think, in order to form a picture more nearly resembling real moral situations' (p.2).

In *Existentialism and Humanism* (1948) Sartre outlines the dilemma of a young man faced with the question of whether to leave home and join the Resistance or stay at home with his aged mother. The dilemma is posed very starkly and briefly; and the point of the story, for Sartre, is that the outcome will be one of mere choice and commitment, for which no justification other than the making of that choice can be found.

Noddings argues that the posing of moral dilemmas in such a way thoroughly misrepresents the nature of moral decisions. Far from making the 'real' issues stand out more sharply, it conceals them. We know nothing about the mother's feelings or situation, about the family history, or about the context of the decision that the young man has to make. If it were argued that however much further information was supplied, *in the end* a decision has to be made on the basis of principles, Noddings would I think reply that the more concrete and detailed knowledge we have of a situation, the less use are general rules and principles. Human situations are so different from each other that a principle of universalisibility (whenever X, then do Y) is either useless or serves to conceal the differences. Noddings also argues that a morality of rules or principles can be dangerous. Principles, for one thing, always imply exceptions to themselves (killing is wrong *except* in defence of one's country, etc.). And they lend themselves to the danger of self-righteousness. The amount of violence and psychic pain inflicted in the name of principle should, she suggests, make us wary.

Noddings' idea seems to be that a judgement *emerges*, as it were, from a more and more detailed look at the situation. Now, insofar as she is criticising what can be called the 'desert-island dilemma' account of moral reasoning, I entirely agree with her. There has been a tendency sometimes, in moral philosophy, to suppose that if you present only the 'bare bones' of a situation, it makes the issues stand out more sharply. If you have one kidney machine and two patients, one a sick child and the other a famous scientist aged sixty, whose life should you save? If you survived an aircraft crash in the jungle, would it be right to leave the wounded to die in order that the fitter might survive? I think the right response to questions like this is to refuse to answer them 'in the abstract', and this is not moral cowardice or fudging, it is a recognition of the absurdity and insensitivity in supposing that a 'right' answer to questions like these could be decided without a detailed knowledge of, and even involvement in, the situation. But I think there is nevertheless something wrong about the sharp distinction between 'abstract' and 'concrete', and about the way this has been used to characterise female moral reasoning. To bring out why, I first want to look again at the notions of 'rule' and 'principle', and then discuss an example in some detail.

Noddings does not really distinguish between 'rules' and 'principles'. What does she take a 'principle' to be? She understands it to be, I think, a rule which prescribes or proscribes a course of action (with possible exceptions). She clearly has in mind rules like 'Don't kill', or 'Don't steal', which, as principles, would be 'Killing is wrong', or 'Stealing is wrong'. She sees rules and principles as functioning to prevent or render more difficult an appreciation of the complexities of a particular situation.

I think, however, that there are important differences which are concealed by this conflation of rules and principles, and I want to suggest a distinction between them as follows. A rule specifies or forbids a certain sort of action, and to follow a rule is to accept a guideline for one's conduct whose purpose is to eliminate the need for reflection, except in marginal or problematic cases. A rule that one should not kill will raise problems about what counts as 'killing'; is abortion killing, for example? No rule can be applied totally 'automatically', for this sort of reason. Nevertheless, to be 'rule-bound' in one's conduct is to seek to order what one does in a way that does not require much in the way of reflection. What I shall call a 'principle', however, functions quite differently. It serves precisely to *invite* rather than block reflection. Principles are, I think, best expressed in the form of 'Consider...'. Consider whether your action will harm others; consider what the consequences for other people will be if you do this; consider whether the needs of others should outweigh consideration of your own.

The distinction between rules and principles is not always easy to draw. Thus it might seem that the injunction not to harm others could either be a rule or a principle, expressed as 'Do not harm others', or as 'Consider whether your actions will harm others'. The notion of 'harm', however, is so unspecific that it would be very difficult for 'not harming others' to function as a rule unless one adopted an extremely narrow definition of what constituted 'harm'. Conversely, it would be very difficult for 'Do not condone homosexual behaviour' to function as a principle, since 'homosexual behaviour' is so much more 'specific' than 'harm'. I am not suggesting that an absolutely hard-and-fast distinction between rules and principles can be drawn; but I am suggesting that there is a real difference between a mode of approaching moral dilemmas and organising one's conduct that tends to invite reflection and attention to the particular, and one which does not; and I think it is useful to draw a distinction between 'rules' and 'principles' to mark this.

A principle, therefore, is a general consideration which one deems important to take into account when deciding what is the right thing to do. In this sense, principles *invite* contextualisation of judgements, consideration of the particular. To have principles is not to be inclined to ignore complexity; it is quite compatible with recognising that the judgement one made in a particular situation was so specific to that situation that other apparently similar situations might require a different one.

Principles may be more or less explicitly held or formulated. I think it is possible sometimes to offer interpretations or 'reconstructions' of someone's behaviour that credit them with adhering to principles which maybe they have not formulated to themselves very clearly or explicitly. If it is possible to make consistent sense of such behaviour, and if the behaviour itself is consistently in line with what would have resulted from explicit appeal to principles, then one is entitled to ascribe such principles. In fact I think one needs to do so; there is a difference between the person who explicitly formulates a principle and one who does not, but there is a more important difference between a person whose behaviour shifts and changes in a random or totally pragmatic way and one whose behaviour can be seen as consistent and coherent in the light of certain principles. I now want to give an example of such a 'reconstruction' which comes from my own experience.

My mother and father both held a strong belief that it was wrong for a woman and a man to live (i.e. sleep) together if they were not married. (I was never aware of any exceptions allowed by them to the wrongness of this behaviour, though doubtless there may have been some). When my sister did this, my father's response was that he would not visit my sister's house, since by doing so he would be 'condoning' behaviour that he thought to be wrong. This, of course, involved him in an interpretation of 'condoning'; thus he did not regard it as condoning what my sister was doing if she visited him, provided it was not in the company of the man she was living with. It was not possible for my mother to behave like this. She too, as much as my father, judged what my sister did to be wrong – but she saw the maintaining of care, of relationships with my sister and her children, as a priority. And she continued to visit my sister. Now, implicitly, I think, in my father's eyes, he was the *real* upholder of principles – and he could safely leave to my mother the 'weaker' (and female) task of maintaining relationships. On this view, she becomes a sort of 'moral pragmatist', thinking contextually and situationally, and more prepared than my father to waive her principles in response to personal feelings.

But I think, in fact, that such an interpretation would be wrong, and that a better one goes like this. My mother and my father both had a rule: 'Don't sleep with someone to whom you are not married'. My father had a principle; roughly, 'Consider whether your behaviour will condone that which you think to be morally wrong'. My mother also had this principle, but she had another one too: 'Consider whether your behaviour will stand in the way of maintaining care and relationships'. This principle overrode the other, although my mother made an effort to reconcile the two, by visiting my sister and *saying* that she disapproved (ceasing to do the latter when it quickly became clear that the relationship could not be maintained on that basis).

This account, as I have said, offers a 'reconstruction', and I do not know whether my parents went through explicit thought processes of this sort. I think, however, that it is legitimate to ascribe principles on the basis of consistency of attitude and behaviour. The reason I have looked at this example in detail is that it suggests to me that a distinction between 'abstract' and 'concrete' judgements, interpreted as a distinction between acting on principle and acting in the context of a particular situation may be misleading.

There is evidence, both from common experience and from the work of Carol Gilligan and others, that women often perceive the maintenance of relationships as very important in their lives, and see it as a moral priority. What I have called a 'principle' is a consideration that one deems relevant and important in making moral judgements. In this respect my mother's behaviour was as principled as my father's. Furthermore, it was not that she, unlike my father, was uncertain about the rule; she was *quite* certain that non-marital sex was wrong. But what she did was different because her principles were different. I suspect that it is sometimes the case, not that women do not act on principles, but that the principles on which they act are not recognised (especially by men) as valid or important ones. Thus, to act so as to maintain relationships, despite belief that certain behaviour is wrong, may be seen as a weakness, as a *failure* of principle. It may, however, more adequately be represented as simply a difference of priorities.

It might be that the behaviour of men tends to be more rule-bound (though I am very uncertain of this). It might be that women do not, so often as men, make their principles fully explicit to themselves, perhaps because they themselves sometimes accept the sort of view that sees them as 'weaker'. But even if either of these were true, it does not follow that women's behaviour is generally less 'principled' in the way in which I have tried to define this. If women are more aware of complexity, or of particularity or ambiguity, it may be because the task of maintaining relationships, of preserving care and love, is one which poses immense problems about how to behave. It is an immensely difficult task. Adrienne Rich (1980) has written of the activity of 'world-protection, world-preservation, world-repair' (p.205), which has been especially the province of women. It has included the daily struggle to 'repair' the dirt and decay which human activity in the world has to contend with; but it has also involved what Rich calls 'the invisible weaving of a frayed and threadbare family life'. I think that is precisely the task to which my mother gave priority; as did Amy, the eleven-year-old girl whose interview was analysed by Gilligan.

I wish to resist, therefore, a view that sees women's moral reasoning, insofar as it may differ from that of men, as context-bound or situational, if these things are understood as sharply opposed to principles or general reasons for action. I think there are real dangers that a representation of women's moral reasoning based on such a sharp opposition will merely become a shadow of the belief that women perceive and act intuitively, situationally, pragmatically, 'from the heart', and that their processes of *reasoning*, if they exist at all, are nebulous or unfathomable.

Differences between men and women have often been mapped onto a series of dichotomies; men are rational, women are emotional; men think logically, women intuitively; and so forth. A sharp distinction between 'abstract' and 'concrete' thinking seems to me to have a tendency simply to replicate some of these other dichotomies. The danger with such dichotomies is that they both misrepresent women's capacities and differences from men, and suggest a false polarisation of such things as reason and emotion. A sharp distinction between 'abstract' and 'concrete' moral thinking could be used simply to defend (yet again) a view that women do not do such things as think out general reasons for acting in certain ways, or that their processes of thought are somehow more mysterious than those of men.

Human Consequences and Experienced Reality

In the second sense of 'abstract', to make an abstract judgement is to be 'distanced' from a conception of the human consequences or actual or potential experienced reality of that which is the object of the judgement.

What is it for a judgement, a concept, a way of thinking, to 'distance' one from some such reality? The best way to explain this is to look at some examples, and the language of warfare provides some of the most striking. In the Second World War, bombs or bomber aircraft were often given 'pet' names, such as 'M for Mother', 'A for Apple', 'P for Popsie', and so forth. During the Vietnam war, the Vietnamese were often referred to as 'Gooks', and military operations were sometimes known as 'zapping the Cong'. Many writers have written about what has become known as 'Nukespeak'; about the use, for example, of terms such as 'limited nuclear warfare' or 'theatre warfare' for the annihilation of Europe.

What is happening in these cases is that an attempt is made (often intentional, as with the training, for example, of American marines) to describe events in a way that is intended to *block* consideration of the often almost unimaginably frightful experienced reality that might underlie the description. The language and context is often homely, jokey; or it is dehumanising. 'Gooks' are not human beings, and to 'zap' the Cong sounds like a cartoon adventure. This sort of distancing happens in many contexts where violence occurs; I suppose it is psychologically easier to rape a woman if you see her as just a 'piece of ass'.

But it happens in other contexts too. For example, the police (where I live at least) call a road accident an 'RTA' (road traffic accident). An event in which people are killed or maimed for life can be referred to bureaucratically as an 'RTA', which might hinder commuters for a few minutes on their way to work. Distancing is not always just a function of language; it may happen, for example, as a result of things like the structure of TV or radio news programmes, where the incessant 'flow' of discrete items, and the juxtaposition of accounts of human disasters such as war or famine with 'lighter' items of news, can have the effect of almost obliterating any real imaginative conception of what it might be like to live through such disasters.

Is it true that men, more than women, are prone to this sort of abstraction or distancing? I think it may be, though I do not know how to substantiate such an assertion. What it *is* possible to say is that wars and military training and the planning of wars have been conducted by men, and warfare provides some of the most horrific examples of this sort of abstraction. Sara Ruddick (1984) argues that this tendency to abstraction is one important factor underlying militarism. Women too have, of course, often supported wars, and men have often opposed them; nevertheless, it is likely, I think, that women have been ambivalent about or appalled by the idea of war more frequently than men. (One problem here is the 'invisibility' of much of what women may have said or thought about war.)

But it is wrong to see 'abstraction' just in connection with militarism. Some capacity for 'shutting off', for refusing to dwell on consequences, is necessary for emotional survival. A surgeon, or an ambulanceman or a nurse have to be able to distance themselves emotionally from the human sufferings and tragedies they may work with in order to be able to do their job at all. Sometimes an incessant emotional dwelling on actual or possible horrors may be counterproductive or oppressive. A dwelling on the horrors of rape, for example, may lead to fears that are out of proportion to the actual risk of being raped. A dwelling on the horrors of nuclear war can lead to the sort of nihilism that sees nothing as worth doing if there is a possibility of the holocaust. Films like 'The Day After' attempt, rightly, to raise consciousness about what nuclear war would mean, to present a vivid picture of what it might be like to survive a nuclear attack. But imaginative portrayals of supposed consequences can also be used to create panics, to inflate fears; think of the language of 'floods' and 'waves' in which black immigration into this country has been described, of the graphic pictures sometimes drawn of white British citizens in fear of the disappearance of their 'culture', of Enoch Powell's speech about 'rivers of blood'.

'Abstraction' as such is neither good nor bad; it all depends who is thinking about or depicting things abstractly, and for what purposes. The reason why abstraction in the case of nuclear war is so chilling is precisely because it is *nuclear war*, and because the language of 'Nukespeak', like that of 'rivers of blood', is manipulative. The objective of 'Nukespeak' is to acclimatise us to thinking of nuclear war as a possibility. It is intended to make the unthinkable thinkable. The objective of the sort of distancing that a casualty nurse might do, however, is not to acclimatise us, or herself, to accepting road accidents as inevitable or not as bad as we had thought. A refusal to dwell on consequences does not necessarily imply a lowered threshold of acceptance of the phenomenon concerned. I have myself stopped watching films depicting the aftermath of nuclear war since I find them unbearable; but I do not think I am any more ready as a result to accept nuclear war as inevitable or tolerable.

In fact, I think that sometimes a distinction between 'abstract' and 'concrete' may conflate a number of things that are different. Consider again a phrase such as 'limited nuclear war'. This is 'abstract' in that it does not give any details about what the 'limitations' are; and one way of rendering it more 'concrete' is simply to remove the reassuring connotations of the word 'limited' by pointing out how many deaths are envisaged, how many cities would be destroyed, how all public services would be destroyed, what problems and agonies those that survived would face. Such a spelling out does not necessarily imply the sort of imaginative emotional living through that might be experienced by watching a film about it. But, as I have suggested, this sort of emotional living through is something that it may be necessary to curtail, and such curtailment does not necessarily imply that one is more prepared to accept or regard with equanimity the possible events on which one refuses, for much of the time, to dwell. Furthermore, a proneness to dwell imaginatively on the consequences of actions either for oneself or for others can create a vulnerability, to which women are perhaps particularly susceptible, and which can sometimes be exploited by others. For example, I have known women who have put up with intolerable behaviour from the men they live with, because they have dwelt on the suffering the man will experience if they leave (usually vividly depicted by the man) and which they will feel responsible for.

In the next section, I shall look at the notions of empathy and caring, and it is clear that there is a connection between these and the notion of emotionally living through the consequences of actions. Here I have suggested that the distinction between 'abstract' and 'concrete' is not always a clear one and that insofar as women have a greater propensity or capacity for conceiving of human actions in terms of the actual or potential experienced human consequences of those actions, these are things which can sometimes work against them, and which it is not always desirable to exercise.

ON CARING

The concept of 'caring' is central to many accounts of a female ethic. I shall first discuss briefly some problems about the meaning of 'caring'. Then I want to look at some ways in which an appeal to 'caring' can be used oppressively, and at the difficulties in supposing that an ethic of 'care' can always provide clear guidelines for human conduct.

The Meaning of 'Caring'

Noddings (1984) rightly points out that the notion of 'care' for another person is complex and has many strands in it. To care for someone thus has connotations of *anxiety*, of a potential burden; it has connotations of *desire*, of wanting to be with or enjoying being with another person; and it has connotations of *carefulness*, in understanding or appreciating the situation of another. The relationship between 'caring' and behaviour is again complex. In some circumstances one might be said to care for someone even if one does or can do nothing practical for them; in other circumstances, claims to care would rightly be greeted with scepticism in the absence of efforts to be with or assist the other person. It is not possible to specify any clear set of sufficient conditions for the existence of 'caring'. And the problem of defining 'caring' is not merely one of how to produce a definition for the sake of clarity of argument; it is also a practical and political problem. I shall try to bring out why in a minute.

Central to Noddings' conception of 'caring' is the notion of 'apprehending the reality of the other'. 'Caring', she argues, involves *engrossment* in another, a putting aside of self and an entering into the experience of another as far as is possible. Thus she gives the example of a maths teacher who tries to enter into the experience of a child who hates or fears maths; what is it like to feel like that, what possible reasons could there be for the child ever to want to learn maths? This engrossment in another does necessarily need to be long-term or part of a sustained or intimate relationship. It is possible to care for another in this sense without having deep personal feelings for them. Noddings suggests that a failure to apprehend the reality of the other in some way may be seen as constituting a failure of care, no matter how deep in other respects the involvement with the other person may be. Thus the parents of Laing's patients in *Sanity, Madness and the Family*, despite their constant anxiety about and involvement with their daughters, could be said in a certain sense not to have achieved the ability to care; the object of their care was often a projection of their own fantasies and bore little relation to the experiences and feelings of the daughters themselves.

The Politics of Caring
I want now to bring out three of the ways in which appeals to 'caring' can be used oppressively, or can serve to disguise social relationships of exploitation or domination.

First, it is very common indeed for women to be accused of failure to care. Recently, for example, I listened to a radio phone-in on the question of women who went out to work. (The way the topic was defined suggested already that there was something deviant or unusual about this.) A number of callers, both men and women, argued that women who went out to work usually did so for 'selfish' reasons, and at the cost of not caring adequately for their husbands or children.

Arguments against abortion are often conducted in terms of 'caring'. Women who want abortions are (again) seen as 'selfish'; as putting their own selfish interests above care for human life or the potential human being they want to get rid of. A common feature of attacks on abortion is the thin-end-of-the-wedge argument; that is, if we care so little for human life that we are prepared to abort a foetus, then the next step might be a careless and unthinking support for euthanasia, a general sliding into lack of respect for others if they interfere with our selfish purposes.

The problem here is often how to define 'care'. What does care for children entail, for example? Is it a failure of care not to be available on demand to one's children twenty-four hours a day for the first five years of their lives? Is it a failure of care not always to find their company rewarding, however much one may love them? Is it a failure of care to insist on a holiday alone away from one's elderly parents? Is it a failure of care for a woman sometimes to refuse sex on demand to her partner? Women in particular are often prone to feelings of guilt if they try to seize a bit of space, time or privacy for themselves, away from other people. They are especially vulnerable to charges of not-caring, since they are so often seen as defined by their caring role and capacities.

Second, it is very common for debates about industrial action to be conducted on the basis of an implied sharp opposition between self-interest and caring, especially where those taking such action have jobs where this is likely to have a direct or immediate effect on the public. If nurses or ambulancemen go on strike, radio and TV reports almost invariably focus on what it is thought will be the immediate human consequences — longer hospital queues, possible deaths, and so on. If teachers strike, there is a focus on the disruption of children's examinations. If it is the power workers, questions are raised about old people dying of hypothermia. The largely female profession of nursing has suffered particularly from this opposition between selfishness and caring. How can nurses, who are doubly defined as 'caring', both by being female and by the nature of their work, possibly entertain the idea of causing inconvenience, let alone suffering, to others, by selfishly striking for some rudimentary form of social justice when all other means fail?

Third, claims about 'caring' can be used ideologically to conceal other more fundamental objectives. There was an advertisement, for example, for Texaco, which showed a tanker delivering fuel supplies to a remote village community; the message of the advertisement was 'Texaco *cares*'. We are thus invited to imagine that what underlies the policy of a large multinational corporation is not primarily the pursuit of profit but a desire to meet the needs of small communities. Programmes of aid to developing countries often conceal objectives of political domination under an official pretence of caring. Programmes of improving industrial relations by policies of greater 'care' for the psychological needs of workers generally have the objective of preventing industrial unrest in the interests of greater profits for the company. One of the most common features of relationships between men and women has been the way in which male 'experts', such as doctors or psychiatrists, have, in the name of a paternalistic care or concern for the welfare of women, reduced women to a state of passivity and dependence on men.

All of this suggests that claims to care or accusations of failure to care may serve to divert attention from issues of injustice or oppression, or to conceal other objectives which have nothing to do with care.

Now, in all attempts to change exploitative or oppressive relationships, someone is going to be deprived of something. They may be deprived of some attention, service or amenity to which they are accustomed. They may undergo some hardship or difficulty and experience this as lack of care. Consider the following examples:

1. A woman is accused of not caring by her husband because she wants some time to herself.
2. A person who is committed to political activity spends less and less time with his or her family, who feel that she/he is neglecting their needs.
3. A nurse knows that industrial action will have the effect of lengthening hospital queues for 'non-urgent' operations, and will inevitably cause hardship to some people.
4. Rebels against an oppressive military government take action which leads to military confrontation, and the certainty of deaths and injuries which will cause immense grief and distress.

In all of these cases a course of action might be seen to be uncaring; to be entered into without due regard for the immediate human consequences. In none of them can an appeal to 'caring' settle the question of what is to be done.

To what sorts of considerations might one appeal to try and resolve the dilemmas posed by the above situations. There are several. Sometimes it might be important (as in example 1), to redefine 'caring'; to argue, for instance, that it does not constitute a failure of care to refuse to spend all one's time serving, or in the company of, those with whom one is intimate. It might be important to suggest that such care may be damaging or destructive, both to the carers and the cared-for. Sometimes it is relevant simply to insist that care for oneself is legitimate. I noted earlier Carol Gilligan's observation of the difficulty women often had in overcoming the feeling that basing a course of action on one's own needs or desires was selfish or reprehensible.

The question of caring, however, also involves the difficult question of the relation between means and ends. One of the strong feelings underlying Sara Ruddick's critique of abstraction and Nel Noddings' critique of a morality based on principles is that of the danger of engaging in any struggle where 'abstract' or large-scale goals, whether they be obedience to God or the dictates of a nationalistic militarism, or a fight against social injustice or exploitation, are pursued without consideration of the damaging consequences to human beings that may occur on the way. The rationale of such a setting aside of consideration of the immediate human consequences may be that in the long run the goal is that of a more just or humane society. Thus, for example, the exploitation of nurses may be closely related to a general failure to provide an adequate health service which is responsive to human needs, and to the distorted priorities which spend billions on armaments while paying nurses a pittance.

There are problems, however, in distinguishing, ultimately, between means and ends. There are many cases where the use of certain means can corrupt or vitiate the end. This is above all, perhaps, true of the nuclear state. The supposed objective of nuclear weapons is the defence of 'freedom'; in fact, however, the nuclear state itself undermines and erodes freedom, by processes of increasing surveillance and restriction, of deception and doublethink, and of escalating fear and terror, quite apart from the possibility of the elimination of all 'freedom' in the event of a nuclear war itself. The same is true in other cases. Peace and security worth the name are unlikely to be achieved by police violence and repression, or by the ruthless elimination of political opponents.

In fact, the notion of 'means' and 'ends', with its picture of a clearly envisaged end-state which is sharply demarcated from the processes that lead up to it, is often a very misleading one. The processes by which change is brought about are themselves often an essential *part* of the sorts of change that are needed or envisaged. One of the strengths of the women's movement has been the way in which it has often perceived this. Thus, for example, in many women's health groups, the processes of sharing knowledge and encouraging participation, in a relationship of equals, are not simply *means* to enabling women to become more healthy. Often, it is precisely the means-end model, based on a mystique of expertise and the reduction of people to the status of powerless 'patients' that has been the object of a great deal of feminist (and other) criticism. Similarly, women have often rejected 'efficiency', if this is seen as something which can only be achieved by authoritarian or hierarchical methods.

Thus appeal to 'caring', to concern for the immediate human consequences that a course of action may entail, cannot of itself solve any problems or answer questions about the right thing to do. But I think that it can suggest two principles which should always be taken into account. First, it suggests a rejection of any sort of *quantitative* approach to human suffering. The suffering of a human being should never be regarded as a negligible thing, or of no consequence, no matter whose it is and no matter what ends this suffering is seen as a means to achieving. It may be that at times the options facing people are such that they have little choice but to cause human suffering in the pursuit of some goal. But this should never be dismissed easily as of little consequence. Second, it suggests a constant consideration of the relation between means and ends; a recognition of the impossiblity of holding these apart, and of the unlikelihood of achieving any liberation worth the name by methods based on authoritarianism, violence or terror, or on the disregard of the principle that, no matter what course of action is eventually chosen, the consequences for all those likely to be affected should be taken into account.

The idea of 'caring', then, if interpreted as concern for the human consequences of a course of action and for the 'reality' of those who will be affected by it can, I think, suggest principles which should be taken into consideration, even though it cannot by itself provide answers on all occasions to dilemmas about the right course of action to take. These principles imply a critique of the sharp distinction between a 'public' and a 'private' morality, one of which is appropriate to personal or intimate relationships, and one of which is appropriate to wider or impersonal concerns.

'Caring' is, as I have said, a concept which needs interpreting before it can be applied, and I want to conclude this chapter by giving an example of a way in which an application of such an interpretation of caring would necessitate quite radical changes in institutions and social practice. It is not possible to care for all those people with whom one comes into contact in a deeply personal way, and any definition of caring which is applicable only to intimate personal relationships is not going to be useful when considering broader problems of social organisation or practice. But there is an aspect of Noddings' account of caring which I think *can* be given an important sense when thinking about such problems. Noddings talks, as I have said, of trying to 'apprehend the reality of the other', of trying to grasp what the other is experiencing and how she sees things, and behaving towards her in a way that recognises and is appropriate to that apprehension. Now such apprehension is a matter of degree; one may apprehend the reality of another more or less well, and that may be a function of things such as the time and energy at one's disposal, as well as the disposition to do so in the first place.

But I think it is possible to argue that a great many institutions tend to work directly *against* such an attempt rather than facilitating it. The example I have chosen here is that of health care and the medical profession.

Above all others, perhaps, the medical profession likes to see itself as a 'caring' profession; and none of what I am about to say implies, of course, that there are not many individuals working within it who are deeply committed to the welfare of those who seek its services. But a number of critiques of the way the medical profession has developed institutionally can be read as arguing that care for patients, in anything like Noddings' sense, happens *despite* rather than because of institutional structures (see, for example, Ingleby, 1981, Mitchell, 1984, and Ehrenreich and English, 1979). The history of the medical profession over the last hundred years has not simply been one of 'progress' in the overcoming of disease, aided by scientific discoveries. It is a history which can be read partly as the attempt to establish white male hegemony over medicine, and what are seen as medical priorities can sometimes been seen as serving to legitimate status and hierarchies within the profession (the emphasis on prestigious 'high-tech' medicine, for example, rather than on other aspects of health care). Jeannette Mitchell (1984) shows how hospitals are often subject to quasi-industrial criteria of 'efficiency' and 'productivity', defined simply as the rate of throughput of patients in the hospital, and how hospital policy can be dominated by this requirement.

The aspect of this system that people most often encounter experientially is its tendency to reduce the patient to the status of a *body* to which things need to be done by medical experts. The cult or mystique of medical authority and expertise, as it permeates much of medical practice, tends to objectify or infantilise people, to deny them the status of participants in discussion or decisions about their condition or welfare and to render them powerless or fearful to ask questions or insist on information or participation. There have been many critiques, for example, of the medical handling of childbirth and the way in which women have often been reduced to a state of drugged passivity, unable in any way to participate in or control their own labour. But it is not just women who are thus objectified. The 'infantilisation' of much hospital procedure was brought home to me sharply when my father was in hospital, in great physical and mental distress after suffering a stroke. The mode of address to him by the staff, both nurses and doctors, often resembled that of 'play-school', and he was routinely described as 'naughty' if, for example, he was restless or uncooperative or made a noise in the night, and 'good' if he was docile. The attempt to preserve any shreds of human dignity in such a situation was well nigh impossible.

Criticisms of the objectification and infantilisation of patients point to a need both to redefine caring and to consider how a medical system might facilitate rather than work against such care. Questions of 'care' in the medical profession are all too often linked with assumptions of paternalism, a mystique of expertise and the incompetence in all respects of those who are the objects of care. Caring might, however, be conceived of as intrinsically involving the participation of a client or patient, facilitating their understanding, regarding consultation as mutual rather than always as a confrontation between expertise and ignorance. It might be thought of as 'apprehending the reality of the other', in the sense of seeing the patient's illness or problem as something inextricable from their consciousness or life situation. And taking these things seriously would involve radical changes in medical training, medical practice, the organisation of hospitals, the relations between the roles of 'nurse' and 'doctor', the hierarchies in the medical profession and the priorities not only within health care but also between health care and other things, such as spending on armaments.

To talk of a principle of caring here, then, is not to put forward a sentimental view of making health care more 'personal'. It is, first, to offer a conception of care that avoids both sentimentalism and paternalism and that is appropriate to the context; second, it is to engage in the very difficult task of seeing how such a conception might be put into practice. Applying a notion of care to any aspect of personal relationships or social life involves both these problems. Nevertheless, it is possible to see, at least in broad outline, the sorts of changes that a principle of caring of the sort that I have described might make. I think that it is in fact this sort of approach to caring which has underpinned many feminist critiques of things such as health care, and the attempts which have been made by many women to develop alternatives.

In this chapter I have suggested that some conceptions of a 'female ethic' raise great problems. In particular, I have argued the following:

1. There is no consensus among women, hence there is no one view of ethical priorities or moral questions that can unproblematically be seen as female.

2. The idea that women 'reason differently' from men about moral issues should be questioned. Insofar as there are differences between men and women, it is better to see these as differences in ethical concerns and priorities, rather than as differences in mode or style of reasoning. The idea that women 'reason differently' rests on problematic oppositions between concepts such as 'abstract' and 'concrete', or on the notion that a morality of 'principles' can be sharply opposed to one in which judgement is contextual. In addition, it tends to recapitulate old polarisations, between 'reason' and 'intuition' for example, which should be challenged rather than assumed.

3. It is important, when considering notions such as 'caring', which have sometimes been thought to be particularly associated with women, to recognise the ways in which these can be used oppressively, and the ways in which they may need transforming before they can guide any re-evaluation of social policy.

I have suggested, however, that the life experiences and activities of women, centred as they have tended to be, more than those of men, around the 'microcosm' of household, family and the physical and emotional care of others, may provide space more easily than those of men for questioning some dominant social priorities. In particular, they may provide space for questioning the split between a 'public' world whose concerns or constraints tend to exclude the personal, and a 'private' world of care for others whose constraints and concerns are not suppose to impinge on the 'public' realm.

If ethical concerns and priorities are related to life-experience and activities, then it follows that questions about the sexual division of labour are crucial. It is very important that men should participate more fully in and take more responsibility for the tasks of physical and emotional maintenance which have been seen as especially the province of women. But feminism needs to engage, too, with questions which are not just about the sexual division of labour. Women, as much as men, are situated within capitalism; their lives are affected, as are those of men, by such things as the sharp division between mental and manual labour and by the criteria of profit and 'efficiency' which govern industrial enterprises and much of public life. It is true that a great deal of socialist and Marxist thinking has been blind or insensitive to the particular situation, needs and aspirations of women, and has often failed to challenge the sexual division of labour. But the sexual division of labour is related in complex ways to the general division of labour within capitalism. Neither the *particular* forms that the sexual division of labour or the oppression and subordination of women takes, nor *particular* conceptions of the public/private split, can be understood by looking at the situation of women in isolation from the ways in which capitalism may often be oppressive to men too. In this sense, I do not think that there can be a viable 'autonomous' feminist criticism which merely considers the situation of women, or ascribes the relegation of common female activities and priorities to an assumed set of 'male' priorities which are believed to characterise men simply because of their maleness. The construction of current conceptions of masculinity and of a male 'sphere' of life has gone hand in hand, for example, with the development of the sort of 'rationality' which subordinates other human needs or concerns to goals of profit, 'productivity', or 'efficiency'. To write all these things down simply to 'maleness' cannot explain the *specific* forms that 'masculinity' has taken, nor the *specific* ways in which the sexual division of labour has been characterised. The relationship between feminism and socialism is a very problematic one but I think it is one which needs to be at the heart of any feminist critique of dominant social priorities.

8 Maternal Thinking

One of the central features of women's lives has been their responsibility for the care of children. Some feminists, as I indicated earlier, have argued that women have often been trapped by the burden of mothering, and some have argued that women should refuse, for the time being at least, to become mothers at all. But others have refused to accept this purely negative view of motherhood and have argued that it is women's mothering which has been one of the main sources of their distinctive priorities and approach to ethical problems.

Many women, of course, are not mothers. But it is sometimes argued that the sort of nurturant or caring or empathic qualities which women are so often expected to display, and the sorts of priorities that they often give to the maintaining of intimate human relationships, are so closely related both to the expectation that a woman will be a mother and to the capacities for mothering that women develop, that these qualities can be called 'maternal'.

I want to look at the account of 'maternal thinking' that is given by Sara Ruddick (1980 and 1984). It is of particular interest in many respects. First, she offers a detailed analysis of what she sees as the priorities and ethical concerns of maternal thinking rather than simply making vague claims about women's 'nurturance'. Second, she tries to identify some elements of struggle and conflict in maternal thinking and does not assume that it is always coherent. Third, her account is anchored in a critique of a certain philosophical tradition of thinking about facts and values and the nature of ethical decisions. This critique is sometimes implicit rather than fully spelled out; but I think it is essential to understanding fully what Ruddick has to say that something of this tradition is appreciated. So the first thing I shall do is explain in some detail the sorts of philosophical views against which Ruddick's account of maternal thinking needs to be read, and try to evaluate her implicit critique of these. Then I shall discuss her account of maternal thinking and ask some questions about the problems there might be in identifying any characteristic female priorities or ethical concerns with maternal ones. Finally, I shall discuss the view (not adhered to in any simple way by Ruddick herself) that the maternal relationship can provide a model or paradigm for all other relationships.

FACTS, VALUES AND THE DEMANDS OF A SITUATION

Ruddick acknowledges a particular debt to Iris Murdoch's book, *The Sovereignty of Good* (1970), and some of the concepts that are central to Murdoch's work are also central to Ruddick's analysis of maternal thinking. So I shall now outline and discuss something of what Murdoch argues in her book. (Murdoch is not concerned with issues of gender; she uses the word 'man' throughout the book and does not in any way suggest that her analysis and critique of certain ways of thinking about ethical decisions might have any relevance to questions of gender or sexual differentiation. Ruddick's use of her work, however, is a good example of the way in which a philosophical view which apparently has nothing to do with gender can be relevant to a feminist analysis or debate.)

In *The Sovereignty of Good* Murdoch is concerned with questioning an influential conception of 'man', and a related conception of morality and of values, that has been around in moral philosophy since the time of Kant. This conception is radically different from, say, that of Plato. In Plato's philosophy, knowledge of the Good is seen, precisely, as *knowledge;* the search for the Good is the search for truth, an arduous quest of the soul. Plato uses *vision* as a metaphor for knowledge of the Good. In the *Republic* Plato told a famous parable of the prisoners in the cave. The prisoners had taken for reality what was in fact merely the shadows flickering on the wall that were cast by the fire in the cave, and it is only when they emerge into the sunlight that they are able to realise the illusory and deceptive nature of what they had seen before.

In a great deal of moral philosophy since the time of Kant, however, morality or 'the good' has been pictured not so much in terms of vision, but in terms of action, choice and will. Kant believed in 'the moral law within', which could be discovered by human reason, and in this sense he accepted a form of belief in a moral reality external to the choice or decision of the self. Adherence to the moral law has, however, to be *willed* by the individual, and Kant argued that the only thing in the world which can be taken as good without qualification is a good will. Thus, he says, 'Intelligence, wit, judgement, and any other talents of the mind we may care to name, or courage, resolution and constancy of purpose, as qualities of temperament are without doubt good and desirable in many respects: but they can also be extremely bad and hurtful when the will is not good which has to make use of these gifts of nature' (Paton, 1948, p.59). Furthermore, 'A good will is not good because of what it effects or accomplishes – because of its fitness for attaining some proposed end: it is good through its willing alone – that is, good in itself' (p.60).

The good will, according to Kant, was the will which acted *out of duty,* not merely in conformity to duty. Kant believed that the good will could discover a rational principle which would serve as a test for determining the morality of any other proposed principle. This was what he called the 'Categorical Imperative', which was valid for all rational beings. One of his formulations of this was as follows: 'Act only on that maxim through which you can at the same time will that it should become a universal law' (p.84). Kant also argued that morality was essentially related to freedom. He drew a sharp distinction between the *empirical* self and the *transcendental* self. A person belongs to the 'sensible' world, and insofar as they are known to themselves by 'inner sense' or introspection, they must regard themselves as determined, as subject to the laws of nature. From the point of view of morality, however, they must conceive of themselves as rational beings, as possessing a will which is free from determination by empirical causes, and as obedient to laws having their ground in reason alone. The rational will is *autonomous,* which meant to Kant that it acted on reason alone. So, on the one hand, we have the messy (and determined) empirical self or psyche; on the other, the pure will, acting on reason alone.

Kant believed, as I have said, that reason could discover a moral law valid for all rational beings. But in a great deal of post-Kantian moral philosophy, the notion of a *rational* will dropped out, and values or morality were seen as a function of will, pure and simple. This is seen at its starkest in Existentialist accounts of morality. In *Existentialism and Humanism* (1948) Sartre argued that in the realm of values there was no excuse behind us and no justification before us. Any appeal to standards conceived of as independent of our own will or choice is nothing but inauthenticity or bad faith. It is a denial of our freedom and the total individual responsibility we have for the actions or values we adhere to. Existentialism thus in some ways retains the Kantian emphasis on the human will, while breaking with the notion of a universal rationality.

But here, I think, there is a coalescence with another view of morality which in many respects is utterly different from the Kantian, and it is that which can be seen as deriving in many ways from the work of David Hume. In his discussions of morals, Hume's particular target was the work of a group of British moralists who argued in general that to act morally was to act in accordance with the nature of things, and that to act immorally was to act irrationally. Thus William Wollaston wrote: 'A true proposition may be denied, or things may be denied to be what they are, by deeds, as well as by express words or another proposition' (Raphael, 1969, p.275). Similarly, John Balguy wrote: 'If by truth be meant the *truth of things,* then I think it may properly be said, that the moral goodness of an action consists in a conformity thereto. It may therefore be called either a *true* or a *right* action' (p.452). Here, a clear link is made between goodness and knowledge, between virtue and reason. Wollaston and Clarke both argued, in fact, that immorality was a sort of *contradiction*. And Balguy wrote: 'To treat men in the same way we treat brutes, and to treat brutes in the same way as we do sticks and stones, is manifestly as disagreeable and dissonant to the nature of things, as it would be to attempt the forming of an angle with two parallel lines' (p.452).

Now one of the main objects of Hume's critique was to demolish this idea of virtue as conformity to reason, and the idea that morality can be rationally discerned. Hume was led to this conclusion for a number of reasons. Morality, he said, is often thought of as a conflict between reason and passion, and men are thought of as moral only insofar as they obey the dictates of reason rather than passion. This, however, Hume believed to be wrong. Reason alone, he argued, can never move us to action. Reason, according to Hume, consisted in the ability to judge 'the abstract relations of our ideas, or those relations of objects, of which experience only gives us information' *(Treatise,* 1740: 1972 p.155). Reasoning concerning the abstract relations of ideas, as in mathematics, can never of itself move us to action. As to reasoning concerning objects of experience, reason, Hume argued, was the 'slave of the passions'. Passions are 'original existences', and not in themselves capable of 'disagreement' with reality. It is the passions which provide the impulse to action, and all reason can do is show the connections which the object of the original impulse has to other objects.

It is from the prospect of pain or pleasure that the aversion or propensity arises towards any object, and these emotions extend themselves to the causes and effects of that object, as they are pointed out to us by reason and experience. It can never in the least concern us to know, that such objects are causes and such others effects, if both the causes and the effects be indifferent to us. Where the objects themselves do not affect us, their connection can never give them any influence; and it is plain, that as reason is nothing but the discovery of this connection, it cannot be by its means that the objects are able to affect us [p.156].

Hence, 'the understanding' as such can neither justify nor condemn the passions, and, Hume argued, 'It is not contrary to reason to prefer the destruction of the whole world to the scratching of my finger' (p.156).

Hume argued that vice and virtue were 'perceptions in the mind'. They were not qualities of objects, nor relations between objects:

> Take any action allowed to be vicious: wilful murder, for instance. Examine it in all lights, and see if you can find that matter of fact or real existence which you call *vice*. In whichever way you take it, you find only certain passions, motives, volitions and thoughts. There is no other matter of fact in the case. The vice entirely escapes you, as long as you consider the object. You never can find it, till you turn your reflection into your own breast, and find a sentiment of disapprobation, which arises in you, towards this action. Here is a matter of fact; but it is the object of feeling, not of reason. It lies in yourself, not in the object. So that when you pronounce any action or character to be virtuous or vicious, you mean nothing, but that from the constitution of your nature you have a feeling or sentiment of blame from the contemplation of it. [p.203]

Hume is arguing that moral judgements are not true or false, and do not attribute any sorts of characteristics to objects. He locates morality and moral judgement in what he called 'sympathy'. By this he meant that the idea of the experience of another person could become 'enlivened'. It could become a real internal impression, by a principle of a sort of communication of the passions. A certain objectivity in our evaluations was gained, Hume thought, through a habit, derived from experience, of being able to consider a person's character in general, without reference to particular interests. But the foundation of morality itself is nevertheless the passions.

In many respects, therefore, Hume's moral philosophy is the antithesis of that of Kant. It stresses passion and emotion, breaks the connection between morality and reason. There is, nevertheless, an aspect of Hume's thinking that is similar to Kant's. Neither of them were in any sense radical subjectivists. Kant believed in a rational universal moral principle. Hume in no sense *reduced* morality to individual feeling, and was at pains to argue that the *mere* experiencing of like or dislike was not sufficient to constitute morality. Nevertheless, in both Hume and Kant, value and morality is seen to reside in the human individual; in the good will or in the passions.

This implies a radical distinction between fact and value. Famously, Hume queried the propriety of deriving an 'ought' from an 'is':

In every system of morality, which I have hitherto met with, I have always remarked that the author proceeds for some time in the ordinary way of reasoning, and establishes the being of a God, or makes observations concerning human affairs; when of a sudden I am surprised to find, that instead of the usual copulation of propositions, *is* and *is not*, I meet with no proposition that is not connected with an *ought* or *ought not*. This change is imperceptible; but is, however, of the last consequence. For as this *ought* or *ought not* expresses some new relation or affirmation, it is necessary that it should be observed and explained; and at the same time that a reason should be given for what seems altogether inconceivable, how this new relation can be a deduction from others which are entirely different from it. [p.203]

According to the most common interpretation, Hume is here saying that just as vice and virtue are not 'real existences' but are impressions in the mind of human beings, so duties and obligations are not demanded by the *nature* of things.

The distinction between 'fact' and 'value', and the critique of any form of 'naturalism' in ethics, has been a dominant feature of much moral philosophy (and much else, including a great deal of social science). The 'natural order' is how things are. The 'moral order' is how we value them and what we ought to do about them, and values are seen as a function of human choice, will, emotion, rather than a function of how things are. The fact/value distinction has permeated deeply, too, into commonsense conceptions of moral discourse. 'Values', or moral judgements, are often seen merely as matters of personal opinion. Thus Tony Skillen (1977) describes as follows his experiences in teaching moral philosophy;

On the one hand, 'the moral' is seen to reside in the private breasts of individuals; at the level of their 'personal feelings' about things; to endeavour to persuade another, let alone to coerce him or her, is just to impose your values on them. On the other hand, 'morality' is seen to reside at the level of 'norms' by which 'society' induces conformity in individuals...Thus, in my experience, students tend to hover between a merely formal libertarianism ('Live by your own values') and a purely formal collectivism ('It depends what is right in your own particular society') [pp.127–8]

'Good' therefore becomes, as Iris Murdoch puts it, a 'movable label affixed to the world'. It is not an object of insight or knowledge. It is a function of the human will (or of human emotions, or social norms). Metaphors of *vision* become totally inappropriate. There cannot be *knowledge* of what to do, only choice or decision (or the promptings of feelings or of society).

There have been critiques of the fact/value split by philosophers, however, and attempts to reinstate some form of ethical naturalism. Thus Philippa Foot (1967) and Geoffrey Warnock (1971) both argued that the notion of 'good' cannot intelligibly be applied to just *anything;* it must have a connection with human welfare, human good or harm, and difficult though it may be to say what these things are, there are some things which could not intelligibly be called 'good'. Iris Murdoch's book, *The Sovereignty of Good* also argues, though rather differently, for a form of ethical naturalism; that is to say, for the view that 'facts' and 'values' are *connected* and that duties or obligations may follow from 'how things are'.

Murdoch argues for a reinstatement of the connection of goodness with knowledge, and for the usefulness of metaphors of vision when thinking about the good. The emphasis on will, choice and freedom in much moral philosophy has, she suggests, wrongly diverted us away from the idea that it is possible to *attend* to a situation, to try and see it accurately or justly, such that the outcome – what one does or thinks one ought to do – is ill-described by notions of 'choice' or 'decision'. And the process of attention is itself part of the moral struggle, not merely the final choice or the behavioural outcome. It is a moral task, a moral requirement, to try to *see* reality, undistorted by self.

The idea of 'attention' is central to Murdoch's work. She writes, 'I have used the word "attention", which I borrow from Simone Weil, to express the idea of a just and loving gaze directed upon an individual reality. I believe this to be the characteristic and proper mark of the moral agent'

(1970, p.34). In this process of attention, a person or a situation will come to be seen as making *demands,* and acting on those demands will be experienced as something more like obedience than choice. If I attend properly, then I may have no choice, since the demands of the situation are such that I can do no other:

One is often compelled almost automatically by what one *can* see. If we ignore the prior work of attention, and notice only the emptiness of the moment of choice, we are likely to identify freedom with the outward movement, since there is nothing else to identify it with. But if we consider what the work of attention is like, and how imperceptibly it builds up structures of value round about us, we shall not be surprised that at crucial moments of choice, most of the business of choosing is already done. This does not imply that we are not free, certainly not. But it implies that the exercise of our freedom is a small piecemeal business which goes on all the time, and not a grandiose leaping about unimpeded at important moments'. [p.37]

We have continual slight control, she argues, over the direction and focus of our vision; and we can make what she calls 'small peering efforts of the imagination' to see a person or a situation more accurately, lovingly or justly.

'Reality', Murdoch argues, is a *normative* word. To see a person or a situation in a certain light, to perceive it as thus-and-thus, cannot be abstracted from the view that there are certain forms of response or action that the situation demands. She sees the virtue of humility as a central (and greatly misunderstood) one. It is not, she says, a peculiar habit of self-effacement, rather like having an inaudible voice. Rather, it is a capacity for 'self-less' perception of the world; self-less in the sense that attention to and perception of a person or a situation are, as far as is possible, undistorted by fantasy or by the desires of self.

Now, I think that Murdoch is entirely right to criticise the idea of a radical split between facts and values. The fact/value split depends not only on a view of values as created in some way merely by choice, but also on a certain view of facts. It depends on the belief that there are 'neutral' or value-free ways of describing social reality that are objective in the sense that they could in principle be accepted by any 'disinterested' person. Human knowledge, however, is never 'disinterested' in this sort of sense.

It is clear that it is often impossible to separate out the 'descriptive' from the 'evaluative' meaning of a word. Consider, for example, describing someone's behaviour as 'rude'. The word is clearly a pejorative one; it makes an evaluation. It also has a descriptive content: not just *any* behaviour could be seen as 'rude'. But there are nevertheless disagreements about what sorts of behaviour are rude. When I was a child, I can remember being told that it was rude to argue; but 'arguing' was defined as any form of disagreement with adults, especially parents. The equation 'disagreement equals arguing equals being rude' depended on an evaluation of my behaviour, but this evaluation was dependent on a particular understanding of parent–child relationships and of parental knowledge and authority. Given a change in that understanding, I might not have been described as 'rude' at all.

I remember watching a TV discussion about families where the wife went out to work and the husband stayed at home to look after the children. The argument between the participants got extremely heated, and the chairman attempted to remove the heat by asking them to forget their *personal* opinions about the rights or wrongs of such a situation, and just say *what they thought would actually happen* if the woman went out to work and the man stayed at home; in other words, to concentrate on facts and forget values. But, of course, there was no 'neutral' descriptive language available. One man commented, 'If my wife went out to work and earned money, she would get too domineering'. Involved in that remark was a perception not just of the individual woman or family, but of gender relationships more generally. And the response was not just to argue that women did not, in fact, become domineering, but to question the whole perception of social relationships in which that word was anchored.

Examples like these bear out Iris Murdoch's belief that reality is a normative concept. To see a situation as one of a certain sort *is* often to see reasons for evaluating it in certain ways, and probably for behaving in certain ways as well. If a man sees his wife as 'domineering' if she earns money, he has already evaluated the situation, and he has a reason for wanting to prevent her doing so (though not necessarily a compelling one – a need for her earnings might, for example, force him to put up with her being out at work).

But there are problems with Murdoch's version of naturalism. Consider now the following. It has been a common experience for women to go through a process of fundamental re-evaluation of male behaviour towards women and of their own behaviour towards men. In Chapter 3 I mentioned Sandra Bartky's discussion (1977) of the experience of developing what she calls a feminist consciousness and of the ways in which this can lead to an experience of radical doubt. First, there is the doubt about the validity of some of one's 'readings' of social behaviour, especially male behaviour. Second, there is the doubt about one's own behaviour and responses. People grow up with a repertoire of behaviour and responses towards the other sex; if they learn to conceptualise or understand social reality differently, they may come to wish to 'unlearn' some of these responses, to behave differently. And new or appropriate responses to a changed perception of social reality may not lie ready to hand. This is true for both men and women; a woman who has tended to present herself in a manner of engaging childishness to men, or a man who has consistently patronised women, may have equal difficulty in knowing *how* to change in response to an awareness of these things.

This radical doubt may be a result of a process of 'attention' of the sort that Murdoch describes. Attending to a situation, trying to perceive it accurately or justly, may not always lead to a feeling that there is no choice, that 'I can do no other'. Sometimes it may; thus, for example, the attention of a parent to the suffering of a child may lead to a feeling of absolute obligation that the alleviation of the suffering has priority over all other things, and sometimes to an absolute clarity as to what the situation demands, what has to be done. Sometimes, however, the feeling of obligation may be combined with a complete lack of clarity about what is the right thing to do, which no amount of attention to the child or the situation seems able to resolve – in which all choices seem wrong.

Sometimes, in fact, the experience of a situation as *demanding* a particular response, and of obedience to that demand, may be associated with a way of thinking which is far removed from any process of detailed attention. A situation that is conceived of in a habitual or stereotypical way may present itself to consciousness as posing demands; so may one which is conceived of according to some rigorous or inflexible code of ethical behaviour. Codes of behaviour or morals in which notions of personal honour have figured largely, have often created such demands. Thus 'honour' may demand that one avenge the death of a relative by a reciprocal murder; that one sack a pregnant maid or send away a pregnant teenage daughter so as not to besmirch the honour of one's household; that one commit ritual suicide rather than admit defeat. Such 'demands' are in direct contradiction to the idea that one should painstakingly seek to adjust one's behaviour and perceptions in the light of the unique or particular features of a situation.

The process of learning, with difficulty, to understand a person or a situation in a new way, to reconceptualise it or see it differently, is commonly one in which the inexorability of what were previously seen as demands may disappear, and in which there may be the sorts of radical doubt I have described. This process does indeed require attention, of a detailed and sustained sort. But if a new understanding is to emerge, that attention cannot always *just* be focused on the details and nuances of the particular situation. Murdoch describes the way in which one might try to apprehend, honestly and accurately, the state of mind and situation of another person, and in so doing perceive that one's previous judgements had been hasty and unjust. But in many cases such attention could not achieve a change in perception unless it drew on some more general (and perhaps newly acquired) ways of making sense of human behaviour. Knowing more about someone's life is not a matter of the mere accumulation of information; it is a matter also of a perspective within which that information can be understood. From one point of view, someone might appear to be stupid, selfish, narrow and prejudice-ridden; put that behaviour, however, in the context of a life lived in drearily oppressive circumstances and a new understanding of these, and the behaviour may be seen differently. This is not to say that to understand all is necessarily to forgive all. Nevertheless, there are occasions when such a changed understanding may change one's perception of a person; thus, for example, ways of behaving once seen as stubborn or stupid or destructive may come to be seen as part of a structure of coping, of defence against hardship and invasion of self, of self-protection.

What I am suggesting is that the process of attention, if it is to result in a changed evaluation of a situation, may have a political dimension. It may require an understanding of a person or a situation that is informed by a much broader conception of the nature and oppressiveness of, for example, class or gender relationships. And the same is true of an understanding of one's own situation. Feminists have often pointed out how it is frequently not until a woman can come to see her situation as shared, as connected with much more general features of social relationships between the sexes, that she can either begin really to understand it or cease feeling constant guilt or failure because she does not live up to certain expectations.

Now, I think that Murdoch's account of attention fails to note this political dimension it may have. In her account, attention appears primarily as an individual task, almost sometimes as a spiritual quest, a heroic (though not grandiose) attempt to transcend self and see the world aright. 'Reality' appears here not just as normative, but as given. Murdoch's link between goodness and knowledge and discussion of the aptness of metaphors of vision is underpinned by an almost Platonic conception of knowledge as that which is 'real' independently of human perception or value and simply has to be grasped or discovered or attended to.

As against this Platonic conception of knowledge and of reality, I think it is crucial to stress the way in which 'reality' is socially constructed. By this I mean that what is seen as 'real' will depend on the conceptions of the world that are socially available, and these conceptions themselves are not independent of human interests and human values. Thus, for example, an apprehension of certain aspects of social

reality as 'sexist' will depend on understandings of these
which are not radically separable from an evaluation of them
as oppressive and damaging. To say this is not to lapse into
the sort of relativism which argues that since all human
perceptions of the world are inflected by interests and by
values, there is nothing to choose between them. That sort
of view is merely a shadow of the sharp distinction between
fact and value which I have been discussing.

I have looked at Iris Murdoch's critique of the fact/value
distinction, and at the use she makes of the concepts of
'attention' and of the 'demands' a situation may make on us
in her characterisation of morality. I have suggested that
there are some problems with this characterisation. I think
that some of these problems are replicated in Sara Ruddick's
use of Murdoch's work in her discussion of maternal
thinking, and I now turn to look at this.

MATERNAL THINKING

Maternal thinking offers, Ruddick argues, a distinctive way
of caring and knowing. It is not that mothers are especially
wonderful people, or that simply being a mother leads to the
possession of maternal virtues and capacities. Rather, she
says, maternal thinking *identifies* priorities, attitudes and
virtues; it conceives of a certain sort of achievement.
Mothers respond to a reality – namely that of bringing up
children – which appears as *given,* as making certain
demands. Ruddick suggests that despite the immense variety
of childrearing practices, a cross-cultural understanding of
maternal practice is possible.

The demands of childrearing are for the preservation,
growth and acceptability of children. Mothers are concerned
that their children should survive and thrive physically, grow
and develop emotionally and intellectually, and be
acceptable to the society in which they are reared. The
conflicts and tensions generated by these demands inform
maternal practice, and the desire to achieve them generates
a conception of maternal virtue. In her article 'Maternal
Thinking' (1980) Ruddick identifies the following maternal
virtues: *a responsiveness to growth* (and acceptance of

change), along with a sort of learning that recognises change, development, and the uniqueness of particular individuals and situations; *resilient good humour and cheerfulness,* even in the face of conflict, the fragility of life, and the dangers inherent in the processes of physical and mental growth; *attentive love,* which is responsive to the reality of the child, and is also prepared to give up, let grow, accept detachment; *humility,* a selfless respect for reality, a practical realism which involves understanding the child and respecting it as a person, without either 'seizing' or 'using' it.

In a later article, *Preservative Love and Military Destruction* (1984) Ruddick sees a connection between maternal thinking and pacifism or opposition to militarism. She sees maternal thinking as opposed to 'abstraction'. It is concerned with the care and preservation of unique human individuals; militarism, on the other hand, involves the sacrifice of human individuals in the name of 'abstract' causes, the destruction of the objects of maternal care.

Now there are, as Ruddick recognises, immense difficulties in seeing any sort of connection between mothering and opposition to militarism. Women have often been as patriotic as men, and as keen as men that their sons should fight; they have urged them to go to war and scorned those who did not. Many women are ardent supporters of nuclear 'deterrence' and oppose disarmament. Given this, is there any meaning at all in the claim that mothering is opposed to militarism?

If there is, it cannot involve, as Ruddick recognises, any claim that all women are pacificists or oppose war, or that women are 'naturally' peaceful just because they have children. And it is not this claim that Ruddick wants to make. She is arguing, I think, that the *task* of mothering is necessarily in contradiction to that of waging war; the objectives of each are in conflict with each other. Imagine a person whose life was occupied with two tasks – first, that of building a city and, second that of making a bomb to destroy the same city. The objectives of the first task are in contradiction to the objectives of the second. The bombing aims to destroy what the building achieved.

Now, someone might try to reconcile these contradictions

in various ways. Building the city might be seen merely as a means of testing the bomb. Bombing the city might be rationalised on the grounds that it was a bad city. Both the building and the bombing might be seen as subordinate to some further end, such as obeying the will of God. Nevertheless, the objectives of the two tasks are still in conflict. And I think it is this sort of conflict that Ruddick sees between the task of mothering (and the skills and capacities it requires) and the task of waging war. War destroys what mothering achieves; there is an essential conflict between a mother's concern to preserve and care for a child, and the destruction of that child in war. If mothers send their sons to war, this is not part of mothering, of what it is to be a mother. The enterprise of building a bomb intrinsically requires that the *aim* is for the bomb to work – otherwise it would have to be described as building a fake bomb, or pretending to build a bomb. The task of mothering intrinsically requires that one desire one's child to survive and grow, otherwise it is not mothering but something else.

But, of course, just as someone might try to reconcile the tasks of building and bombing, so mothers try to reconcile the tasks of mothering and waging war. Thus, waging war may be seen as a *means* of preserving one's children – making the world safe for democracy, deterring the enemy, and so forth. Or the sacrifice of one's own child might be seen as a means of preserving other children. But what I think Ruddick would also want to claim is that *in fact* mothers *do* often tend to oppose the sacrifice of their sons in war, and to be sceptical about claims that war is simply a means to great or good ends; more than many men, they refuse to accept the notion that *any* objective can require or be worth the sorts of suffering and loss inflicted in war.

Women's lives have often been dominated, as I have already said, by the 'dailiness' of care and concern for others, by the work of preserving, sustaining, repairing and mending both the physical and emotional fabric of life. And I think that it is probably right to suggest that, for this reason, they can sometimes find it easier than men to question those ways of thinking which see wars as legitimate means of attaining highly abstract ends. Nevertheless, the connection between women's lives and opposition to militarism remains, as much as anything, a hope. It is the hope that women, more easily than men, can be brought not only to recognise the contradictions between the task of waging war and the tasks of daily life, but to reject attempts to explain away and rationalise these contradictions. But the evidence that there is, such as that of Greenham Common, of women's opposition to and scepticism about war, and of their dislike of the relegation of personal and emotional ties with others to second place, suggests to me that there are some grounds for supposing this hope to be a reasonable one.

There are, however, some further questions that I want to ask about Sara Ruddick's account of mothering and of maternal virtues. The first arises as follows. If the task of mothering in its most general sense can be defined as that of preserving and caring for the growth of children, it is nevertheless true that conceptions of what is involved in the task of mothering have varied enormously. There is plenty of evidence for historical changes in conceptions of what mothering requires. One view was, for example, that the main task of the parents in the first years of life was to chastise the child constantly, almost to beat the original sin out of him or her (John Wesley held to such a view). It has been questioned whether, in eras where infant mortality was extremely high, parents either could or did care for individual offspring in the intense way envisaged by Ruddick's account of maternal thinking. But even in the twentieth century, when such emotional involvement with one's children has usually been accepted, there have been great differences in what it has been thought that the care of children 'demanded'. And most theories of how to bring up children, of what adequate mothering demanded, have been put forward by male 'experts'. Men (and some women) have not only told women that their only real hope of happiness and fulfilment lay in having children, but have told them in great and often contradictory detail how to bring up those children. Ehrenreich and English (1979) chart the course of childrearing theories, from those which stressed, above all, the importance of schedules and routines, to those which stressed the importance of an all-pervasive, permissive and supposedly instinctual maternal love. Behaviourist theorists such as J.B. Watson (1928) stressed the importance of a 'scientific' approach. Watson fulminated against parents who played with a child or cuddled it, and warned that such things would spoil the child's character for life. Spock (1957) told mothers, on the other hand, to 'trust your instincts' Time and again, mothers have been blamed for things that were believed to have gone wrong; thus the revolt of middle-class youth in America in the 1960s was often blamed on permissive and indulgent methods of childrearing. Women have therefore constantly been faced with the sort of 'radical doubt' that I discussed earlier. Clearly, being a mother is a task of immense importance, and the 'demands' that it makes must be met. But what *are* these demands? Was it abnormal, or a sign of inadequate mothering, not to wish to be with one's child all the time? Did children need their mothers with them all the time to be able to form adequate attachments to other people? Would a child be spoiled for life if it was picked up regularly when it cried, or would it be spoiled for life if it was *not* picked up? Did children need to be entertained and amused and taken on trips all the time if their educational achievement was not to suffer? Amid the contradictory theories of what it is to be a good mother, and the more general feeling that not to be a mother, or to want to be something *more* than a mother, showed a failure of femininity, women have constantly been anxious and mystified.

In 'Maternal Thinking', despite Ruddick's recognition that women may *fail* to achieve the maternal virtues they identify, an impression is given that there is at least some consensus as to what these virtues are or what the maternal task entails. I think this tends to ignore two problems. First, it ignores the extent to which conceptions of mothering have not just been developed by women out of a concern for children, but have often been foisted on them by 'experts' whose interests have not just been in the welfare of the individual child. J. B. Watson, for example, explicitly saw his work on childrearing as having the aim of producing disciplined and well-behaved workers for American industry. The schedules according to which mothers were supposed to bring up their children were to induce habits of order and regularity and the disciplining of impulses. Second, it ignores, as I have said, the sorts of radical doubt that women themselves have faced about the nature of the maternal task and the ways in which it should be carried out.

Conceptions of mothering have not *simply* been a response on the part of mothers to the needs of children, and mothering as a practice cannot be considered in isolation from the other social relations and institutions in which it is embedded. Motherhood has often been ideologically constructed in ways that have served to legitimate the dependence of women on men. Conceptions of mothering have also sometimes legitimated class-based assumptions about the working-class family, and racist assumptions about the 'pathology' of certain ethnic groups. Norms of white middle-class motherhood have been taken as standards by which to judge as deficient the often very different patterns of working-class or black family life.[1]

Ruddick sees mothers as responding to the *needs* of children. But questions about a child's needs are not always answerable just by a process of patient attention to the individual child. There are times when it might seem strange or even myopic to say this; when in particular circumstances, a child's need seems so clear and so demanding that it is difficult to see how that need could be questioned. The need of the starving child, the need of the severely institutionalised child for personal care and love, the need of the terrified child in hospital for the presence of its mother, seem to fall into this category. But despite the clarity of perceptions of need that we might have on such occasions, in a broader sense conceptions of needs are complex, problematic and raise political questions.

Consider, for example, Shulamith Firestone's (1979) view of childhood. She identified the main need of the child as to be 'left alone', without the oppressiveness of constant maternal concern, to develop in its own way. She is clearly suggesting a mode or style of mothering which is radically different from that depicted by Ruddick, and which is anchored in a quite different conception of children's needs.

And it seems to me in fact that Firestone's conception of these needs is scarcely derived at all from any real attention to children; she is simply 'reading back' into childhood a conception of children's needs which is extrapolated from her vision of a society based on contractual, voluntaristic relationships.

Now, I think it is crucial that a view of children's needs should not adopt the sort of 'distance' from attention to children that Firestone does. She is not alone in this distance; it was not uncommon for feminists at one time to shelve questions about the needs of children and simply assume that twenty-four-hour crèches would solve the problem. But is is not a simple choice between *either* looking carefully at children *or* making assumptions about them which are simply derived from some political theory or programme. There are many empirical studies which are of great relevance to questions about children's needs – studies of institutionalised children, studies of 'attachment' behaviour in children and of mother – child relationships, and so forth. We ignore these at our peril, or at our children's peril. But the assumptions that underlie these studies, the use that is made of them, the implications they are seen as having, the policies they are seen as suggesting, may depend on much broader social or political beliefs or priorities. The work of John Bowlby (1953), for example, on attachment and loss, was often read, by him and others, as showing that children would be 'deprived' if they did not have more or less continuous maternal care in the first years of life. Such a reading was reinforced by assumptions and beliefs about the role of women that were by no means derived simply from the observation of children. To read Bowlby's work differently, to reject some of its assumptions and some views of its implications, is not to say that it is of no value; it is to say that empirical evidence does not just speak for itself.[2] Interpretations of children's needs are informed by conceptions of the maternal role which are themselves related to conceptions of the sort of society we should be endeavouring to realise or maintain. But these in turn need informing by a detailed and realistic understanding of children. And this is where, I think, a notion of 'attention' comes into play. Children should not be pawns in a political scheme, and one reason for *querying* a political scheme like that of Firestone is that it lacks this attention, and that there is evidence that children have needs that Firestone does not consider. On the other hand, neither are children beings whose lives and needs can be conceptualised in abstraction from broader social questions. There is (or should be) a dialectic between these things. If Firestone overpoliticises childhood, in that the demands of childrearing are simply derived from a political scheme in which this dialectic is largely absent, Ruddick, I think, underpoliticises it. She is right to see that childhood makes demands and that mothering is a response to what those demands are seen to be. But her use of Murdoch's notion of 'attention' and of the 'demands' of a situation suffers, as does that of Murdoch, from paying insufficient recognition to the ways in which the demands of reality are not just given but are related to the ways in which reality is socially constructed. Ruddick's account tends to isolate mother and child as a self-contained unit of demand and response which is sometimes very like that of Bowlby or Winnicott, and other theorists who have seen women as defined solely by their maternal role.

Furthermore, as Kate Soper (1981) has pointed out, concepts which are often used in the delineation of human needs, such as those of 'autonomy' or 'self-development' are capable of bearing very different interpretations. Thus, she says:

I am...concerned to stress how circumspect we must be in proceeding to any claims about universal needs for 'autonomy', 'security', 'self-development', and so on. For appeal to such needs is made to justify the most heterogeneous political programmes, and it is all too likely that the concepts of 'autonomy', 'individuality' and the like that are involved in such claims will themselves derive their particular content *from* the social-political theory which wants to appeal to them as if they were external to it and represented 'neutral' facts about needs...We must consider, for example, that thinkers as diverse as Marx and Mill both insist upon the need for the development of individuality, and yet argue for utterly different political programmes on its basis. [p.13]

In 'Maternal thinking' Ruddick presents maternal thought as essentially giving, attending, responding, accepting, patient.

It is entirely outgoing, focused on the welfare of the child. And there is something missing from this picture. The problem for many women, after all, is how to *limit* demands: when is it all right *not* to attend, when and in what ways may 'acceptance' be withdrawn, and how is one to resolve the guilt feelings that all of these may bring? A central 'demand' of mothering is how to negotiate these conflicts between the demands of self and the demands of the child. Of course, a child's interests are not radically separable from those of the mother, and the worst thing one may be able to imagine befalling oneself is some disaster to one's child. But in day-to-day living there may be sharp conflicts.

Furthermore, it is not just that mothers need to preserve their own identity; it is also crucial that children recognise that there may be limits to the demands that can be made on other people. Children need, in other words, to learn themselves the sorts of capacities for responsiveness, good humour and attention to others that Ruddick identifies as maternal virtues. In the later article (1984) Ruddick recognises this. Attentive love, she says, may necessitate *moments* of self-denial, but:

Attentive love calls for a realistic self-preservation on the part of the mother, a mother-self that can be seen and identified by the child who is itself learning attentive love...Maternal thinking identifies attentive love as the fulcrum, the foundation of maternal practice; at the same time as it identifies chronic self-denial in its many forms as the characteristic temptation of mothers and the besetting vice of maternal work. In naming the virtue and its degenerative form, it points to a struggle [p.283]

There is a shift in Ruddick's thinking here. In the earlier article there was a stress on the way in which the demands of childrearing can appear as given. In the later article, the demands no longer seem so clear, and Ruddick suggests that maternal thinking may misidentify maternal virtues. But it is not made clear how this 'misidentification' might happen; and the problem arises because of the way in which Ruddick tends at times, as I have said, to conceive of mothering as a task whose demands arise simply within the mother–child nexus and to adopt an ahistorical view of the ways in which these demands are understood.

ON 'MATERNALISM'

I use the word 'maternalism' here to represent two beliefs: first, that insofar as there are distinctively female understandings of social relationships or female ethical views, they should be seen as arising principally out of the practice of mothering; second, that the relationship between mothers and children can provide a model or paradigm for other relationships.

It has been quite common, in recent feminist thinking, for mothering to be seen as a central or paradigm case of the practices out of which arise what are seen as distinctively female understandings. Sometimes the practice of mothering is associated with others, seen as similar. Thus Caroline Whitbeck (1983) says:

By 'practice' I mean a coherent form of co-operative activity...that not only aims at certain ends but creates certain ways of living and develops certain characteristics (virtues) in those who participate and try to achieve the standards of excellence peculiar to that practice. The practice that I consider to be the core practice is that of the (mutual) realisation of people. I take this practice to have a variety of particular forms, most, if not all, of which are regarded as women's work and therefore largely ignored by the dominant culture. Among these are the rearing of children, the education of children and adolescents, care of the dying, nursing of the sick and injured, and a variety of spiritual practices related to daily life. [p.65].[3]

This picture is, however, very problematic. Apart from the lack of history evident in the notion of a coherent 'core practice' spanning the very varying historical manifestations of the 'practices' Whitbeck discusses, it is not true at all to say that these have been simply ignored by the 'dominant culture'. It is true that many aspects of the work associated with these practices have been allotted to women, and regarded as of low status, in the sense that men would have felt demeaned by performing them. But practices such as those of education and the rearing of children have been the focus of constant ideological concern and struggle, and the 'standards' which should govern these have been constantly contested and redefined.[4] And they have often been defined by men in ways that have been damaging to women.

Education, motherhood or the nursing of the sick are not practices where a consensus about 'virtues' or 'standards of excellence' can be identified even among those who participate most fully in these practices – namely, women.

In the late 1960s and early 1970s a great deal of feminist writing was highly critical of the way in which women had been seen solely as mothers or as nurturers of other people, at the expense of what was seen as their own personal development and self-realisation. In the writing of Ruddick and Whitbeck, however, mothering is again taken to be at the centre of women's lives. Ruddick argues that it is in practice impossible conceptually to separate the 'womanly' from the 'maternal', and throughout her work, female ethical concerns and priorities tend to be identified with maternal ones. She argues, too, however, that it is not only mothers who can think maternally. By this, I think she means to suggest two things. First, women who have not borne children can often care for them in a maternal way; this is clearly true. But second, Ruddick wants to suggest that maternal thinking can inform relationships other than those with children, and even *transform* them.

Now there are some versions of this sort of 'maternalism' which seem to me to be quite unacceptable. Shanklin and Love (1983), for example, argue that *all* relationships should be modelled in some way on the 'nurturant' relationship between a mother and her child (or at least on the idealised version of this that they present). Such claims ignore the fact that there are features of parent–child relationships which are quite inappropriate as a model for relationships between adults. Responsibility in mother–child relationships is not mutual. A baby is not at all responsible for its mother's welfare; an older child will hopefully have learned some responsibility and care for others, but full mutuality is not attainable until the child is able to live without parental care. The needs and demands of children, however they are conceptualised, are different from those of adults, and many childish needs are only really paralleled in adults if the adults themselves are childish or childlike. There is a lack of equality, too. The small child is not yet the parents' equal in knowledge or competence in most things, and the parental role is necessarily, among other things, a teaching role. It is also one that may often require one to tolerate, accept, and try not to be hurt by, behaviour that would be quite intolerable or a cause for anger in most adult relationships. Insofar as some of these features characterise an adult relationship, it is quite likely to be a damaging and destructive one. Mother–child relationships can only be seen as a model for all others if children themselves are seen as 'miniature adults' (Shulamith Firestone, I think, tends to see them in this way).

I do not think that Ruddick wants to suggest, like Shanklin and Love, that the maternal relationship can in any simple sense be used as a model for all other relationships, and she says that maternal thinking will need to be transformed before it can inform other relationships. Nevertheless, it still seems to me important to question the extent to which the label 'maternal' should be applied to ways of entering into or thinking about relationships which might be argued to characterise women more commonly than men.

Ruddick's description of maternal thinking is derived from an analysis of the capacities and achievements that she thinks women display or recognise in the task of mothering. But, as I have said, she also argues that women who are not mothers can think maternally, and that women learn to think maternally not just because they are mothers but *because they were daughters*. It may be that she has in mind here Chodorow's theory that capacities for mothering are not just acquired by explicit role-teaching but are formed by the development of a sense of self-in-relationship with others which, Chodorow argues, is a feature of the way girls, rather than boys, develop in a system where mothering is undertaken by women. But insofar as women have these capacities, they are by no means developed *just* in the task of mothering. It is true that girls are often expected to become mothers, but their mothering capacities are only one aspect of a more general sense of the importance of relationships to the self.

The sorts of attitudes and capacities which Ruddick sees as maternal do not, I think, figure just in maternal relationships. Consider, for example, the notions of care, responsiveness, attentive love and resilient good humour. Women's relationships with men have often been characterised by these things, and they have sometimes taken damaging forms. As I have said before, a woman who is dependent on a man may develop great skill in attending to and caring for him, in 'reading' his behaviour and learning how to interpret his moods and gratify his desires before he needs to ask. She may put his needs or desires before her own and selflessly do what he wishes. And she may need a lot of resilience and good humour to be able to do this at all, and perhaps put up with neglect or violence. This is the worst sort of case. More positively, women often form supportive networks of friendship with other women; sometimes these constitute the emotional centre of their lives. Thus Caroll Smith Rosenberg (1975) shows, for example, the importance of friendships among women in nineteenth-century America. And women living in close-knit communities where there was poverty and hardship have often formed supportive networks of care and assistance without which life would have been insupportable.

Insofar, then, as women give priority in their lives to the maintaining of relationships with others, and to attention to and care for others, such capacities should not be seen just as 'maternal'. In fact, I think such priorities need explaining as a response to the material circumstances of life and as a resource developed in the face of deprivation and oppression rather than just as result of the development of self in infancy and early childhood. And it is a problem in Chodorow's theory that she says so little about women's relationships to women other than their mothers, or about women's relationships to men. The stress in her book on mothering, and the way in which capacities for mothering are seen as requiring a very particular sort of explanation, may simply tend to reinforce the view that what really defines a woman is her capacity to mother. I think the same may be true of Ruddick's account of maternal thinking, and her identification of female ethical priorities with maternal ones. It may be as Ruddick says, a *problem* to separate the 'womanly' from the 'maternal'; but I think it is important to challenge any tendency to equate the two, on a number of grounds. First, it actually misrepresents women's lives to suppose that they have been always or exclusively dominated by mothering. Second, the description of any characteristically female ethical priorities or concerns as maternal may lead to difficulties in recognising the ways in which these priorities may have sometimes worked against women's interests. Children cannot reciprocate care equally, they require a degree of selflessness and attention that is specific to them. To see female 'virtues' or priorities as arising mainly out of relationships with children may lead to a tendency to gloss over the ways in which resilience has become resignation and acceptance, attention has become chronic anxiety, and care and responsiveness chronic self-denial.

Afterword

In this book I have tried to identify what I see as some central tensions in feminist thinking, the particular forms these have tended to take in recent feminist debate, and some of the ways in which they have generated both a use and critique of philosophical theories and traditions.

In a considerable amount of recent feminist philosophy, as I have tried to show, a central theme has been that of the idea of a 'woman's voice' in philosophy. Thus it has been suggested that women's experience, and the social practices which have been especially the province of women, can provide a source for a distinctively female (or feminist) approach to philosophical problems.

There are tensions, however, in feminist thinking, about the way in which the lives and experiences of women should be conceptualised. And the general form of the tension which I have seen as most central is that which leads, on the one hand, to a stress on the way in which women have been oppressed and victimised by the forms of domination and exploitation to which they have been subjected, and that which leads, on the other, to a celebration of the strengths, values and priorities that are seen as having arisen from the ways in which the lives of women have differed from those of men.

Thus, on the one hand, one finds in much feminist writing an emphasis on the needs of women for autonomy, self-realisation and self-affirmation, and for liberation from what are seen as the bonds of servitude to others and domination by men. Along with this stress on autonomy has often gone a stress on the victimisation of women, and the ways in which they have been 'damaged' by the forms of subordination to which they have been subject. The images of robotitude in Mary Daly, of dehumanisation and degradation in Andrea Dworkin, of victimisation and the disintegration of self in Marilyn Frye, of infantilisation in Betty Friedan, of woman as scarcely a human 'subject' in Simone de Beauvoir, are anchored in this perception of the harm inflicted on women by their subordination and oppression. This stress on degradation and dehumanisation, however, is often implicitly rejected by those who see in women's lives and in the activities which have been particularly theirs a source for a critique of dominant 'male' values or social priorities.

There is an interesting parallel between these tensions in feminist thinking, and a controversy about the understanding of black slavery in the United States. In a book first published in 1959, the historian Stanley Elkins (1976) discussed the ways in which he thought that the personality of black slaves had been affected by the conditions of their servitude, including the trauma and shock of the brutal detachment from their native cultures in Africa. Elkins argued that the prevalence of the 'Sambo' stereotype in American literature about slavery was not replicated in the same form elsewhere (e.g. in the literature on South American black slavery). He suggested that this stereotype should not be seen *simply* as white falsehood or propaganda. Drawing on a number of arguments from social psychology and on a comparison of the situation of black slaves in the southern states with concentration camps in the Second World War, Elkins argued that the social system of slavery tended to lead to a degree of 'infantilisation' in the behaviour and personality of black slaves. Apart from the brutal initial shock of detachment and loss, slaves were subjected to an arbitrary system of authority in which survival was dependent on the will of a master; slavery tended to be, Elkins argued, a 'closed system', in which the authority of the master might well become internalised, and in which a working adjustment required of the slave a childlike conformity and docility.

Now, there were many problems with Elkins' arguments,

such as the validity of the comparison with concentration camps, the accuracy of his understanding of the social system of slavery, the adequacy of the psychological concepts that he used. But, a controversy developed not so much about the details of Elkins' argument but rather about the nature of any approach to slavery which saw it simply in terms of brutality and oppression. During the 1950s and 1960s, Elkins argued, 'damage' had been the predominant theme of most discussions of slavery, and it underlay the political programmes of civil rights, integration, restitution and the sweeping away of race separation in the early 1960s. But a great deal of work was also produced (mostly by white scholars) to try and show that slavery had produced not merely hardship but 'pathology' of various forms in the black personality and in black social life, which was seen to underly such things as low black educational performance and high crime rates.

However, during the late 1960s (contemporaneous with the emergence of what is sometimes called 'new-wave' feminism) there was a demand, both from black historians and activists and from white radicals, for a new vision of the black American experience. This involved a study of the forms that slave culture had taken and the ways in which slaves had resisted oppression. It involved, as Elkins (1976) says, a denial of two things:

One is that the collectivity of blacks must be seen as essentially inert; the other, that when all this prejudice and discrimination is removed, blacks would become undifferentiated Americans. Their past - by definition an ugly pathological blot - would be wiped out, their distinctive character, experience, contributions and culture would in effect be denied, would no longer really exist. (p.275)

From the early 1970s the new literature on American slavery was mainly absorbed with documenting such things as the existence of a rich, variegated and diverse slave life and culture on the plantations, the importance of the slave family, the strategies by which slaves resisted oppression, and so forth.

Elkins, however, suggested that the problem with much of the newer literature was that it began to make brutality and oppression appear to be a mere 'backdrop' to the existence of this culture.He argued as follows:

Any group that has been dispossessed of liberty by another group, and subjected to daily assaults on its dignity, on the personalities of its members, and on their very physical being, is by the primal laws of life going to do something to protect itself. It brings to bear whatever individual and communal resources it has in order to make its condition tolerable; it develops patterns of response; it fashions a body of lore and a picture of itself that makes its own existence in some way comprehensible, predictable and tolerable. The product — as with any other people seeking collectively to make sense out of the world — is 'culture'.

But it does not follow that simply in locating culture we have automatically found something *ipso facto* positive, in and of itself. No theory of culture I know of claims that much, though the point is by no means clear in much of the recent discussions of American black slavery. Culture, under such conditions as those of black slavery, is not acquired without a price; the social and individual experience of any group with so little power, and enduring such insistent assaults (of cruelty, contempt and, not least, uncertainty), is bound to contain more than the normal residue of pathology. Any theory that is worth anything must allow for this. It must allow, that is, for damage. (p.300)

Comparisons have often been drawn between women and slaves; thus southern women writers in the United States in the nineteenth century, some of whom were struggling towards forms of feminist consciousness, not uncommonly drew analogies between their own situation and those of slaves. More recent feminist writers such as Mary Daly and Marilyn Frye have again explicitly drawn the comparison. It is clearly one which needs using with caution. But the problems about giving an account of slavery to which Elkins draws attention are also raised by the feminist enterprise of celebrating 'womanculture', and of seeing in it a source of distinctively female values, strengths and priorities.

Women's 'culture', the skills, capacities, priorities and goals which women have produced (which have, of course, historically taken extremely varied forms) should not be seen *simply* as a reaction to the ways in which they have often been dominated, oppressed or defined by men. On the other hand, the social practices of women are not autonomous, isolable things, which can be considered apart from the context in which they exist. Motherhood, for example, as Adrienne Rich (1977) pointed out, is not just an experience but an institution, and an institution which has been embedded in things such as class differences, conceptions of the roles of men and women, conceptions of the needs of an industrialised society, and so forth. And the norms which have governed women's lives and women's practices have not just been developed autonomously by women. Furthermore, the *characterisation* of these norms is often very problematic (as, for example, in the representation of women's lives as governed by feeling rather than by reason, or in the representation of women as not, like men, acting on principles). Equally problematic has been the representation of women's activities — as based on 'biology' or 'nature' rather than on 'culture', as not qualifying for inclusion in the realm of 'fully human' activities. It is not simply men who have characterised women's capacities and activities in these sorts of ways; such characterisations have often been reiterated by women themselves, including a number who are within the feminist tradition.

Thus insofar as it is true that women's social experience, sense of self, priorities or goals have differed from those of men, these things cannot be appealed to in a simple way as a source of alternative values or priorities. This is for a number of reasons. First, as I have said, these have often been developed in a context of powerlessness and oppression, and, as Elkins puts it, culture, under such conditions, is acquired at a price. Thus, for example, if it is true that women's sense of self and identity is commonly more orientated around relationships with others and care for others than is that of men, it is also true that these things have worked in ways that have been damaging to women. Second, characterisations of the particular capacities and activities of women have always been, (and remain) contested. The problem with some of the characterisations that women themselves have produced is that they tend not only to marginalise the extent to which these things are not simply the autonomous creation of women, but also to repeat, in their characterisation, polarisations or dichotomies which have often had a long and oppressive history. Third, even if it is often true that women's priorities may differ from those of men, and that taking them seriously would require a fundamental re-evaluation of human priorities more generally, the problems of translating such priorities into broader social and political terms remains. So an appeal, for example, to an ethic of 'caring' raises, rather than solves, the problems of how to define 'care' in ways that do not demand damaging forms of self-sacrifice, and how to translate the notion of 'care' into wider social contexts.

The history of philosophy needs to be understood against a background of historical problems and tensions which come to predominate at certain times. In this sense I am in agreement with Jane Flax's view (1983), which I discussed in Chapter 2, that philosophy represents a 'stream of social consciousness' and that philosophical theories cannot be understood apart from the historical experiences which give rise to the problems which lie at the centre of those theories. What I disagreed with in Flax was what seemed to me be the ahistorical and over-monolithic nature of her account of male experience, and the problem of locating all the essential features of this experience in the unconscious development of infancy and childhood.

Feminism, too, is anchored in the problems, contradictions and tensions in women's lives and the different historical forms these have taken. Some of the divergences within feminist thinking can be seen against a background of differences in female experience. Thus the problems and tensions in the lives of, say, American black or Hispanic women will be very different from those in the lives of white middle-class women. There may of course often be common ground, recognition and similarity, and it is essential both that these be found and that women listen to each other and try to understand the differences between them. But the divergences in the lives of women and in feminist thinking mean that there is no non-contested or isolable paradigm of female values or priorities which can be seen as a source for feminist philosophical thinking.

In this sense, just as I have argued that it is not possible to identify a paradigmatic or typical 'male point of view' in philosophy, so it is not possible to identify a 'woman's point

Notes

Introduction

1. *See*, for example, Susan Okin, *Women in Western Political Thought* (1980). Okin charts in detail the assumptions about women in the work of Plato, Aristotle, Rousseau and Mill, and the ways in which these assumptions affected their philosophy.

   A useful collection of essays on women in the work of political philosophers is *The Sexism of Social and Political Theory*, edited by Lorenne Clark and Lynda Lange (1979).

2. *See*, for example, the collection of essays *Feminism and Philosophy*, edited by Mary Vetterling-Braggin, Frederick Elliston and Jane English (1977). The essays in this volume discuss topics such as language, equal opportunity, marriage, rape and abortion.

1. Feminism and Philosophy

1. In her book *Women of Ideas* (1982), Dale Spender notes the ways in which the work and writing of many women has been 'lost' and has had to be 'recovered' by contemporary feminism.

2. The question of changing conceptions of home, family and personal life under capitalism is interestingly discussed by Eli Zaretsky in his book *Capitalism, the Family and Personal life* (1976).

3. Mary Daly, for example, in *Gyn/Ecology* (1979), often writes as if *all* theories produced by men should be rejected by feminism.

4. *See*, for example, Juliet Mitchell, *Psychoanalysis and Feminism* (1975), in which she argues that Freud's work is essential for understanding the social construction of masculinity and feminity.

   One of the best accounts of the (problematic) relation between feminism and socialism is provided by Alison Jaggar in *Feminist Politics and Human Nature* (1983).

5. Two recent books can serve as an indication of the current feminist interest in the question of mothering: *Mothering: Essays in Feminist Theory*, edited by Joyce Trebilcot (1984), and *Why children?* edited by

Stephanie Dowrick and Sibyl Grundberg (1980). The latter is a collection of essays by women on the question of why they decided to have or not to have children. In the Introduction the editors write: 'Even to ask this question is to start a revolution. Motherhood — that great mesh in which all human relations are entangled — has been for so long the central fact of women's lives that the idea of *choice*, deceptively linked with such familiar concerns as contraception and the option of abortion is almost beyond our grasp...In asking this we encourage each other to face a major and often painful confrontation with self, upon a battlefield shared with family and custom, church and state, mythology, economic reality, and an increasing anxiety about the quality of the future.' [p.7]

6. For a more extended critique of Janet Radcliffe Richards' book, *see* my article, 'Feminism, History and Morality' (1982).

7. One of the most interesting discussions of the ways in which the meanings and associations of words change historically and are anchored in changing understandings of society is Raymond Williams, *Keywords: A Vocabulary of Culture and Society* (1976).

2. The 'Maleness' of Philosophy

1. There is a very useful collection of the writings of philosophers about women, *Philosophy of Woman: Classical to Current Concepts*, edited by Mary Mahowald (1978).

2. For a discussion of Aristotle's biology, *see* Lynda Lange, 'Woman Is Not a Rational Animal', in *Discovering Reality*, edited by Harding and Hintikka (1983). Lange argues that Aristotle's biology is relevant to an understanding of his ethics and politics.

   For an excellent general survey and discussion of the central but changing relations in western philosophy between ideals of reason and conceptions of masculinity and feminity, *see* Genevieve Lloyd, *The Man of Reason: Male and Female in Western Philosophy* (1984).

3. Reproduced in Mahowald (1978).

4. It is interesting to note that while symmetry might lead one to expect that Stern would see the problem for women as that of rejecting the 'masculine' in themselves, in fact he sees the problem for women *too* as a 'rejection of the feminine'!

5. A detailed discussion of Locke's political theory and his view of women can be found in Okin (1980) and Clark (1979).

6. Chodorow draws heavily on the work of such psychoanalytic theorists as D.W. Winnicott, W.R.D. Fairbairn and H. Guntrip.

7. For critical discussion of Chodorow's work, see the papers by Iris Young, 'Is Male Gender Identity the Cause of Male Domination?', and by Pauline Bart, 'Review of Chodorow's "The reproduction of Mothering"'; both can be found in Trebilcot (1984).

See also the discussion in Peter Leonard, *Personality and Ideology* (1984), of the extent to which psychical development should be understood as determined by infantile experience.
8. I am in agreement with Flax that philosophical theories cannot be understood apart from the historical experiences which give rise to the problems which lie at their centre. What I shall argue is problematic is the way in which Flax gives, I think, an ahistorical and over-monolithic account of the male experience that she sees as underlying philosophy.
9. The *Confessions*, translated and introduced by J.M. Cohen. Rousseau wrote, 'My purpose is to display to my kind a portrait in every way true to Nature, and the man I shall portray will be myself' (p.17). In the introduction, Cohen points out the historically novel nature of Rousseau's enterprise.

3. Experience and Reality

1. For a wonderfully vivid and perceptive discussion of the ways in which notions of 'sexuality' have figured in contemporary discourse, and of the ways in which the idea of 'sexual liberation' can be oppressive, *see* Stephen Heath, *The Sexual Fix* (1982).
2. See, for example, the paper by Freud, 'Some Psychical Consequences of the Anatomical Distinction between the Sexes'.
3. My criticisms of Winnicott should not be taken to imply that I think there is nothing illuminating or of value in his work on infancy and childhood. There is, for example, a great deal of interest in his discussion of 'transitional objects' in *Playing and Reality* (1977).
4. For a discussion of the relationship between black women and feminism, and a statement of the view that much white feminism has been racist, *see* Bell Hooks, *Ain't I a Woman? Black Women and Feminism* (1982).
5. There is an interesting discussion of the political implications of theories of society and theories of human behaviour in Brian Fay, *Social Theory and Political Practice* (1976).
6. An example of this approach is H.J.Eysenck and D.K.B.Nias, *Sex, Violence and the Media* (1980). For a critique, *see* a discussion of the debate about violence and television by Murdock and Mc Cron (1979).
7. For discussion and critique of Kuhn's theory of paradigms and the philosophy of science, *see* I.Lakatos and A.Musgrave, *Criticism and the growth of knowledge* (1970).
8. There is a discussion of this in Barbara Ehrenreich *The Hearts of Men* (1983), Ch.10.

4. Human Nature and Women's Nature

1. *See*, for example, Richard Dawkins, *The Selfish Gene* (1978). For a critical discussion of sociobiological theory, *see* Martin Barker, *The New Racism* (1981).

2. See Erich Fromm *The Sane Society* (1963), Ch.3.
3. *See*, for example, Maslow (1970, 1973).
4. There is a comprehensive and excellent discussion of the relation between feminist politics and conceptions of human nature in Alison Jaggar, *Feminist Politics and Human Nature* (1983). Also useful is a collection of essays edited by Ian Forbes and Steve Smith, *Politics and Human Nature* (1983).
5. A very useful collection of essays discussing the question of biological determinism is *Not in Our Genes*, edited by S.Rose, L.Kamin and R.Lewontin (1984).
6. *See* John Stuart Mill's essay 'On the Subjection of Women', in *Essays on Sex Equality*, edited by Alice Rossi (1970). Rossi's volume also contains an interesting introduction, and the writings of Mill's wife, Harriet Taylor, on the question of the subordination and situation of women. The writing of Harriet Taylor are not as well known as those of her husband, despite the fact that Mill himself constantly acknowledged his debt to her. Many feminists have seen this as yet another example of the way in which the views of women have tended to become 'invisible' (*see*, for example, Spender, 1982).
7. There is a wonderful discussion of historical contradictions in conceptions of woman in Simone de Beauvoir, *The Second Sex*, (1972), Pt 3, Ch.1.

5. Women and Autonomy

1. This is not merely a view held by men. One aspect of the reaction of some women to feminism has been an almost aggressive reassertion of the values of femininity and the role of women in serving men. In Britain there is an organisation called 'The Campaign for the Feminine Woman'. In America, a book called *The Total Woman*, by Marabel Morgan (1973), was a best-seller, and Morgan taught classes orientated around the ideas of the book. The gist of these is summed up by the chapter headings of Part 2 of the book. These are : 'Accept Him', "Admire Him', 'Adapt to Him', 'Appreciate Him'.

   Some of the essays in *Women Who Do and Women Who Don't Join the Feminist Movement*, edited by Robyn Rowland (1984), give insights into why many women reject feminism.
2. There is, I think, no question that conceptions of 'childhood' have changed, and Aries work shows this convincingly. But to show that conceptions of childhood have changed (or to argue that they *should* change or be questioned) is not at all the same thing as to argue that in previous ages there was no distinction between adults and children at all.
3. Roger's basic ideas are spelled out most clearly, I think, in *On Becoming a Person* (1961).
4. *See*, for example, Allan Buss, 'Humanistic Psychology as Liberal Ideology: The Socio-historical Roots of Maslow's Theory of Self-actualization' (1979).

5. Steven Lukes, in *Individualism* (1973), discusses the historical emergence of the concept of 'individualism' and the many different meanings it can have.

6. The Critique of Individualism

1. Wittgenstein in the *Philosophical Investigations* (1953) argued that there must be shared criteria for the use even of a concept such as 'pain'. The precise meaning of what Wittgenstein said, and the nature of the relationship between 'mental' concepts and concepts which refer to outward behaviour has been the subject of a very great deal of debate in the philosophy of mind.
2. Scheman's view raises, I think, all the problems that I discussed in Chapter 2 about identifying large-scale, transhistorical 'themes' in philosophy and seeing them as typically male. Steven Lukes (1973) argues that it is both possible and necessary to give a sense to the concept of 'individualism' in ways that do *not* assume doctrines such as those of psychological egoism or the classical liberal belief in the 'pre-social' nature of persons.
3. This is neither to deny that there are many problems with the way in which Hegel characterised social relationships, nor that there are problems with the way in which he characterised women. (For a discussion of this, *see* Genevieve Lloyd, (1984). Nevertheless, it is undeniable that Hegel sees the self as essentially social.
4. One might instance here much of the work of the two Oxford philosophers, Peter Strawson and Stuart Hampshire. Hampshire's book *Thought and Action* (1959), for example, defends a view that concepts which refer to 'inner' mental states or processes are essentially dependent on shared interpersonal criteria, and Hampshire would oppose any view of human beings which saw them in any way as having a 'pre-social' nature. Nevertheless, his conception of social life and politics is a recognisably liberal one; it is anchored, for example, in a 'pluralist' view of what he calls 'ways of life', which he sees as consensually chosen by those who participate in them. (See, for example, *Public and private morality*, Cambridge University Press 1978). See also P.F.Strawson, 'Social Morality and Individual Ideal', in *Freedom and Resentment and Other Essays*, Methuen, London 1976.
5. For a very interesting discussion of the ways in which class can affect personality and sense of identity in damaging ways, *see* R.Sennett and J.Cobb, *The Hidden Injuries of Class* (1977).
6. There is a good discussion of Laing's work in Andrew Collier, *R.D.Laing: The Politics and Practice of Psychotherapy* (1977).

7. The Idea of a Female ethic

1. *See* for example, E.Erikson, *Identity, Youth and Crisis* (1968) and J.Piaget, *The Moral Judgement of the Child* (1977).

Lawrence Kohlberg originally published his theory of stages of moral development in a PhD dissertation from the University of Chicago in 1958: 'The Development of Modes of Thinking and Choices in Years 10-16'. Many questions have been raised about Kohlberg's work which I do not discuss in this chapter. It has, for example, been suggested by C.M.J.Braun and J.M.C. Baribeau (1978) in their article 'Subjective Idealism in Kohlberg's Theory of Moral Development' that Kohlberg's approach simply exemplifies an ethical theory derived from the work of Kant and from the contemporary liberal philosopher John Rawls. There is a critique of some of the philosophical assumptions underlying Kohlberg's work in an article by Owen J. Flanagan Jnr, 'Virtue, Sex and Gender': Some Philosophical Reflections on the Moral Psychology Debate', *Ethics*, April 1982. This issue of *Ethics* also includes a reply by Kohlberg to Flanagan.

2. For a discussion of Gilligan's work which argues that she tends to depoliticise questions about the differential development of men and women, and points out some of the ways in which ideas of distinctive female 'virtues' or capacities can be used in non-feminist or anti-feminist ways, *see* Judy Auerbach, Linda Blum, Vicki Smith and Christine Williams, 'Commentary on Gilligan's 'In a Different Voice' in *Feminist Studies* 11, no. 1, Spring 1985.

3. The idea that moral principles should be universalisable is one that is very much a Kantian one. One of the best-known modern defenders of a view that sees universalisability as essential to moral judgements is Richard Hare (*see*, for example, *The Language of Morals (1952) and Freedom and Reason* (1963).

8. Maternal Thinking

1. Discussions of this can be found in the collection of essays edited by Nell Keddie, *Tinker, Tailor...the Myth of Cultural Deprivation* (1973).

2. For a discussion of Bowlby's work, *see* Michael Rutter, *Maternal Deprivation Reassessed* 2nd edn, Penguin, 1981.

3. I do not, of course, want to deny that women's social experience and life activities have often differed greatly from those of men; in fact, I have stressed this at various points in this book. What I am questioning is the view that these differences give rise to 'women's practices' which can be considered as if they were quite 'apart' in some way from other aspects of the culture in which they exist.

4. Think, for example, of the perennial political debate about the notion of 'standards' in education and of the constant right-wing critique of so-called 'permissive' parents or lack of 'responsibility' in parents.

Afterword

1. *See*, for example, the book by J.Blassingame *The Slave Community: Plantation Life in the Ante-bellum South* (1972).

Bibliography

Allen, J. (1984), 'Motherhood: The Annihilation of Women', in Trebilcot (1984)

Aries, P. (1973), *Centuries of Childhood*, Penguin, Harmondsworth (1st edn, 1962)

Aristotle, *The Politics*, trans. T.A. Sinclair, Penguin, Harmondsworth, (1962)

Auerbach, J., Blum, L., Smith, V. and Williams, C. (1985), 'Commentary on Gilligan's 'In a different voice', *Feminist Studies* 11, no. 1, Spring 1981

Baker, R. and Elliston, F. (1975), *Philosophy and Sex*, Prometheus Books, Buffalo, NY

Baker Miller, J.(1978), *Toward a New Psychology Of Women*, Pelican, Harmondsworth. (USA, Boston Beacon Press, 1976)

Barker, M. (1981), *The New Racism*, Junction Books, London

Barnes, B. (1977), *Interests and the Growth of Knowledge*, Routledge and Kegan Paul, London

Bart, P. (1984), 'Review of Chodorow's "The Reproduction of Mothering"', in Trebilcot (1984)

Bartky, S. (1977), 'Towards a Phenomenology of Feminist Consciousness', in Vetterling-Braggin, Elliston and English (1977)

Berger, P. and Luckmann, T. (1971), *The Social Construction of Reality*, Penguin, Harmondsworth

Blassingame, J. (1972), *The Slave Community; Plantation Life in the Ante-bellum South*, Oxford University Press

Blum, L. (1980), *Friendship, Altruism and Morality*, Routledge and Kegan Paul, London

—— (1982), 'Kant's and Hegel's Moral Rationalism: A Feminist Perspective', *Canadian Journal of Philosophy* XII

Bowlby, J. (1953), *Child Care and the Growth of Love*, London

Bradley, F.H. (1927), *Ethical Studies*, 2nd edn, Oxford University Press (1st edn, 1876)

Braun, C and Baribeau, J. (1978), 'Subjective Idealism in Kohlberg's Theory of Moral Development', *Human Development* 21

Brownmiller, S. (1975), *Against Our Will: Men, Women and Rape,*, Bantam Books, New York

Broverman, I., Broverman, D., Clarkson, S., Rosencrantz, P. and Vogel, S.(1981) 'Sex-role Stereotypes and Clinical Judgements of Mental Health', in Howell and Bayes (1981)

Buss, A. (1979), 'Humanistic Psychology as Liberal Ideology: The Socio-historical Roots of Maslow's Theory of Self-actualization', *Journal of Humanistic Psychology* 19 (3), Summer

Cartledge, S. (1983), 'Duty and Desire: Creating a Feminist Morality', in Cartledge and Ryan (1983)

—— and Ryan, J. (1983), *Sex and Love: New Thoughts on Old Contradictions*, the Women's Press, London

Chodorow, N. (1978), *The Reproduction of Mothering: Psychoanalysis and the Sociology of Gender*, University of California Press, Berkeley

Clark, L. (1979), 'Women and Locke: Who Owns the Apples in the Garden of Eden?', in Clark and Lange (1979)

Clark, L. and Lange, L. (1979), *The Sexism of Social and Political Theory*, University of Toronto Press

Collier, A. (1977), *R.D. Laing: The Philosophy and Politics of Psychotherapy*, Harvester, Brighton

Cooper, D. (1976), *The Grammar of Living*, Pelican, Harmondsworth

Daly, M. (1973), *Beyond God the Father: Toward a Philosophy of Women's Liberation*, Beacon Press, Boston

Daly, M. (1979), *Gyn/Ecology: The Metaethics of Radical Feminism*, The Women's Press, London; Beacon Press, Boston, 1978

Dawkins, R. (1978), *The Selfish Gene*, Granada, London

De Beauvoir, S. (1972), *The Second Sex*, Penguin, Harmondsworth (1st edn, 1949)

Dinnerstein, D. (1977), *The Mermaid and the Minotaur: Sexual Arrangements and Human Malaise*, Harper Colophon, New York

Dowrick, S. and Grundberg, S. (1980), *Why Children?*, The Women's Press, London

Dworkin, A. (1981), *Pornography: Men Possessing Women*, The Women's Press, London; Perigree Books, New York

Ehrenreich, B. (1983), *The Hearts of Men: American Dreams and*

the Flight from Commitment, Pluto Press, London; Anchor Press/Doubleday, New York
—— and English, D. (1979), *For Her Own Good:150 Years of the Experts' Advice to Women*, Pluto Press, London; Anchor Press/ Doubleday, New York, 1978
Eisenstein, H. (1984), *Contemporary Feminist Thought*, Allen and Unwin, London
Elkins, S. (1976), *Slavery: A Problem in American Institutional and Intellectual Life*, 2nd edn, Chicago University Press
Elshtain, J. (1981), *Public Man, Private Woman: Women in Social and Political Thought*, Martin Robertson, Oxford; Princeton University Press, 1981
Erikson, E. (1968), *Identity: Youth and Crisis*, Faber, London
Eysenck, H. (1977), *Psychology Is About People*, Pelican, Harmondsworth
—— and Nias, D. (1980), *Sex, Violence, and the Media*, Granada, 1980
Fay, B. (1976), *Social Theory and Political Practice*, Allen and Unwin, London
Firestone, S. (1979), *The Dialectic of Sex*, The Women's Press, London (1st edn, 1970)
Flanagan, O. (1982), 'Virtue, Sex and Gender: Some Philosophical Reflections on the Moral Psychology Debate' in *Ethics*, 92, April
Flax, J. (1981), 'The Conflict between Nurturance and Autonomy in Mother–Daughter Relationships and within Feminism', in Howell and Bayes (1981)
—— (1983), 'Political Philosophy and the Patriarchal Unconscious: A Psychoanalytic Perspective on Epistemology and Metaphysics'. in Harding and Hintikka (1983)
Foot, P. (1967), 'Moral Beliefs', in Foot, P., (ed.), *Theories of Ethics*, Oxford University Press
Forbes, I. and Smith, S. (eds.) (1983), *Politics and Human Nature*, Frances Pinter, London
Freud, S. (1977), *On Sexuality, ed.* A. Richards, Pelican Freud Library, vol. 7, Penguin, Harmondsworth
Friedan, B. (1965), *The Feminine Mystique*, Penguin, Harmondsworth; W.W. Norton, New York, 1963
Fromm, E. (1963), *The Sane Society*, Routledge and Kegan Paul, London
Frye, M. (1983), *The Politics of Reality*, The Crossing Press, Trumansburg, NY
Gilligan, C. (1982), *In a Different Voice: Psychological Theory and*

Women's Development, Harvard University Press, Cambridge, Mass

Golding, W. (1954), *Lord of the Flies*, Faber, London

Gould, C. ed.(1983), *Beyond Domination*, Rowman and Allanheld, NJ

Gramsci, A. (1971), *Selections from the Prison Notebooks*, ed. and trans. by Q. Hoare and G. Nowell-Smith, Lawrence and Wishart, London

Griffin, S. (1982), *Made from This Earth*, The Women's Press, London

Grimshaw, J. (1982), 'Feminism, History and Morality', *Radical Philosophy*, no. 30, Spring; reprinted in *The Radical Philosophy Reader*, Verso, London, 1985

Hampshire, S. (1959), *Thought and Action*, Chatto and Windus, London

—— (1978), *Public and Private Morality*, Cambridge University Press

Harding, S. and Hintikka, M. (1983), *Discovering Reality: Feminist Perspectives on Epistemology, Metaphysics, Methodology, and the Philosophy of Science*, D. Reidel, Dordrecht, Boston and London

Hare, R. (1952), *The Language of Morals*, Clarendon Press, Oxford

—— (1975), 'Abortion and the Golden Rule', in Baker and Elliston (1975)

Heath, S. (1982), *The Sexual Fix*, Macmillan, London

Heller, A. (1980), 'The Emotional Division of Labour between the Sexes', *Social Praxis*, 7 (3/4)

Hite, S. (1981a), *The Hite Report on Female Sexuality*, Corgi, New York (1st edn, 1976)

—— (1981b), *The Hite Report on Male Sexuality,* Macdonald, London; Alfred A. Knopf, New York

Hooks, B. (1982), *Ain't I a Woman? Black Women And Feminism*, Pluto Press, London

Horney, K. (1967), *Feminine Psychology*, W.W. Norton, New York

Howell, E and Bayes, M. (1981), *Women and Mental Health*, Basic Books, New York

Hubbard, R. (1983), 'Have Only Men Evolved?', in Harding and Hintikka (1983)

Hudson, L. (1967), *Contrary Imaginations: A Psychological Study of the English Schoolboy*, Pelican, Harmondsworth

Hume, D., *A Treatise of Human Nature*, (1740;1972) books 2 and 3, ed. P. Ardal, Fontana, London

Ingleby, D. ed (1981), *Critical Psychiatry: The Politics of Mental Health*, Penguin, Harmondsworth

Jaggar, A. (1983), *Feminist Politics and Human Nature*, Harvester, Brighton

Keddie, N. (1973), *Tinker, Tailor...the Myth of Cultural Deprivation*, Penguin, Harmondsworth

Kerouac, J. (1958), *On the Road*, Andre Deutsch, London

Koedt, A. (1970), *The Myth of the Vaginal Orgasm*, New England Free Press, Boston

Kuhn, T. (1970), *The Structure of Scientific Revolutions*, 2nd edn, University of Chicago Press

Laing, R.D. (1965), *The Divided Self*, Penguin, Harmondsworth

—— (1967), *The Politics of Experience*, Pelican, Harmondsworth

—— (1976), *The Politics of the Family*, Pelican, Harmondsworth

—— and Esterson, A. (1970), *Sanity, Madness and the Family*, Pelican, Harmondsworth

Lakatos, I. and Musgrave, A. (1970), *Criticism and the Growth of Knowledge*, Cambridge University Press

Leonard, P. (1984), *Personality and Ideology: Towards a Materialist Understanding of the Individual*, Macmillan, London

Lloyd, G. (1984), *The Man of Reason: Male and Female in Western Philosophy*, Methuen, London

Locke, J., *Two Treatises of Civil Government*, Everyman, J.M. Dent, 1924

Love, B. and Shanklin, E. (1984), 'The Answer Is Matriarchy', in Trebilcot (1984)

Lugones, M. and Spelman, E. (1983), 'Have We Got a Theory for You! Feminist Theory, Cultural Imperialism, and the Demand for 'The Woman's Voice', *Women's Studies International Forum* (6)

Lukes, S. (1973), *Individualism*, Basil Blackwell, Oxford

Mahowald, M. (ed.) (1978), *Philosophy of Woman: Classical to Current Concepts*, Hackett, Indianopolis

Maslow, A. (1939), 'Dominance, Personality and Social Behaviour in Women', *Journal of Social Psychology*, no. 10

—— (1942), 'Self-esteem (Dominance Feeling) and Sexuality in Women',*Journal of Social Psychology*, no. 16

—— (1970), *Motivation and Personality*, 2nd edn, Harper and Row, New York

—— (1973), *The Farther Reaches of Human Nature*, Pelican, Harmondsworth

—— (1982), *The Journals of Abraham Maslow*, ed. R. Lowry, abridged by J. Freedman, Lewis, Lexington, Mass.

Masters, W. and Johnson,V. (1966), *Human Sexual Response*, Churchill, London

McClellan, D (1972), *Karl Marx: Selected Writings*, Oxford University Press

Mill, J. and Mill, H. *Essay on Sex Equality*, introduced by A. Rossi, University of Chicago Press, 1970

Millett, K. (1977), *Sexual Politics*, Virago, London (1st edn, 1971)

Mitchell, Jeannette. (1984), *What Is to Be Done about Illness and Health?*, Penguin, Harmondsworth.

Mitchell, Juliet. (1975), *Psychoanalysis and Feminism*, Pelican, Harmondsworth

Morgan, M. (1973), *The Total Woman*, Pocket Books, New York

Murdoch, I. (1970), *The Sovereignty of Good*, Routledge and Kegan Paul, London

Murdock, G. and McCron, R. (1979, 'The TV Violence Controversy', *Screen Education*, no. 30

Nietzsche, F., *Twilight of the Idols* and *The Anti-Christ*, trans R.J. Hollingdale, Penguin, Harmondsworth, 1968

Nietzsche, F., *Beyond Good and Evil*, trans. R.J. Hollingdale, Penguin, Harmondsworth, 1973

Noddings, N. (1984), *Caring: A Feminine Approach to Ethics and Moral Education*, University of California Press, Berkeley

Oakley, A. (1972), *Sex, Gender and Society*, Maurice Temple Smith, London

—— (1974), *The Sociology of Housework*, Martin Robertson, Oxford

—— (1984), *Taking It Like a Woman*, Jonathan Cape, London

O'Brien, M. (1981), *The Politics of Reproduction*, Routledge and Kegan Paul, London

Okin, S. (1980), *Women in Western Political Thought*, Virago, London; Princeton University Press, 1979

Paton, H. (1948), *The Moral Law: Kant's Groundwork of the Metaphysic of Morals*, Hutchinson, London

Piaget, J. (1977), *The Moral Judgement of the Child*, Penguin, Harmondsworth

Plato, *The Complete Dialogues*, ed. E. Hamilton and H. Cairns, Princeton University Press, 1963

Poole, R. (1985), 'Morality, Masculinity and the Market', *Radical Philosophy*, no. 39, Spring

Radcliffe Richards, J. (1980), *The Sceptical Feminist: A Philosophical Enquiry*, Routledge and Kegan Paul, London

Radcliffe Richards, J., (1982), Letter to *Radical Philosophy*, no. 32, Autumn

Raphael, D. (1969), *British Moralists 1650-1800*, Oxford University Press
—— (1976), *Problems of Political Philosophy*, revised edn, Macmillan, London
Rawls, J. (1972), *A Theory of Justice*, Oxford University Press
Reich, C. (1971), *The Greening of America*, Penguin, Harmondsworth; Random House, New York, 1970
Rich, A. (1977) *Of Woman Born: Motherhood as Experience and Institution*, Virago, London; W.W. Norton, New York, 1976
—— (1980), *On Lies, Secrets and Silence: Selected Prose, 1966-1978*, Virago, London; W.W. Norton, New York, 1979
Rogers, C. (1961), *On Becoming a Person*, Constable, London
Rogers, C. (1978), *Carl Rogers on Personal Power: Inner Strength and Its Revolutionary Impact*, Constable, London
Rorty, R. (1980), *Philosophy and the Mirror of Nature*, Basil Blackwell, Oxford; Princeton University Press, 1980
Rose, S., Kamin, L. and Lewontin, R. (1984), *Not in Our Genes: Biology, Ideology and Human Nature*, Pelican, Harmondsworth
Rousseau, J.J., *The Confessions*, trans. and introduced by J. Cohen, Penguin, Harmondsworth, 1953
—— *The Social Contract and Discourses*, trans. G. Cole, J.M. Dent, 1973
—— *Emile*, trans. B. Foxley, Everyman Library, J.M.Dent, 1974
Rowan, J. (1976), *Ordinary Ecstasy: Humanistic Psychology in Action*, Routledge and Kegan Paul, London
Rowbotham, S. (1973), *Woman's Consciousness, Man's World*, Pelican, Harmondsworth
Rowland, R. (ed.) (1984), *Women Who Do and Women Who Don't (Join the Feminist Movement)*, Routledge and Kegan Paul, London
Ruddick, S. (1980), 'Maternal thinking', *Feminist Studies 6*, Summer
—— (1984), 'Preservative Love and Military Destruction: Some Reflections on Mothering and Peace', in Trebilcot (1984)
Ruth, S. (1981), 'Methodocracy, Misogyny and Bad Faith: The Response of Philosophy', in Spender (1981)
Sartre, J. -P. (1948), *Existentialism and Humanism*, trans. P.Mairet, Methuen, London
—— (1969), *Being and Nothingness*, trans.H.Barnes, Methuen, London (1st edn, 1948)
Scheman, N. (1983), 'Individualism and the Objects of Psychology', in Harding and Hintikka (1983)

Sennett, R. and Cobb, J. (1977), *The Hidden Injuries of Class*, Cambridge University Press

Seve, L. (1978), *Man in Marxist Theory and the Psychology of Personality*, Harvester, Brighton

Skillen, A; (1977), *Ruling Illusions: Philosophy and the Social Order*, Harvester, Brighton

Skinner, B. (1972), *Beyond Freedom and Dignity*, Jonathan Cape, London

Smith-Rosenberg, C. (1975), 'The Female World of Love and Ritual: Relations between Women in Nineteenth-Century America', *Signs: Journal of Women in Culture and Society* 1 (1)

Soper, K.(1981), *On Human Needs*, Harvester, Brighton

Spelman, E. (1983), 'Aristotle and the Politicization of the Soul', in Harding and Hintikka (1983)

Spender, D. (1980), *Man-made Language*, Routledge and Kegan Paul, London

—— (ed.) (1981), *Men's Studies Modified: The Impact of Feminism on the Academic Disciplines*, Pergamon Press, Oxford, New York

—— (1982), *Women of Ideas (and What Men Have Done to Them)*, Routledge and Kegan Paul

—— (1985), *For the Record: The Making and Meaning of Feminist Knowledge*, The Women's Press, London

Spock, B. (1957), *Baby and Child Care*, Pocket Books, New York

Stanley, L. and Wise, S. (1983), *Breaking Out: Feminist Consciousness and Feminist Research*, Routledge and Kegan Paul, London

Stern, K. (1966), *The Flight from Woman*, Allen and Unwin, London

Timpanaro, S. (1980), *On Materialism*, Verso, London

Trebilcot, J. (ed.) (1984), *Mothering: Essays in Feminist Theory*, Rowman and Allanheld, Totowa NJ

Vetterling-Braggin, M., Elliston, F. and English, J. (1977), *Feminism and Philosophy*, Littlefield, Adams and Co., Totowa, NJ

Warnock, G. (1971), *The Object of Morality*, Methuen, London

Watson, J. (1928), *Psychological Care of Infant and Child*, W.W. Norton, New York

Whitbeck, C. (1983) 'A Different Reality: Feminist Ontology', in Gould (1983)

Williams, R. (1976), *Keywords: A Vocabulary of Culture and Society*, Fontana, Glasgow

Williams, R. (1985), 'Mining the Meaning: Keywords in the Miners' Strike', *New Socialist*, March 1985

Willis, P. (1977), *Learning to Labour: How Working-Class Kids Get Working-Class Jobs*, Saxon House, Farnborough, Hants

Winnicott, D. (1964), *The Child, the Family and the Outside World*, Penguin, Harmondsworth

—— (1974), *Playing and Reality*, Pelican, Harmondsworth

Wittgenstein, L. (1953), *Philosophical Investigations*, Basil Blackwell, Oxford

Wollstonecraft, M. *Vindication of the Rights of Woman*,. introduced by M. Kramnick, Pelican, Harmondsworth, 1975

Woolf, V. (1979), *Women and Writing*, introduced by M. Barrett, The Women's Press, London

Young, I. (1984), 'Is Male Gender Identity the Cause of Male Domination?', in Trebilcot (1984)

Zaretsky, E. (1976), *Capitalism, the Family and Personal Life*, Pluto Press, London

Index